Socially
Constructed
School Violence

Studies in the
Postmodern Theory of Education

Joe L. Kincheloe and Shirley R. Steinberg
General Editors

Vol. 281

PETER LANG
New York • Washington, D.C./Baltimore • Bern
Frankfurt am Main • Berlin • Brussels • Vienna • Oxford

Kimberly M. Williams

Socially Constructed School Violence

Lessons from the Field

PETER LANG
New York • Washington, D.C./Baltimore • Bern
Frankfurt am Main • Berlin • Brussels • Vienna • Oxford

Library of Congress Cataloging-in-Publication Data

Williams, Kimberly M.
Socially constructed school violence: lessons from the field /
Kimberly M. Williams.
p. cm. — (Counterpoints; v. 281)
Includes bibliographical references and index.
1. School violence—United States—Prevention. 2. Behavior modification.
3. Alternative schools—United States.
I. Title. II. Series: Counterpoints (New York, N.Y.); v. 281.
LB3013.32.W56   371.7'82–dc22   2004026609
ISBN 0-8204-7129-1
ISSN 1058-1634

Bibliographic information published by **Die Deutsche Bibliothek**.
Die Deutsche Bibliothek lists this publication in the "Deutsche
Nationalbibliografie"; detailed bibliographic data is available
on the Internet at http://dnb.ddb.de/.

Cover design by Joni Holst

The paper in this book meets the guidelines for permanence and durability
of the Committee on Production Guidelines for Book Longevity
of the Council of Library Resources.

Table of Contents

Preface..vii

Acknowledgments.. xxv

Introduction..1

PART I: PERSONAL VIOLENCE

Chapter 1: The Important Role of Personal Violence at WANTS 37

Chapter 2: Social Location and Perceptions of Personal Violence 53

Chapter 3: Personal Violence and Feelings: Pain, Fear, Passion, Love,
Anger, and Revenge..71

PART II: STRUCTURAL VIOLENCE

Chapter 4: Power and Structural Violence: Controlling Resources......................89

Chapter 5: Prep Jails: Alternative Schools Preparing "Delinquent Students"
for the Next Step..131

PART III: SOLUTIONS AND RECOMMENDATIONS

Chapter 6: Conclusions, Implications, and Recommendations............................145

Appendix A: Promising and Demonstrated Violence Prevention Programs....169

Appendix B: Checklist for Schoolwide Approach 179

Appendix C: A List of References for School Violence Prevention 181

Appendix D: The PEACE Approach to Violence Prevention Framework.......185

References..187

Index...189

Preface

Violence is a social construction. I approached this project from the perspective that our way of understanding violence is socially constructed and that people from different social locations (i.e., gender, race, social class, geographic location, religions, and so on) will have varied perspectives on what is violent. In this project, teachers, administrators, parents, community members, and students defined violence differently, and, therefore, approached the "problem of violence" in a different manner. I am putting "problem of violence" in quotation marks because various groups viewed the problem of violence in such different ways depending on their social location. For example, most male students did not consider sexual harassment as a form of violence unless it was physical. In fact, when I asked teachers, students, and others what constituted violence, sexual assault and harassment were mentioned rarely. Bullying behaviors and ostracizing behaviors were also mentioned infrequently as violence by those working in inner-city high schools but more often described by those within suburban elementary schools. However, some found these ostracizing behaviors problematic, although they were not associated with "violence" or the "violence problem." Mostly teachers, other adults, and young people who did not engage in antisocial behaviors focused their talk about violence around fighting, gangs, and the carrying of weapons. Conversely, students who carried weapons and belonged to gangs did not see these behaviors as necessarily associated with violence. They often saw these behaviors as ways to *prevent* violence—or to keep themselves safe. Although I began with the notion that violence was socially constructed, I did not end with it. I examined how the structures and processes (e.g., schools and school policies) affected individuals' lives.

The first section of this book focuses on personal violence. Specifically, I began by asking how individuals made sense of violence around them. I found that when questioned about violence in their lives, individuals frequently commented on episodes of personal violence (i.e., violence that was directed at a person by another person or people). However, I wanted to take this project a step further. I examined schools and school policies and how some of these policies affected the individuals who participated in this project. Two examples were how "zero tolerance" policies affected students and how alternative school experiences for "violent youths" can be set up to fail the neediest students by providing insufficient resources and underprepared teachers.

The second section of this book examines the connection between policies and issues of structural or systemic violence. Specifically, I observed particular programs designed to remedy the "problem of school violence" (mediation, alternative schools, and other approaches) and how these programs were perceived. From these observations and the literature on various programs, I drafted a proposal for a "school-wide approach" to violence prevention.

The third and final section of this book discusses promising practices and strategies to reducing violence in school that were implemented at the alternative school which served as the primary case study for this project.

Theoretical Framework

Dorothy Smith's (1987) work served as a guide to help examine both personal and structural violence in this project. Like Smith, I sought to find out how "situations are organized and determined by social processes that extend outside the scope of the everyday world and are not discoverable within it" (p. 152). Although Smith's focus is on a sociology for women, I have extended her definition to oppressed groups—particularly teenage boys and girls who are labeled "violent" or "aggressive" and often are poor and likely to be students of color (primarily African American). I wanted to understand how social processes, especially school structures (administrations, districts, alternative school placements), affected the lives of this oppressed group of young people. Therefore, this book revolves around the situation of a group of young people who do not usually receive media coverage or the attention of those in power but who experience personal and structural violence on a daily basis.

My investigation did not end with discussing the lives of those children in the margins of society. Because of personal experiences in school and my professional and personal desire to better understand the causes of school shootings in affluent America (e.g., Littleton, Colorado), I began to conduct ethnographic research in a relatively small, affluent, suburban elementary and middle school, renamed Lorenzo Hill Central School for the purposes of this book. I chose these schools because I wanted to focus on how violence was constructed in these sites among young children.

Ethnography was the primary tool to examine the structure and function of an urban alternative school for students who had been caught with a weapon at school. For Smith (1987, p. 153), "ethnography does not mean here, as it sometimes does in sociology, restriction to methods of observation and interviewing. It is rather a commitment to an investigation and explication of how 'it' actually is, of how 'it' actually works, of actual practices and relations." I wanted to find out how young people labeled "aggressive" or "violent" were treated in their school environments, how these labels influenced their education, and how they interpreted this treatment. How did these children make sense of violence in their lives and their relationships? In addition, I wanted to investigate how children in affluent schools made sense of relationships and violence. Was the nature of violence truly different in these sites? Was the nature of caring relationships truly different? Were the structural processes in place dramatically different?

My project began as an ethnographic case study of an alternative school for young people who had been caught with any dangerous object that could be construed as a weapon in school (the weapon of choice was most often box cutters or the blades from them). For the purposes of this study, the weapons school has been renamed WANTS (Weapons Are Not Tolerated in School). I quickly realized that the structure of the district (e.g., having alternative schools with insufficient resources for children who had "behavioral problems"; for pregnant or new mothers; and for "violent," "aggressive," or "dangerous" students, who brought weapons to school) and the policies of the district (e.g., zero tolerance for violent behavior) powerfully shaped the meanings students and staff attached to the school. Furthermore, teachers were affected by these institutional policies, thus, comparable to a domino effect, impacting students. Smith (1987) described in her research design moving from

> the experience of women at work as mothers in relation to children's schooling to an explication of the school organization and the administrative relations of the state of which that school organization is a local agent. The aim of analysis has been to disclose a social organization implied but not spoken of in the original narratives, a social organization that is presupposed but not explicit. (p. 202)

Smith began with the words of mothers talking about the work they did with their children and their children's schooling. I started with children and school personnel who had been placed in an alternative school site. By observing and talking with students, I realized to what extent their days were organized by teachers, and to what extent they resisted the school structure to lead their own lives and have their own relationships–generally outside of adults' gaze. Teachers' lives were organized by the restrictions placed upon them by the administration, but teachers also resisted the structure imposed upon them. They worked to develop strategies that made their lives more manageable. Administrators were limited by budget restrictions decided by the district and the school board, but they also felt the pressure from parents to "do something about violence." The district and the school board were limited by the state budget, and so on. The social organization quickly became complicated. Students' lives are supposed to be the focus of schooling; however, life decisions are often being made by those in power who do not live in their communities, go to their churches, play at their parks, or shop at their grocery stores–or are involved with any aspect of their complex lives.

At the WANTS school, teachers and students felt like victims of "the system." The *system* was vaguely defined–the district administration, the school board, the state. The teachers and the students alike complained about "the district." One teacher said, "the district should be ashamed of themselves." One teenage male student said in response to a comment I made about district policy, "[expletive] the district . . . They don't give a [expletive] about us; they put us down here in this so-called school." There was a great deal of anger and frustration directed at this vague, ill-defined notion of "the district." The social processes, controlled by policies developed by the school board and the central administration, influenced the ways the participants in this project felt about themselves, their jobs, and their education.

After my experience at WANTS, I shifted my focus to examining how violence gets constructed at an affluent suburban school 20 miles away from WANTS. I wanted to see how these students made sense of personal violence and how the structures and processes shaped their lives and relationships and the role of violence in their schools.

How I Came to This Project

The first part of this book discusses my personal experiences with, my struggles to understand, and my attempts to reduce school violence. Persons attempting to better comprehend the perceptions of others about school violence should begin by assessing their own perceptions regarding it. In other words, we have to examine our own perspectives, biases, and thoughts on school violence before we can begin to understand those of others. More specifically then, we need to ask questions about the context of violence within the respective school before we can create workable solutions to reduce and ultimately eliminate school violence at a particular school. Some of these questions may be: What is considered violent? What is considered problematic? What strategies may work to reduce violence and keep people safe? What are students', teachers', administrators', and others' perspectives on what these strategies are? After examining my own standpoint, I tried to find out the ways that school violence is socially constructed—particularly in school sites often labeled "violent" such as WANTS. Because I started from the premise that school violence was socially constructed, I realized I had to understand my own perceptions of violence in general, school violence in particular, and my own social location to work on this project. All research is undertaken from a perspective—a view from somewhere, despite efforts of many researchers to deny their own social location and its influence.

I came to this work as a white woman of privilege. I state this because I believe that those of us working in violence prevention and strategizing for solutions must acknowledge our own privilege and how this privilege has influenced our perspectives about what is violent and who is violent. I grew up in a nurturing, loving, middle-class family. We lived in the country with horses and other animals—far from city life. This life, despite my initial thoughts to the contrary, was far from violence-free. My first exposure to guns was as a young girl riding my pony through the woods during hunting season and hearing gunshots. I knew there were parts of the year when we needed to be careful and stay away from certain areas of the woods. At these times of year the woods behind my house sounded like a war zone, but I never really paid much attention to the sound of gunfire. Guns and violence were not subjects I thought much about. I was not afraid of being shot. After all, the bullets were not intended for me but rather for animals and criminals. However, there were places we could not go during hunting season because we knew we could be killed. Not unlike the young people in the inner-city war zones, parents and other adults attempt to keep them safe and prevent them from being shot by making them stay inside during certain times (usually evenings and weekends) when they are at highest risk.

The first time I was truly afraid of being shot was when I was followed home by a man carrying a gun—chasing my sister, a couple of friends, and me because we were trespassing on his property. This was perhaps the most terrifying experience of my young life. We had been following the river down to the falls. As we came closer to the waterfall, a man who looked very scary to me came out of the woods pointing his gun at us and said, "git goin.'" I ran with the dog as fast as I could. My defiant young sister and the two teenaged boys walked more slowly than I did. Out of breath, I ran into my parents and the parents of the two boys. The boys' father was a police officer. They told me to run home, and they went to go find my sister and the two boys. I waited at home by a window for their return, facing the road that led to the river. There was no sign of my family. Suddenly, from over the hill I saw the angry man with the gun. He was walking toward my house! He saw the dog in the driveway and headed toward the door. I ran and hid in the closet as my heart felt as though it would pump itself right out of my chest. I heard him break the outside latch and enter into the porch. He was fiddling with the knob to the door of the kitchen where I was shaking in the closet when all of a sudden, from the other door I heard, "Kim, where are you?" I heard him run off the porch. I ran toward my father's voice and cried hysterically. They asked me what had happened, and I couldn't speak. I could barely breathe. They told me that they had to take the long way home because the madman stood in the road with his gun and would not let them pass in their car. My friends' police-officer father grabbed the intruder's gun that he'd left on the edge of the property—apparently he knew there was a law against bringing it onto the property. As I blubbered and gasped for air, I told them the story. They called the police. As far as they were concerned, he had done nothing illegal, or at least that was what the police report said. He legally owned the gun. He never shot at us. He did not bring the gun onto the property. There was no sign of forced entry. Ever since this experience, the sight of guns makes my heart stop for a brief moment. The thought of children handling guns is as terrifying as the madman-recluse who lived at the waterfalls. However, children carry guns and threaten to use them in part for the same reason that my father and the man who threatened me did—to protect what they see as theirs: territory, their block, their turf, their families, themselves, or sometimes to protect all they have, self-respect. When self-respect is all that one can call one's own, as is the case for so many poor children, one becomes more willing to fight to the death to protect it.

Until the experience at the waterfall when I was sixteen, I never really thought that actual people shot and hurt or killed other people—at least nobody I had ever known personally. I had heard about war and watched battles on television, but I never actually knew anybody who was killed at the hands of another or even anyone who was seriously injured at the hands of another. I went to a public school in an affluent area, but lived in a rural area, close to rural poverty. There were rarely fights, except on the bus. Furthermore, there was a clear separation between those who lived on or near the lake (the wealthy students or "preppies" or "popular kids") and those who lived in the rural communities (the "trailer park kids" or the "dirts"). I was somewhere in between, and sometimes I could "pass" in each culture. When I did, I faced the physical wrath of the bullies (who were from the "dirts"), or the emotional wrath of the "preppies" (being outcast or not invited to the "popular" girls' parties). These are pervasive forms of violence that many young people experience in our schools—violence that never gets labeled as such.

This type of behavior and dealing with it on your own or with your peers is just part of being a teenager and going to school. As students at Lorenzo Hill told me about being scared on the bus, "it's just the way it is." Some people were mean or jealous, but I was just told (as many children are in middle-class worlds) to mind my own business and not do anything to deserve victimization. As I began this project, I remembered my own experiences with violence (that I never considered violence as a child)—being bullied in gym class by two girls who were bigger than I was (at 95 pounds, most people were bigger than I was). They would hit me with floor hockey sticks and push me hard against the wall. Sometimes I was afraid on the school bus that they might try to hurt me, but they rarely rode the same bus. These girls were considered "dirts." They were poor. One had been pregnant twice (the only girl I knew in school who was pregnant). In my privileged life girls like these were likely to be the topic of conversation, but they were rarely included in the conversation. They were to be avoided.

I never thought much about poverty. I never thought much about guns. I almost never thought about race. However, race and social class become complicated within any discussion of school violence. Those from privileged social locations rarely think of violence until it affects them personally—or people who look like them (as was the case for affluent white Americans when Columbine happened). Despite my own experiences, I rarely thought about violence—except sexual violence, which had been hammered into my head in college as something of which to be very afraid. We had "safe walks" in college where people would come and walk you home when it was dark—rapists and attackers were still viewed as lurking out there—not in our own homes and schools. Similar to many women I have encountered in my life, I was living in fear of the stranger rapist who, in fact, is much less likely to hurt me or anyone else than our own partners and loved ones.

I have written this book to explain the way many privileged people are able to avoid seeing and experiencing the pain of poverty and racism firsthand. We even deny the aforementioned kinds of violence that are directly around us: bullying, cruel treatment, ostracizing, and segregation based on socioeconomic status. Violence in affluent America simply does not happen. We delude ourselves into believing violence is a poor person's problem. We separate ourselves from "violent" or "unsafe" places instead of trying to make these places safer. It becomes easy to turn a blind eye to those who grow up poor or those from different racial groups because these are the not-so-subtle messages affluent schools teach. Avoid those who are different because they are to be feared. They are dangerous. I mistakenly believed, not unlike most privileged folks, that stranger violence was more common than acquaintance violence. As I found out throughout the course of

this project, individuals are at a far higher risk of being hurt by someone they
know or even once loved than by a stranger.

I never thought about the role of guns and other forms of violence in intimate relationships such as families and romantic relationships, schools, and
community. I never thought about gangs. These were not problems for me to
worry about. I learned how to pretend that our culture isn't that bad—that somehow the victims of poverty, racism, and violence are not real people—or that they
are somehow bad people who deserve this plight. I never questioned how it could
be that hugely disproportionate numbers of African American males are imprisoned or killed during their teenage years. We have convinced ourselves that in our
land of opportunity, anyone can pull himself or herself out of poverty if he or she
works hard enough. I realized that this might be true for some, but certainly not
for all. It is almost always easier to avoid painful reality if you can. If you can alarm
your home in your gated community, send your children to private schools, park
your car in an attended lot, you can almost think that the violence and poverty
that plagues so many young people is not real.

I know I wanted to protect myself from the pain of poverty and violence. It is
difficult to face, and as educators we struggle to adjust and teach within more violent and poorer environments than the ones in which we grew up. When I first
started this project, I would regularly come home crying. My husband would say,
"you don't have to do that job if you don't want to." My boss would see the de-
feated look on my face and say, "you can work in another neighborhood, in
another school." While these comments were made to comfort me, I knew that I
could not hide from this reality any longer. I felt that I had to tell the story in a
way that would make other privileged folks like me—others who had shut out the
reality of poverty for so long—listen, understand, and internalize.

Early on in this project, in an effort to gain a perspective on what life on the
street was like and the violence that teenagers experience who live in that life, I
interviewed one of the college students with whom I had worked for four years
who managed to escape urban poverty and gangs and go on to college. He told me
about his high school experiences. He had been a street fighter who would fight
for money—sometimes until his rival was near death. As he said, "they may have
been dead for all I knew—I usually just took off." He grew up in a poor, large, urban ghetto. He went to an inner-city public school. He was the leader of one of
the most influential Latino gangs in his school. He told me why. When he entered
high school, there was a ritual unknown to the adults in the school where ninth-
grade boys would be picked up by older students, have their legs spread, and be
rammed into a flag pole. My student was a large ninth grader, over 200 pounds,
and he said he was not going to let that happen to him. So as he left school after

his first day he was chased to the subway station by a group of older kids. They shouted after him. They caught him and one said, "what's your problem?" He told them he was just trying to get home. He did not flinch. One member of the group put a gun into my student's ribs, and said, "what's your problem, man?" Hector was convinced that he could not show any weakness or fear—a popular phenomenon for young people in cultures where violence is pervasive. "I got no problem. I'm just trying to get home . . . what are ya gonna do—shoot me right here in this open place with the cops right across the street?" They said that they had a problem with him running away from them. After more words were exchanged, Hector thought he was going to break down, but he kept up the front that he was unafraid. Then, he heard the one young man pull the trigger. Hector did not look down, or show any emotion, he just thought to himself, "oh my God, I've been shot and I'm bleeding. I'm going to die right here on the street." Suddenly, he looked down and the group started to laugh and praise Hector for his toughness. It was a starter pistol. The group of young men was impressed with Hector's bravery, so they wanted him in their gang. He knew that if he did not join he would be harassed daily. Within a year he was a leader. As he said, "there are thugs and there are smart folks, but few smart thugs. The smart thugs become the leaders and figure a way out—college was my way out." To get to college, however, he had to lead a double-life. He kept a pile of books and notebooks in his locker at school so his fellow gang members would think he was blowing off his school work, and he had a separate set at home that he would use to teach himself because he rarely went to class. The science teacher, who knew he was bright but doing what he needed to do to survive, spotted Hector roaming the halls. She asked him to help her clean test tubes. She got him interested in science. She helped him apply to college. He was accepted and graduated near the top of his engineering class.

Despite stories such as Hector's, nothing could have prepared me for my first few experiences with the group of "disadvantaged" and "at-risk" youngsters at WANTS. These labels quickly became problematic. We use these terms indiscriminately and frequently to describe young people of color who are poor.

Thinking About the Meaning of "At-Risk"

Many researchers have attempted to create an operational definition of "at-risk," or at least identify what places a young person at-risk. For example, Garmezy (1991) describes risk factors and the notion of "cumulated risk" (the more of these factors one has, the greater risk they have for a psychiatric disorder): "(1) severe marital discord, (2) low SES [socio-economic status], (3) overcrowding or large family size, (4) paternal criminality, (5) maternal psychiatric disorder, and (6) foster home placement of children in the family" (p. 128). Some of the at-risk college students with whom I worked had many of these risk factors, and they would have been labeled "resilient" by Garmezy's and others' standards. What these students had in common was that they each described having at least one person in their lives who believed in them and who stood by them unconditionally. I tried to be that person to the college students with whom I worked, but the truth was, they had already found that special person or people long before they met me. I wondered what happened to the young people who had nobody who believed in them or encouraged them—or at least felt as though nobody was there to protect them or help them. I embarked on a journey where I found out what happened to some of them.

My journey started with my awakening to the violence that was part of the daily life of some and my realization that there were many youngsters in my city who did not believe there was any hope for their futures.

My First Awakening:
Discussing Violence With "At-Risk" Kids From the "Hood"

I was asked to give two presentations on conflict resolution to a group of 20 seventh and eighth graders from a subsidized housing community. This group was on the local university campus for a residential four-week summer program. These children went to different middle schools, and some were about to enter high school in the fall. All of them were African American, and, as one young boy put it, they were from the "hood." Most felt that I, as a white woman, would not understand what their lives were like because as another boy said matter-of-factly, "she don't know what it's like in the 'hood.'" He was right, and I agreed with him. I told them that I was there to learn from them. I told them that I wanted to talk about ways they thought they could prevent fights and shootings from happening. Most of them wanted to share their experiences and did not seem to mind too much that the person they were telling did not look the way they did or did not come from the same neighborhood. In fact, the openness of many of them suggested that they enjoyed having someone listen to them and hear about their experiences. It seemed as though they were not used to someone asking them about their lives and genuinely caring about their answers.

I had read books about what life was like in the "hood" for young people. I watched disturbing media representations such as "Boys in the 'Hood.'" I thought I had some idea, but I had no idea. Nothing was as alarming as hearing about violence firsthand from the mouths of the children who were living it every day—

unwilling to hear some textbook solution such as conflict resolution or empathy training. They learned to accept that "it's just the way it is." They were at the age when they were learning how to survive in their worlds without adults to protect them, as well as the reasons to fight and rules of the game. They shared with me the violence that surrounded them every single day and how they learned to survive in it. I taught them communication skills and what it was like to be listened to and respected and have personal experiences matter. However, I wondered if they thought this was at all useful for them in their daily reality where one hit first and never had a chance to listen, even later.

Reasons to Fight. There were more boys than girls in each of the groups, and the boys seemed to dominate the conversation. I tried as much as possible to get the girls to speak, but this was not easy. However, the young girl who told me why people fight said succinctly as she counted on her hand, "money, drugs, and someone talking shit." Based on my discussion with these young people, I broadened the categories a bit. Money (because few of these young people actually have it) also meant turf or territory—whatever they felt they could claim as their own. Drugs often actually meant drug money because fights over drugs were rare, but fights over not paying for drugs were frequent. Someone "talkin' shit" meant someone talking about the other person in a bad way. This was also referred to as "he said/she said" that was frequently cited as a reason for fighting. If he or she was thought to have said something negative about another person either to that person's face or that they heard about (hence the he said/she said label), or if he or she got in the person's face (basically picking a fight face-to-face "talkin' shit"), then you had to fight or else you would risk being "jumped" by a group that the person would "hang with" (gangs) or you could get "punked," which was to be made to look like a fool.

The girls seemed to get into fights most often because someone was talkin' shit about them or over boys or boyfriends. One of the women, who was a college student charged with chaperoning these students, wrote a story of a typical fight she saw when she was in high school in the same local area:

> There was a girl who was minding her own business but because another girl was jealous she started talking about her. This girl—let's call her Jenny. Jenny was telling anyone who would listen that Keisha was a Ho [whore]. Well it got back to Keisha, and she confronted Jenny. Jenny wanting to look good in front of her friends started talking more trash and put her hands in Keisha's face. A fight started. Weave was flying. Well, when Keisha's boyfriend saw her get hit in the stomach and knowing that she was pregnant got mad and jumped in . . .

She told this story to the group as well and was immediately bombarded with questions such as "who won," "what happened to them," "what'd she do?" These seemed to be the questions that surround most fight stories. In this world of competition, fighting was about winning and losing. Winning was a sign of strength and an indication that one was worthy of respect—at least temporarily. However, one's strength was always being challenged, and these children felt that they had to keep fighting to prove that they were tough.

Guns and Gangs. Most of the boys agreed that the older boys were carrying guns. When I asked how much older, they said "high school boys." They knew some kids their age who carried BB guns that looked like real guns. One young boy said that he had been in a fight with a kid he had "beef " with (a reason that many gave for fighting, but when pressed to articulate what the "beef " was about, it often was about someone "talkin' shit" about them), and the kid had a BB gun and shot him in the shoulder. He said he wasn't scared because he knew it was not a real gun. When I asked him how he knew he said, "I knew because I knew the kid—we hung out in the beginning of the year." I asked, "so you used to be friends and he showed you his BB gun?" He said, "yes," and I asked him why they were no longer friends. He responded that he had "beef with him." When I asked why, he said he didn't know (also a common response to why one had beef or what kind of shit was being said).

Many talked about gangs but did not use the word *gang*. Because I was using their words as much as I could get away with, I did not use the word *gang* either. Nevertheless, "your boys" or the "people you hang with" were certainly gangs. They named some of the popular gangs in the area, so I knew they were talking about gangs. One asked me whom I hung with, and one of the girls, who had a bad attitude through the whole discussion and hardly contributed to it, said, "probably Brentwood or something" (Brentwood is a predominantly white suburb of the city).

One of the boys said that now that he was getting bigger, he could not walk places that he used to because he would get "jumped" (which frequently meant several boys attacking one person). He said he would always be asked "who are your boys" or "who do you hang with" when he would walk places, and when he was younger he would say nobody, and for the most part he was left alone. Now, he was saying this was no longer the case, so he felt that he had to "have some boys" to protect him. Being in a gang was seen as essential to survival in this environment, and a young man's allegiance was to his boys because they would save him and he should save them, even if it meant getting shot in the process. In many ways, one's "boys" were viewed as better able to protect these children than their families.

The Impact of Parents and Family Members. Violence has been taught to these children, some for generations, as the most appropriate way to resolve disputes.

Violence was practiced in the home where hitting and fighting were seen as a common way to resolve disputes. Parents condoned, and in some instances encouraged fighting, especially fighting in self-defense.

To provide an idea of some of the violence that may occur at home, I am quoting directly from what one of the girls wrote as her example of violence she had witnessed lately. I have elected not to put "sic" to denote spelling, punctuation, or grammatical errors and kept the text as it was to give full flavor to how students wrote. This particular young woman did share this text with the larger group as well:

> One time my brother and my father was fighting and my mother side to my brother don't be hitting him so my mother jumped in. Then I said well you is not going to jump my brother so I jumped in and my sister and then my brother girlfriend jumped in so we were all fight the next door people called the police and they came my mom open the door and closed it the police kicked our door down then we started fighting the police my brother girlfriend was throwing plates at them then I hit a police man in the head with the arin (iron) then they took all of us to jail. We all had to stay there over night.

A lot of fighting occurred to protect younger siblings or cousins. One boy described that he fought a kid who was talkin' shit to his little brother who was "really little" so he "snuffed him" (fought him). Also, if your cousin or sibling was in a fight that you witnessed, you had to get involved too. One girl described this in her writing:

> Once when I was in school and my friends were fighting and than my friend had pulled out some mase and tryed to mase my sister cousin than my sister cousin had polled out a knife and stabbed her in the thigh. Than they both went downtown and went to [juvenile detention home] for 2 days.

Family was important to many of these children. In fact, fighting to protect family members was crucial to demonstrating the importance of family. Some of these children learned about violence within their families through personal experience. Violence was a part of family life and encouraged. One of the boys said, "some kid was following me home wanting to fight. I told him I wouldn't. My grandmother wouldn't let me into the house 'til I fought him." In this case, walking away (an option preached frequently by schools) was not acceptable to what was being preached at home—if someone threatens you, you fight him or her.

The Impact of Peer Mediation and Other School Programs. I asked the students in each group if they had peer mediation programs in their schools. I knew that almost all of the schools in the district had peer mediation programs, but these youngsters did not know what peer mediation was—except for one of the girls who had been trained to be a peer mediator at her school. She said that she did not think it did any good because "as soon as the girls were out of school, they just started fighting again."

Many white privileged administrators and teachers like peer mediation because they think it makes a difference in reducing violence. For these children, mediation was not viewed as able to make a difference. It is not viewed as the best way to resolve disputes—fighting was. Mediation may buy some time, but the minute the tough conflicts were out of the sight of adults, they were likely to be resolved violently by children who did not see the value in finding a peaceful resolution to conflict.

Race. Race was never directly mentioned in discussions in the focus group or class. Perhaps because I was white and they were black. One of the girls did write about race playing a role in violence however:

> This white boy in my school was real prejudice and didn't like blacks. I was walking down the hall w/a few friends and he called me a Black B-tch. I got upset and punched him and gave him a bloody nose.

She gave two other examples. Both involved race. Interestingly, she did not share any of her stories with the group:

> This white girl in my school was big and a bully. We were outside playing football. She threw the ball and it hit my face. I jumped on her back and started kicking her. . . One day while I was walking down the hall in school this white girl called me a bitch. I got upset stepped to her and beat her down.

Race seemed to play an important role in both personal and structural violence to be discussed in greater detail later in the book.

The Perception of the School's Response to Violent Behavior. Most of these boys and girls seemed unafraid of the school's response to their violent behavior, or at least they did not seem to think about getting in trouble when they were in the "heat of the moment" of retaliation. One girl wrote:

> One day when I was in fourth grade I was sitting down talking to this girl while the teacher was out the class. This boy came up and hit me on the back of my head so I got up and chased him out the class and pushed him then I turned around and he hit me in the head agin and we started fighting in and out of classrooms and up and down the stairs. The boy went in the classroom and got a stick and hit me over the back so I started ramming his head into a locker. Then the teacher came and brook it up we had blood all over our faces and we got suspended but first we got in trouble by the prencible and superintendant. We got suspended for the first three mothes of the school year.

The girl's expectation after being attacked seemed to be that the school personnel would not protect her. Thus she had to do it herself and risk the consequences—although neither she nor the other student seemed to consider the consequences before engaging in the fight. Generally speaking, when students were angry, their first automatic response would be to fight back: "I was sitting on the floor and this boy was playing over me. I told him to stop playing over me and he kicked me in my head. And I got very upset and it got kind of violent."

The stories of violence were nearly always told as though the person telling it was the victim initially and needed to fight to avoid further victimization. Fighting was done regardless of the consequences. What frequently goes unnoticed by adult gaze is that many children who fight and behave aggressively learn these behaviors at home and in the neighborhoods—most often as victims. As children become more independent (as they enter adolescence), they determine ways to take the matter of their own safety into their own hands.

What About the Affluent School?

What was happening 20 miles away at a far more affluent place as these marginalized youths were learning strategies for protecting themselves from potentially deadly violence? I noticed the dramatic differences immediately between the urban schools where I had been conducting my ethnographic investigations and Lorenzo Hill, a much more wealthy suburban/rural school district. The schools within this district were clean, bright, and had newly renovated physical environments. They were quieter, and instances of obvious personal violence were much rarer. I found myself examining more subtle forms—bullying, ostracizing, and teasing. Even these behaviors occurred with little frequency. For the most part, teachers told students to do something, and they did it. Fights and hitting and other forms of physical violence happened outside of adult gaze—particularly on the buses and on the playground.

As far as structural violence in the wealthier district, it was rare to hear teachers or administrators talk of a student they felt should be placed on homebound instruction. I heard of only one in the elementary school and one in the middle school. In both cases, the school was considering this alternative only as a last resort. The district had an alternative high school for students who were thought to have drug problems and aggression problems. Most of these students tended to come from lower socioeconomic classes, but there were sometimes wealthy students there, too. These students were separated from the mainstream high school in many of the same ways as the WANTS students, and there were some similarities to be discussed later. However, it is important to mention that this school did not serve as the primary case study of this project—WANTS did. I learned about the alternative high school at Lorenzo Hill because I served on the board of directors. The more I learned about the students there through my participation on the board, the more I realized there were many similarities between it and WANTS, thus validating some of the theories espoused throughout this book.

There was poverty at Lorenzo Hill (13% qualifying for free or reduced lunches and breakfasts). These students were usually the same students who were in trouble more often, labeled as "special ed kids" and those "lacking in social skills." The boys from the lower socioeconomic groups were in trouble for physical violence far more often than the girls, but it was extremely rare to hear of girls fighting in any physical way. In fact, it was rare to hear of girls getting in serious trouble, which meant being sent to the principal's office. As the principal observed, "once girls get a detention once, you'll never hear from them again." The same boys seemed to cause the bulk of the problems with fighting and bullying and other forms of aggression.

Students at Lorenzo Hill did not have conversations that revolved around violence as I heard so frequently in the urban schools when children were having conversations without adults around them. Children's conversations were about parties and clothes and what they did in or after school. These activities and issues were what contributed to being "popular"—the most important concept in the affluent school. Being accepted and popular was incredibly important, and students who were not popular knew it and felt left out. These students tended to have the problems with violence and aggression.

I talk about myself and the experiences that brought me to this study because this background information is relevant to understanding how I framed this project and made sense of the experience as an ethnographer. In addition, I wanted to acknowledge how difficult it was for me, as it is for many others, to deal with school violence. Even so, we must accept the challenge and work collaboratively to reduce and ultimately eliminate school violence. We must start with our own experiences, perspectives, and biases before we undertake the challenging work of examining the context of each school and its respective school violence.

When adults create strategies to curb violence among young people, it is critical that we have a better understanding of the roots of the violence and how social processes increase the levels of personal and structural violence. We need to listen and examine how young people make sense of violence in their lives. This project focuses on a particular school within one particular poor urban district that I renamed WANTS and examines an affluent suburban school that I renamed Lorenzo Hill Central School.

This project began from the perspective of the researcher—entering into it from a social location with specific ideas, developed within a particular history. My goal was to understand how certain groups of people made sense of violence in their school lives. The information from the WANTS school was taken to create intervention strategies that were implemented during the second year of this project. During the second year, observations and interviews continued to be used to improve the interventions. Finally, after spending two years at WANTS, I conducted an ethnographic investigation at Lorenzo Hill Central School. I examined the effectiveness of a school-wide intervention conducted there—the "No Put-downs" Program.

The focus of the book is on the site where violence was more pervasive and dangerous—the WANTS school. It served as the primary case study. In this preface, we read the voices of young people from the same community as the WANTS students. Some ended up at WANTS. Many had relatives at WANTS. These youths from the community told us the meanings they attached to youth violence. I use their words to set up the book because they had been important in shaping my own thinking during the WANTS project. After listening to these groups of young people, I have realized how important it is to listen to what youth say they think violence is and why they behave violently. If we know that young people perceive themselves as victims—fighting back when they fight—then this issue needs to be addressed in violence reduction programming. If we hear from young people that they are fighting over drugs, money, turf, and self-respect and that they join gangs and carry weapons to keep themselves safe, then we can begin to address some of these issues related to violence. If we know that some young people grow up in families where violence is a part of daily life, then we need to make every effort to work with families and communities to develop alternatives to violence.

My journey to understand the experience of school violence remains unabated today. Most recently, I have considered it important to continue my quest by observing school violence issues in a more affluent school. I have included some of what I have seen in this district in this book because we need to examine what is happening at suburban wealthier schools to determine if the causes for students' violence there are fundamentally different from the causes of violence at urban schools. If the roots of students' violent behavior in wealthier schools are a lack of popularity, being ostracized, or a feeling of inadequacy, then we need to develop programs to address these issues for young people. It is difficult and time-consuming to listen to the voices of those living in a school community (students, teachers, administrators, and other staff—especially recess monitors and bus drivers), but we need to develop a deeper level of understanding within a community to determine why people are behaving violently. Survey instruments alone do not allow the kind of depth of information we need—qualitative methods help. We need to listen to individuals living in violent communities to understand how they make sense of violence in their lives. This is a difficult goal to meet, but it is important and necessary if we want to better understand the causes for violent behaviors and to begin to change them.

Acknowledgments

First and foremost, I would like to acknowledge and thank my family for their love, patience, and support throughout the creation of this book—specifically my husband Jon and my daughters Whitney and Dalton Jane. Without them this book would not have been written.

Many projects at several schools (the names have been changed to protect their anonymity) have culminated in the writing of this book. I would like to thank all of the administrators, parents, teachers, staff, and students who worked with me on gathering data for this project. In addition, thank you to my colleagues and funding agencies. Some of the funding for the research described in this book was made available from the Hamilton Fish National Institute on School and Community Violence. The funding was from Grant No. 97-MU-FX-KO12 (S-1) from the Office of Juvenile Justice and Delinquency Prevention, Office of Justice Programs, U.S. Department of Justice.

Furthermore, some funding was made available from Contact, Inc., of Syracuse, New York. Points of view or opinions in this book are those of the author and do not necessarily represent those of the U.S. Department of Justice or Contact, Inc.

The author also wishes to thank Scarecrow Press for permission to reprint portions of my previously published book "The PEACE Approach to Violence Prevention: A Guide for Teachers and Administrators." (*Portions of Part 3 and the Appendix are reprinted with permission from the publisher Scarecrow Press from chapters 4, and 5 in Williams, 2003. The PEACE Approach to Violence Prevention: A Guide for Administrators and Teachers. Scarecrow Press: Lanham, MD. For more detailed information about the approach, how to use the PEACE strategy step-by-step please refer to Williams, 2003.*)

Introduction

The Problem of Definition:
What Is Violence?

Any book about violence needs to address the issue of definition. What is violence? Who decides? Why is definition important? Which definition of violence do we use? There are no simple answers to these questions. Several attempts have been made to create comprehensive definitions of violence. Organizations such as the Centers for Disease Control and the American Psychological Association have come up with definitions of violence as have peace activists, authors, researchers, and others.

Despite efforts to create universal working definitions, there is no one correct or true definition of what violence is, but then, a single uniform definition is unnecessary. Violence is socially constructed, and the ways individuals construct meaning about violence are affected by aspects of social location (e.g., race, class, gender, age, geographic location, ability, religion, and so on). After all, it is the perceived threat of violence that often justifies decisions to behave violently. Improving our understanding of young people's perceptions of violence is essential to reducing violence in our schools.

This book presents a description and an analysis of how students and school personnel at the WANTS (Weapons Are Not Tolerated in School) alternative school for students who had been caught with weapons at their neighborhood schools made sense of violence. From the accounts of how violence was constructed by the children and adults at WANTS, this book critically examines both the personal and structural violence that people at WANTS experienced. After analysis of these accounts, methods of intervention were developed to reduce violence at the school. These intervention methods and other promising practices will be discussed in the final section of the book.

When I had completed my work at WANTS, I was hit with the news about Columbine High School in Littleton, Colorado. The events at that school in April 1999 reflect the most horrific single episode of school violence in our nation's history to date. This fact left me wondering as to what we really did know about school violence and its causes. What was different about affluent white suburban American schools and violence within them? I attended an affluent, white, suburban school. I had some thoughts, but I wanted to see for myself. What was happening among children at white affluent schools? How did relationships develop at the early ages when students were forming opinions about one another and starting their own cliques? How were students learning or failing to learn nonaggressive ways of behaving with one another? At what point and for what reasons do children begin to ostracize other children in the affluent school? I had so many questions as a result of the Littleton massacre that I felt that we knew so little. I decided to go back to the elementary and middle school levels to see what I could find out.

When I first began my observations at a predominantly white, upper-middle class suburban elementary school and middle school, I was struck by the marked contrast from my experiences at WANTS and the other urban schools. The schools were newly renovated, very bright and clean, and incredibly quiet. I was also shocked by how easily I could just walk in and walk around without anyone saying anything to me or making me sign in and state my purpose for being there. Almost all of the teachers and staff were white women with the rare exception of a white male. The children were all white with the very notable exception of a couple of darker-skinned students (there were no African American or Latino children that I ever saw).

I focused my observations on the most problematic areas—those where the most discipline referrals came from—recess and the bus. I also examined places where students had the most freedom from adult supervision such as in physical education class and in the hallways. However, in the elementary school, aides escorted the students quietly in rows to the appropriate classrooms when they needed to change classes. In addition, students sat with their homeroom teachers during lunch, and thus, they did not have freedom from adult gaze during lunch either. Even though buses and recess periods were supervised, the ratio of children to adults was higher than at any other time, and children acted free and more like children—silly and sometimes aggressive. If violence was going to happen, it was most likely to happen at these sites.

Interwoven into the analysis and discussion throughout the book is an examination into the underpinnings of violence within the more affluent suburban school and the implications for educators. More specifically, it is examined how students at these schools made sense of personal violence and issues of structural violence. Coincidentally, a program designed to reduce violence in grades K to 6 was being implemented at the same time when I made my observations. The implications of this program will be described in the final chapter.

Numerous school shootings or threats for intended school shootings that have shocked and frightened the entire nation have been featured in the media—both before and after the massacre in Littleton, Colorado. We have been bombarded with media images of dangerous white, suburban, affluent youths and notions that schools are far more violent places than ever. This is not necessarily the case, but now those in power are paying attention to these images, and they are motivated to do something about the problem. Despite the images, school violence is not just a problem of white, affluent America—violence is pervasive in urban schools. However, the solutions to ending violence in urban versus suburban schools may be somewhat different. The bottom line is we need to tailor programs to meet the specific needs of each individual school.

Violence in the Schools: A Brief Review of the Literature

Nationally, in 1995, according to data compiled by the Hamilton Fish National Institute on School and Community Violence, one in twelve high school students was threatened or injured with a weapon at school. Between 1992 and 1995, one third of all violent crimes against young people between 12 and 19 years of age occurred inside a school building or on school property. In 1995, two in five students between 12 and 19 years of age in urban centers reported that there were street gangs in their schools; one in five in rural areas; and one in four in suburban schools. In 1995, 4.5% of high school students stayed home from school one or more days in a month out of concern for their personal safety. Students in grades 7–12 made 34,200 visits to the doctor concerning injuries sustained in physical attacks at school. Nearly one of five public school teachers in the United States was threatened with injury by a student from his or her school (for more information on these statistics see www.hamfish.org).

According to a comprehensive report commissioned by the Office of Juvenile Justice and Delinquency Prevention published in 1997 and edited by Loeber and Farrington, chronic and serious juvenile offenders represent a very small proportion of the population of youths, but they are responsible for the majority of violent crimes. Schools struggle to identify youths at risk of becoming serious violent juvenile offenders (SVJs) in an attempt to protect other students. Schools adopt zero tolerance policies for weapons and drugs, and many schools remove students indefinitely. School reports of crime and responses to crime vary dramatically across the nation.

Incidents of Crime and Violence in Public Schools: The National Statistics

The U.S. Department of Education, National Center for Education Statistics (NCES) published a report in 1998 entitled "Violence and Discipline Problems in U.S. Public Schools: 1996-97" (see nces.ed.gov/pubs98/violence for more detailed information. This report synthesized the works of Mansfield, Alexander, & Farris, 1991; Bastian & Taylor, 1995; Nolan, Daily, & Chandler, 1995; Kachur, 1996). These authors surveyed administrators, teachers, and students across the country to determine the nature and extent of school violence in the 1990s.

In the NCES (1998) study when public school principals were asked to report the number of violent incidents that were reported in their schools during the 1996-97 school year, only incidents for which the police or other law enforcement officials had been contacted were included. Crimes that occurred in school buildings, on school grounds, on school buses, and at school-sponsored events or activities, but not officially on school grounds were included. According to these data, during 1996-97, about 4,000 incidents of rape or other types of sexual battery were reported in our nation's public schools. There were about 11,000 incidents of physical attacks or fights in which weapons were used and 7,000 robberies in schools that year. About 190,000 fights or physical attacks not involving weapons also occurred at schools in the 1996-97 school year, along with about 115,000 thefts and 98,000 incidents of vandalism. No murders were reported by any of the 1,234 public schools, and only four schools in the sample reported any incidents of suicide. However, in a study published in the *Journal of the American Medical Association* about violent deaths in schools, Kachur (1996) estimated that there were 105 school-associated violent deaths, including 85 murders occurring at schools during a two-year period from 1992 to 1994.

According to the Bureau of Justice Statistics, the following were found in 2001:

- In 2001, students 12 through 18 years of age were victims of about 161,000 serious violent crimes at school, and about 290,000 away from school. Between 1992 and 2001 victimization rates at school and away from school declined.

- In 1993, 1995, 1997, 1999, and 2001 about 7% to 9% of students in grades 9 to 12 reported being threatened or injured with a weapon such as a gun, knife, or club on school property in the past 12 months.
- In 2001, about 6% of students carried a weapon such as a gun, knife, or club on school property in the past 30 days, a decline from 12% in 1993.
- Sixteen school-associated homicides were of school-age children between July 1, 1999 and June 30, 2000.
- In 2001, 20% of students reported the presence of street gangs in their schools.

Despite recent downward trends in school violence, schools are still far from "violence-free." There is still a lot of work to be done to address the issue.

What Happens When Students Are Caught: The National Data

A survey conducted by the U.S. Department of Education, National Center for Education Statistics 1997, entitled "Principal/School Disciplinarian Survey on School Violence" asked respondents to indicate how many of three specific actions were taken against students for each of the following offenses: possession or use of a firearm; possession or use of a weapon other than a firearm; possession, distribution, or use of alcohol or drugs, including tobacco; and physical attacks or fights. Schools were asked to report the number of expulsions, transfers to alternative schools or programs, and out-of-school suspensions lasting five or more days for each of the aforementioned offenses. This list of three discipline actions was not exhaustive, but these were the only three options the survey offered. The results were as follows:

Firearms. Five percent of all schools reported taking one or more of these three actions against students for a total of 16,587 actions for the possession or use of a firearm. Nearly half reported out-of-school suspensions lasting five or more days (49%). Twenty percent of students from the schools surveyed were transferred to alternative schools or programs. Thirty-one percent of students were expelled for possession or use of a firearm.

Weapons Other Than a Firearm. This survey defined weapons other than firearms as any instrument or object used with the intent to threaten, injure, or kill, including knives, razor blades, or other sharp-edged objects, ice picks or other pointed objects, baseball bats, sticks, rocks, or bottles. Twenty-two percent of public schools took one or more of the specific actions (described above) against students for possession or use of a weapon other than a firearm. About 58,000 actions were reported: 23% of the students using such weapons were expelled; 22% were transferred to alternative programs or schools; and 55% were suspended out-of-school for five or more days.

Physical Attacks or Fights. About 40% of all public schools reported having taken at least one of the actions against students for fighting for an estimated total of 331,000 actions. Most schools reported suspending students out of school for five or more days (66%). The remainder of the schools transferred students to alternative schools or programs or expelled them (19% and 15%, respectively).

Clearly there was great diversity among schools in the nation in the treatment of violent and violence-related behaviors. While some schools expelled students for fighting, drug use, and carrying weapons, others did not. During the time of the WANTS project (1997–99), and for the year prior, the federal government applied pressure on schools to create "zero tolerance" policies for drugs and violence. At least 75% of all schools reported having zero tolerance policies for various student offenses (U.S. Department of Education Statistics). The U.S. Department of Education defined "zero tolerance policies" as school or district policies that mandated predetermined consequences or punishments for specific offenses. Ninety-four percent of schools reported zero tolerance policies for firearms and 91% for weapons other than firearms. Eighty-seven percent had policies of zero tolerance for alcohol and other illegal drugs, and 79% had a zero tolerance policy for tobacco. Seventy-nine percent had generalized zero tolerance policy to punish any form of violence (see U.S. Department of Education Statistics). However, these punishments have been far from uniform, ranging from suspension to expulsion. Schools with no crime reported were less likely to have a zero tolerance policy for violence (74%) than schools that had reported one or more serious crimes (85%) (U.S. Department of Education Statistics, 1998). This book will discuss some of the problems associated with zero tolerance policies and how students and others at WANTS experienced their effects.

An Introduction to the WANTS Alternative School

The national statistics set the stage for the national climate and diversity of policies around weapon-carrying, zero tolerance policies, violent behavior, and drug use. To illustrate how these national and local policies are experienced every day, I have drawn upon the results of a qualitative, ethnographic case study I conducted at Weapons Are Not Tolerated in School (WANTS) alternative school.

WANTS is a pseudonym—all identifiable characteristics including names have been changed.

The WANTS school is located in a medium-sized urban area of about 250,000 people. According to the police reports for juvenile arrests in the city, there had been an increase of 24% in offenses 15 years of age or younger (from 830 in 1996 to 1031 in 1997) with the largest increases in aggravated assault (90% increase), arson (100%), and sexual assault (111%).

The WANTS school was developed in response to the growing number of students caught with weapons in school. The perception that weapon-carrying was on the rise was so pervasive that the district attorney's office offered a $50 reward to students who reported that other students had weapons in school. The result within this poor urban school district was that students would set up other students for the money by planting weapons on others and then reporting them. The WANTS school was created as an alternative to expulsion for students who were caught with weapons because it was cheaper to educate all the students together than to educate them all individually at home (as mandated by the state that all students were to be educated until age 16, even if this meant providing individual homebound instruction).

I met the school counselor for WANTS in a class I was auditing on school violence. After speaking with her about the school, I wanted to learn more about it, the students, and the staff. I set out to conduct an ethnographic research project in the school starting in September 1997. My goal was to understand how the students and staff made sense of violence in their lives because only a few studies on violence have included the perceptions of those most likely to be victims or victimizers. The students at WANTS were considered at high risk of violence because they had already been caught with a weapon at school. This "at-risk" label quickly became problematic because many students indicated they were carrying weapons because they were trying to protect themselves. I began to question whether these children were more at-risk of being perpetrators, as the label was meant to suggest, or victims. Nevertheless, the popular perception among those least familiar with the students at WANTS (myself included when I first started observing) was that the students there were dangerous criminals—somehow deserving to be removed from the mainstream educational experience.

First-Day Jitters

I still remember how I felt the first day I went to WANTS. I was nervous and slightly scared because I knew that these students had been caught with *weapons* in school. It was not particularly comforting that students caught with firearms had

been expelled from their neighborhood schools and now resided in the local juvenile detention facility (if they were younger than 16 years) or in jail (if 16 years
or older) and were not sent to this school instead. I was still concerned about what
students who would bring other weapons (knives, blades, box cutters, and other
dangerous objects) to school would be like.

As I drove through the neighborhood to get to the school, I was troubled to
see a lot of houses with boards over the windows and trash strewn in the yards. I
saw a young girl, probably kindergarten age, get off a bus in the middle of the afternoon. A woman, presumably her mother, came out of a house that I was sure
was condemned, and took this little girl inside. This image suggested such poverty
that persons, I was sure, who didn't work or live here usually didn't see.

A young blonde woman driving alone in a brand new car with a CD player
made me, I thought, the perfect target for a robbery or an attack. The voice of my
friend Jules—my friend who had grown up and still lived in this neighborhood—
echoed through my brain, "it will be a wake up call for you Kim—no more cushy
little university office with all your clean-cut college kids . . . you'll see what it's
really like down here in the 'hood.'" My heart sank when I realized that I would
probably be unwelcome at first, partly because of my affiliation with the university
and partly because of my social location (age, gender, race, geographic location,
and so on). Assumptions would be made about me in the same way I was making
assumptions about those whom I would meet.

The guidance counselor, April, had given me good directions and I drove
right to the school. I was struck by how close it was to the university—only a few
city blocks. It was attached to a large church—decades before it had been a Catholic school. When I drove into the parking lot, I looked around at the houses.
Some were in pretty good shape, but most were dilapidated large houses—similar
in structure to most of the homes right around the university, and somewhat akin
to the homes where the undergraduates who had the keg parties regularly lived. I
walked into the building and followed the signs to the second floor. I ran into a
man and asked him where the program was. Kindly, he took me right to the office
of April Dempsey.

April greeted me and we talked about the nature of the school, why students
were sent here, and so on. She explained that kids in grades 7 through 12 were
sent here if they were caught with a weapon in school as a result of the district's
zero tolerance policy. Because of this rule many students were sent to WANTS not
because they had necessarily used weapons, but they had carried items with them
that could be construed as weapons. For example, some students may have
brought paring knives to school to cut their apples, while others may have had
metal nail files in their coat pockets for obvious use; still others may have had box

cutters in their jackets from their after-school jobs at the local grocery store for opening boxes. After these items were discovered in the students' possession, they all attended a formal hearing and then were sent to WANTS. It had been in existence for nearly five years—starting in a very small building with a small grant from the state to pay the salaries of one guidance counselor and two teachers. Since the beginning, staff had increased to one guidance counselor, two full-time teachers, eight part-time teachers, hall monitors, a part-time nurse, a full-time administrator, and some other help.

April gave me a tour of the school and introduced me to some of the teachers and other staff. She took me down the dark, musty smelling hallway to the large classrooms. The school was only a lengthy corridor on the second floor of the building. There was a gymnasium on the first floor, but students were only allowed down there during physical education—which they only had every other day.

I observed that some students had their heads on their desks. Some students were standing up as the teacher tried to lecture. Others were laughing and joking together as the teacher worked with another group. I saw teachers trying to lecture, and some were working with small groups of students. I noticed that the overwhelming majority of students were African American, and there was an even split of boys and girls. By contrast I realized that all the teachers were white. As we walked past the main office, April took me in and introduced me to the principal. When I met him, I realized that he was only the second African American adult I had seen in the building (the first was the man who showed me to April). I told him a bit about my project, and he seemed interested in it. He was getting ready for another meeting, and thus we did not have much time to talk.

April took me to the dark end of the hallway and showed me a very small library with books that had been discarded from a public library and those purchased from a small grant that one of the teachers was able to obtain before she left. There was also a computer room with a handful of fairly new machines.

I watched students as they passed from class to class. As with most teenagers, there was a lot of shouting and loud talking, teasing, harassing, poking, and playful hitting. I saw some students pick on one of the smaller boys. The hall monitors were visible and directing students to their next assigned place.

We went back to April's office. We talked some more. I noticed that students did not have lockers. They brought their jackets and packs into the principal's office every morning where they were searched. Some students would be frisked, and sometimes administrators would use the "wand" (a handheld metal detector) on students. Backpacks, coats, and personal belongings were stored in an office until the end of the day when they were picked up again.

The Structure of the School and the School Day

Students were split into "middle school" (grades 7 and 8) and "high school" (grades 9–12), and there was almost an even number in these two groups according to the roster, that included 68 names at the outset of the year. April explained that the high school group was deceptively small because once many of these students turned 16, school was no longer mandatory, and many of them dropped out. Others, though, remained on the roster until they had missed 21 consecutive days and were removed from it by default.

The day was organized around these two groups. There was mandatory community service for two hours per day for all students. The middle school students would attend their community service in the morning from 9 A.M.– 11 A.M. The high school students would attend their community service in the afternoons from 12:30 P.M. – 2:30 P.M. Each of the groups had four half-hour classes. The instruction for most groups included social studies, science, math, and English/reading. These groups rotated so that students could also take physical education and computers/introduction to occupations every other day. All students also had a half-hour break for lunch. This is how the day was supposed to work. However, the transition from theory to practice in this case was not smooth. Most students (roughly 80%) never attended their community service placements. When I asked what happened to them, April told me that they received an "F" on their report card. She said that many of the students did not seem to care about failing a class or two—particularly a course such as community service that carried no credit.

In April's office, which she shared with the part-time school psychologist, she showed me a list of the students. I noticed that there were many more students in eighth and ninth grades than in any of the other grade levels. "What's happening then?" I asked. April told me that students were beginning to figure out that adults could not protect them anymore, and so they felt they needed to take responsibility for their own protection. They shield themselves the way many adults do—they carry weapons. Instead of pepper spray (that I carried, and some of them were caught with it, too), some had knives and box cutters with them. These weapons were almost never raised in anger to hurt anybody—although there were a few cases when this happened—mostly they were meant to protect themselves from rival gangs, ex-boyfriends, ex-girlfriends, bullies, and so on.

After my first day, I thought I had a better understanding and appreciation of these young people. My anxiety was beginning to wane, partly because of April's calming effect. The way she talked about these students was comforting. For the most part, she could appreciate where they were coming from, and she did not assume the worst about them. She saw them as products of an environment of poverty and violence—as children trying to stay alive the only way they knew how. I had only just begun to understand what this school was all about.

I thanked April for her hospitality. We arranged that I would come back to observe a program, "Respect," conducted by an agency that dealt with dispute resolution and that was funded by the United Way. I happened to know the woman who would be the trainer, Annie, from an observation I had conducted at another high school's peer mediation program. She was one of the best trainers I had ever observed and the only person of color I knew who did mediation and violence prevention programs for students. The students in the group of peer mediators seemed to respect and enjoy learning from her. I was looking forward to seeing her interact with the students at the alternative school.

My Introduction to the Field:
The First Middle School Student Observation

The middle school students (grades 7-9) comprised the majority of students at WANTS, and they were the ones going to attend the two-hour Respect program. I met with April and Annie before it began. April told us that there had been a major fight in the cafeteria just moments before because of feuding gang factions. She said these kinds of fights happened frequently in the cafeteria and were usually because of gang hostilities. The group of students who were fighting had just gone through the Respect program that morning. I observed the same phenomenon when I worked with another group of students during one summer (described in the preface). Immediately following my lessons on how to listen and communicate respectfully and how to resort to alternative strategies to violence, there was a huge fight, and consequently some students were removed from the program. Perhaps students in a culture where violence was so important needed to maintain the status quo after such lessons by fighting. In addition, when programs such as these were only given once in a while, students showed their defiance by behaving violently.

The three of us walked to the cafeteria after it was announced to the middle school students that they were to gather in the cafeteria. The only staff members there were the nurse and April despite repeated reminders to the teachers to attend. Most of the teachers had left for the day. When asked to put on name tags, most of the students put on their gang nicknames and another tag with their gang affiliation.

Annie introduced herself and then me so that I would have a comfortable entrance discussing my reasons for being there. She went over the agenda and the rules. The group was segregated by race and gender, although there were only two white boys there and one girl who might have been partially white, and she sat alone on the end—next to a group of boys who seemed to be members of the same gang. When Annie went over the ground rules, some of the students were fidgety. Several boys seemed preoccupied with their name tags, laughing at the gang names and membership. Annie asked if they needed to separate from others who might be distracting to them.

She said we were going to play Bingo and there would be prizes for those who got the most Bingos. "What's the prize?" several asked, but she only responded "you'll see." I participated. The students seemed to take this very seriously and seemed to actively participate in the game. Many came up and asked if I was playing. I was assertive too and sought out others. At this point there were 18 students, nine girls and nine boys, including the two white boys. One girl and one white boy sat outside. The other white boy sat next to me. The health teacher/nurse sat outside and did not participate.

After Human Bingo (where students had to find people who were different from themselves in a variety of ways), the students would not settle down. Annie had to stop talking twice and would not continue until all was quiet—some of the girls shouted for others to "shut up" and let her speak. We played a game called Hurricane, which involved running from one chair to the next, but Annie stopped it after two rounds because kids were tipping over the chairs and pushing each other to the ground. The final straw for Annie was when someone slid into her newsprint. She observed, "obviously we can't play this game without hurting each other."

She had the students return to their seats, and she sat silently and said, "when you're ready, let me know." When they had quieted down, she said, "I want to talk about conflict, and then we'll see a video." She had an agenda that was printed on newsprint with the ground rules clearly identified. On the paper she wrote "conflict" as she had done with the previous group. She said, "give me another word for conflict." Students shouted out: argument, disagreement, problem, fight, war, beef (giggles happened at this one), drama (some girls chanted almost in unison, "save yo drama fo' yo' mama . . .").

At this point there was almost total gender and racial segregation. Some of the girls started saying, "what's his problem?" about one of the boys across the room from them who would not be quiet. Annie stopped again and said to the rowdy group of adolescents that she would wait to continue when she could get the respect that she expected. She added that she did not like to be disrespected and that she had not and would not disrespect them. She sat silently. When there was no sign of the acting out behaviors stopping, she asked, "What needs to happen for this to work?" The girls said they should kick out Ray, who was one of the main trouble-makers, but Annie responded that she didn't want to do that.

Finally, after much shushing, the group settled down somewhat. Annie asked what was positive or negative about each of the things on the newsprint. The students in the group had a tough time articulating why some points were positive and others negative. Annie helped out by giving some examples. I was struck by one girl, who sat next to the group of boys and who was sucking her thumb throughout the session. Nobody said anything to her, but it made me realize how young and insecure these children were despite their attempts to act out and act tough.

> "What's negative about beef ?" Annie asked. (Beef was a popular term in this environment to denote having a serious conflict with a person or group that was expected to result in a fight.)
>
> Ron said, "if you're less than 30 deep . . ." (meaning that if you had less than 30 people in your gang to support you).
>
> "Fighting," Annie asked, "is it positive or negative?"
>
> Fighting was seen as positive and negative. Annie pointed out that you didn't have to use fists to fight—you can use words. Physical fighting was seen as positive and negative also.
>
> Annie asked, "Why negative?"
>
> Students replied, "because someone could get hurt."
>
> "Why positive?"
>
> "Some fight over stupid stuff like if yo' mother gets jumped you hafta protect her," one of the students said.

At this point people were talking over one another, and Annie stopped again. Most teenagers in the group were no longer paying attention. Students had a difficult time focusing on one thing for more than a couple of minutes.

Annie was able to bring them back on task eventually, but it took a few minutes of laughing and hitting and talking loudly. Eventually, they gave examples of the United Parcel Service strike as a positive fight and that verbal fights were negative if they involved cussing and swearing and threatening; some in the group told Ray (the main troublemaker) to shut up. One girl said to Ray from across the room, "what did (someone) ever see in you she must've been ignorant."

The thumbsucker and Ray had words, and April went and sat behind them. Then they were moved. Annie tried her mediation skills on the two of them, but they were not buying into it. Things escalated and became more heated and loud. One girl, who had been quiet throughout, asked whether she could go back to class. Others piped in, too, "Can I go back to class?" Annie said, "Who would rather be in class because I'd rather work with a smaller group of folks who want to participate than those who don't." About half said they would—April led them out, and Annie continued with those who remained. April couldn't find the staff, so she didn't know what to do with the kids. Thus, the principal came in, and the others came back. He scolded them and took those who wanted to leave out of the room.

Annie thanked those who stayed and asked, "How do we fight?"

"Hit, swing, kick, bite, pick up somethin' and bash in the head, weapons, stab, slam, stomp, hair-pulling, grab clothes, jump 'em," were the answers members of the group shouted. Ray said so all could hear, "strip 'em naked and rape 'em." Penny, who was often outspoken (I later discovered she had been sexually molested by her stepfather for years), stood up and screamed, "Who said that—that's not funny—rape 'em—that's disgusting . . . who said that?" She picked up one of Annie's markers and threw it in the direction of the group of boys from where the comment had come. The principal came in at that moment and said, "Penny, you're outta here . . ." Annie pointed to Ray and said, "you're outta here too." The principal escorted Ray out, too—now the group seemed very small.

Annie continued, "When is hitting positive?"

One girl said, "when your mom hits you because you have no business doin' somethin' you're doin'."

"All these," Annie said, "are forms of violence . . . anytime you fight you risk dying. . . what is your goal when you fight?"

Someone answered, "to beat the other person down."

"So this means you win," Annie asked, "can there be a situation where both win . . . are you sayin' that the only thing you can do is fight?" There were nodding heads and words of affirmation before Annie continued, "I believe that there are, and I just want you to think about some of the alternatives . . . and some of the consequences." She had us get into a circle and play the question game before we went to another room to watch a video. I told Annie that I had to get back to campus for another meeting and that I would call her. She, like April, was not disgusted with the students' behavior, but with the staff and the fact that they had taken off for the day when they were supposed to be around to help with the students during the program.

Frustration in these situations was obvious—on both the students' and the adults' parts. Adults want to talk to young people about making rational decisions that consider the consequences of behavior. Some people, including many young people, react emotionally out of passion without considering the consequences. Students think that adults do not understand, and adults cannot understand why young people will not listen to them. This is an age-old struggle of adolescence, but the issue here is that both parties want to stay alive. Young people have weapons, fight, and join gangs to protect themselves in order to stay alive, and adults tell them not to carry weapons or they will end up getting killed or imprisoned. Thus, when our words do not cut it, we send them to watch their favorite medium—television. Whenever I observed students watching television, even the most disruptive students who usually could not sit still, sat still and listened to it. Television provided them a chance to enter another world, albeit temporarily, a world in which they did not have to think too deeply about their lives.

Young people in this environment needed a place to air their feelings with another person. Programs such as the one Annie offered were only one-time educational experiences, and there was rarely any kind of follow-up. Most teachers did not see the classroom as an appropriate place to resolve students' social, emotional, and family problems. Consequently, when these emotions erupted as "discipline problems," teachers removed the students from class or told them to be quiet. "Good students" were the ones who kept their pain and passion to themselves.

There were clear tensions between some students and some staff, between certain members of the staff, and between students. On my first full day of observing, I only began to see the tip of the iceberg. There were many conflicts lurking underneath the surface. Without a real understanding of alternative ways to deal with conflict, many of these students behaved violently toward each other and toward adults in the school. Some withdrew entirely because they did not feel safe (as evidenced by the extremely low 60% attendance rate). Some tried to do what they had to do to survive and hoped to get back to their "regular" school. Teachers had their own challenges. They struggled with the mixed messages that the administration sent them and to meet the needs of their students without having any preparation or training to work with this population. They had difficulty teaching without resources. Teachers felt disenfranchised and frustrated as well. The combination of frustrated teachers and frustrated students resulted in a conflict and violence-laden environment. The students, teachers, and administrators all had unique perspectives about WANTS.

Introduction to Key Informants at WANTS

Throughout my year and a half at WANTS, I had an opportunity to interview most of the staff and many students. There was a bit of staff turnover from the first year of my observations to the second. Most notably, the principal, the social studies teacher, the school nurse, and the sixth-grade teacher left.

Introduction to the Teachers and the Administration

Jerry. Jerry, the social studies teacher, was a white male and somewhat short and stocky. His mannerisms suggested that he was slightly insecure about his teaching and about himself. This was his first regular teaching job, and he was new to WANTS during the first year of my observations. In fact, he was quite paranoid about my role and regularly joked about me being an undercover newspaper reporter. His teaching certification was in social studies, and, after a year of being a substitute teacher, he considered himself "lucky" to have been offered a job at WANTS, although he left the school for a full-time teaching position after only one year. He briefly explained his background preparation as follows, "I spent a few years in the military; that's how I paid for college. I went to the University of B and I got a BA in history, and from there I came back to [this city] because my wife's originally from here, and after working in the business world for a couple of years, I decided to go back to teaching. I went to C State and got my teaching credentials there and got a BS in elementary and early secondary education."

Even though he was a part-time teacher, he taught six *different* courses each day. He claimed that nothing he had learned in his teacher prep curriculum prepared him for what he encountered every day at WANTS. He was known for sending students to the principal's office for offenses other teachers considered relatively insignificant, although he did struggle to reach the students. His frustration, though, was clear on his face and in the tone of his voice when he would describe his "trial and error" method of teaching.

Barry replaced Jerry. Like him, he was another new teacher who had just completed his undergraduate teaching degree. Barry was popular among students. He was tall, white, young, and typically patient with students, and he seemed to get along well with his colleagues. He really enjoyed teaching at WANTS.

Paul. Paul was a thirty-something white male, who considered himself a good math teacher. He was one of the only two full-time teachers who had been at WANTS since it opened its doors four years before my observations. Paul's mannerisms, his way of dressing, and his slicked-back hair reflected self-assurance. He liked to brag about his teaching ability and acted as if he could handle any challenge. As one of the informants said about him after our interview, "Did he break his arm from patting himself on the back?" Other teachers seemed to share this view of Paul as having a somewhat overly inflated opinion of himself. However, upon further analysis, he seemed to be good at playing the same game that students did "frontin' it" (acting tougher, stronger, and more self-assured than one actually was to avoid victimization and to receive respect). He described his thoughts about his teaching as follows:

> I am a teacher. I do teach these kids. I do not just hand out things and say, do it. And I'm teaching multiple subjects, more so than I should be. I'm teaching eight different courses. Now not all the teachers do that. Raji teaches a hand full up there, too, but I think you all understand that most teachers only do preparation for three courses at best. Now whether you have 70 kids or 170 kids its still a lot of work to do the preparation, and when you are prepping for eight different courses you can understand sometimes I might get tongue-tied. I'm teaching multiple courses at once in a few classes. Not all the teachers are doing this. In math, for each grade level, especially in 9th, 10th, and 11th grade, there is like three or four different courses you can take in each grade, which makes my job more difficult. It makes me a better teacher because I understand the content in all areas from 7th through 12th grade where most teachers who have been teaching for a while might just understand 10th grade. It's one thing to know, it's another thing to teach it. And most teachers might just teach 9th and 10th grade all their lives. Some teachers just teach 7th grade for 20 years. Here I'm teaching it all at the same time and all the time.

Paul's demeanor suggested that he had mastered the challenging art of teaching various levels of math to WANTS students. This accomplishment was evident in that he had not sent any students to the principal's office this year because, according to him, he was a well-trained mediator and could deal with conflicts himself as they arose in his classroom.

Sherry. Sherry was an African American woman, a mother of four, and probably in her early forties. She was filling in for a woman who had gone on maternity leave after her first month of teaching. Sherry's assigned subject area was Spanish, but she did not speak Spanish—nor had she ever taken a course in it. Sherry's lack of knowledge in the subject area she was supposed to teach is indicative of the fact that frequently underqualified or inexperienced teachers were sent to WANTS. To remedy her deficit, she was taking a course offered by the district to teach her basic Spanish. As she put it:

> So they [administrators at the district office] say, "well, the only thing available is the weapons program," and they said, "well, do you know Spanish?" And I said, "well, I've had three years of French in high school, and I've learned Italian when I was in the military alert in Italy." And I said, "I probably could just go with what I know."

And they said, "well just wing it." So I came and I thought it was going to be a few days until they got a certified Spanish teacher, and it turned out that they were having difficulty finding a certified Spanish teacher in the district.

Sherry had been at the school for somewhat more than a month when I interviewed her. Ironically, some of the students were more advanced than she was, but she did the best she could. She was a clear example of a teacher in her early days at WANTS trying to learn what would work with her students with no guidance. Like all new teachers at WANTS she described her approach to working with these students as being through "trial and error." She was the only African American teacher at the school.

Raji. Raji was Asian Indian, and she occasionally wore traditional Indian dress. She was in her late thirties, and had been teaching for several years. Raji was at WANTS from the beginning as a full-time teacher with Paul. The two of them seemed to have a bond because of their shared experience at WANTS. She taught all the science courses and admitted that her comprehensive preparations for these courses included biology (two different tracks), chemistry (two different tracks), earth science (two different tracks), and health. For a while, she also taught French and Spanish. She felt she had learned a great deal about teaching these students through trial and error and her time at WANTS. She decided not to apply to a regular school because of her efforts for these courses and for the students at WANTS. At a new school she would have had to prepare new material.

Chris. Chris was a rather large white man. His age was difficult to judge, but he had not been teaching long. He had had his own business and had worked in industry for a while before getting certified to teach business and social studies. He was the business and computer teacher and taught the mandatory "Introduction to Occupations" course. Although this course had the potential to help students set goals and make steps toward becoming productive members of society, he did not consider the curriculum as useful.

Tom. Tom was a white male, short and athletic, and approximately in his mid-thirties. His subject area was English. Tom began teaching at WANTS when the school was started, but he claimed that because he was the third person interviewed and there were only two full-time openings, he was made a part-timer. This part-time situation was a position that he and others obviously resented. He talked about all that he would do if he were a full-timer, but his other part-time job prevented him from becoming full-time. Tom was the only teacher who met with students outside of class. He ate lunch in the cafeteria with them, and he would bring some of them to rugby games on the weekends.

Administration and Other Staff People

Bruce. Bruce was an African American man who had been the acting administrator at the school since its inception. I had very little contact with him until near
the end of the school year when I had a chance to meet with him and ask him if
he would be willing to be interviewed. Bruce was burned out, and he admitted it.
He said that he had many stress-related physical ailments that caused him to miss
many days of school. He saw himself as a pioneer who was creating a school unlike
any other, and like many pioneers, there were times when he wanted to turn back.
There were times when he wished he had kept his job as a teacher. As he said:

> There were just so many things coming at you—myself and the staff. As I think back
> now if I had known that these are some of the things I would have had to handle, I
> probably would have stayed in the classroom. But I guess it's that way with all
> trailblazers. I guess that's the true trailblazer. You don't know what you're blazing
> into. You just blaze in. Sometimes you blaze through things, around things, or under
> things, but you are trying to arrive at some destiny. You try to get to some end point,
> but you just don't know where it is or when it's going to stop. And I'm still making
> progress toward that end point. I guess that's a good statement to make, end point. I
> don't know if there's an end point or when I'm going to get to it.

Bruce was replaced at the end of the year, shortly after our interview. He was
sent to an urban middle school in the district—with almost no warning. Despite
his having built the WANTS school from the beginning, he became a victim of
budget cuts and seniority rules. He was "bumped" by a white female administrator, Catelyn, who was nearing retirement.

Before Catelyn started, teachers were very upset. They thought she was un-
qualified because of her previous position as a library media specialist. However,
they did not know that she had been working in the district for 30 years and had
worked as a teacher, vice-principal, principal, and had a variety of experiences and
knew many of the students, their parents, and other teachers and administrators
in the district. When she took over, teachers grew to appreciate her and like her
"no holds barred" approach to administration. She was clearly an advocate of her
staff and her "babies" as she called the students.

Kelly. Kelly was a white woman, in her thirties and matronly. She had only
been at WANTS for two months when I interviewed her. I interviewed her the
day before she left. She had a two-year-old child at home and said that she was
quitting to spend more time with him because she had seen what a lack of parenting had done for the children at WANTS. She talked about the children in ways
similar to April, the school counselor, and Nancy, one of the key administrators,
not as poorly behaved troubled children but as victims of poor environments. For
her, as for April and Nancy, these were basically "good kids" who just didn't have

a lot of support at home. It was clear to me that she cared about the children at WANTS and said that she was very sad to leave some of them. She had created a place where students could come and feel safe, a space where they could talk about things that were difficult for them. Some, she said, would pretend being ill just so they could come and talk to her. She gave her most recent example, Ron, who knew the latest shooting victim in the city: "He knew the person shot. I asked him what the reason was and I asked him if it was gang related, and he said most probably it was gang related . . . His stomach ache, which turned out to not be a stomach ache but his way out of class to come in and talk. . . . Because I asked him if he truly did have a stomach ache . . . he said, 'well I think this stuff is both-ering me' . . . and that's what I find with a lot of the kids in this program. They don't have true physical illness, but they need to talk." Kelly, in her short time at WANTS had built a rapport of a sense of safety and trust with the students.

Nancy. Nancy was a short, stocky, tough, white woman. She did not take any grief from anyone. She was the acting administrator during the nearly two months early in the year when Bruce, the principal, was out with a bad back. Some of the students remembered her from the middle school where she had previously been an administrator and blamed her for sending them to WANTS. One high school boy suggested, "Send her back to Lincoln [middle school]. Nobody wants her here!" In other words, students were very open about their anger toward her. She did not seem to let their attacks faze her, though. She was tough and fair with them and said on one occasion, "You see I amazingly know a lot of these children because I've been at different schools and I've dealt with many of these kids. I went to the hearings of some of these kids that resulted in them being assigned here." The teachers seemed to think she was the best thing that had happened to WANTS. Eventually, she gained the respect of the students as well.

April. April had really been my primary informant throughout this process. April was a white woman, approximately in her mid-forties, and the mother of two adolescent children who attended one of the high schools in the district. She had been a full-time guidance counselor at WANTS since its inception and had a great deal of input in the decisions that were made at the school. Because April knew the background stories of the children at WANTS, she had been very helpful about sharing some of the pain and suffering she heard about and observed daily. She and I developed a friendship, and she came to enjoy our conversations. She told me on several occasions that she was grateful to have somebody with whom she could discuss the difficult issues related to the school. When she tried to talk to the teachers about these children's lives, they sometimes betrayed her confi-dence and would tell each other or embarrass the students. For example, she related a story to me about the last time she confided in the teachers about a student who was having a difficult time. He was getting ready to testify against a police officer, who was charged with raping him. In the course of the conversation, she mentioned to the teachers that he might be having a difficult time and might need to leave class to come to the guidance office to talk. To her dismay, a few of the teachers said things in front of the other students like, "Are you getting stressed out about your trial? Do you need to go to the guidance office?" Since then, she said, she swore she'd never confide in the teachers again. She did talk sometimes to Kelly, the school nurse, until she left. After her departure (in October 1997), I became April's main confidante. The pain involved in these children's lives is not the kind of information one wants to bring home and share with one's own family after work either, so I could certainly relate to her appreciation of my listening skills. However, it was difficult for me to be a sponge for this kind of heartache without anyone to confide in at my end. I did not want to burden her because I was there to be a listener for her.

Key Student Informants:
The Participants of the Pilot Literacy Project

About two months into my observations at WANTS, I realized I could no longer be a passive qualitative ethnographer. I needed to transform my role to a participant action researcher and to reshape my work in the spirit of Brydon-Miller (1993, p. 125) and other participant researchers, conducting research "to provide participants with useful information and skills to conduct effective self-advocacy work . . . to identify . . . problems experienced by . . . people . . . and to plan and carry out advocacy efforts guided by a shared understanding of the needs of the . . . community." My decision to change the research paradigm was guided by a belief similar to that of Brydon-Miller's. Specifically, she stated, "[M]y conviction that traditional social science research has contributed to the continued powerlessness of oppressed groups. The participatory research approach, on the other hand, demands the active involvement of people in identifying and finding solutions to the problems they face, and requires a commitment from the researcher to make this involvement possible and effective" (p. 126). My goal was for this research to be useful for those involved with WANTS and not just for it to sit on a shelf.

I wondered how I could help at least some of the students who were interested in working on more fulfilling community service projects. Some students felt disconnected from their community service assignments and, consequently, they frequently did not meet their obligation. Often they complained of the menial tasks they were made to do, reemphasizing the punitive nature of the community service project. Thus, I decided I would create a project that would help connect students to their community. I had noticed that students at WANTS had very low literacy rates, which, many teachers felt, contributed to their acting out behaviors in and out of the classroom. I wanted to create an experience that would empower students.

I bounced a couple of ideas off James, a ninth-grade student who helped out in the guidance office. He thought the most promising idea was to teach a group of WANTS students to become literacy trainers and to work with young children. I knew I needed to work out the details—what children? Where? When?

Working out the details was not an easy task. WANTS students were viewed as criminals. They were not permitted on any school property other than WANTS; therefore, the district would not allow me to bring them into an elementary school to work with young children—even carefully supervised. I called the community center that had made such a difference in the lives of some of these young people.

I managed to find a group of elementary school students in an after-school program at the local community center who might be interested in participating. With April's help, we selected six students—five boys and one girl who were involved in the gang scene. One of the boys did not want to participate in the project because he was in a rival gang and felt outnumbered in the group.

I taught the remaining four boys (the one girl showed up for one of the training sessions) how to teach younger children how to read. I brought in and paid literacy experts to work with them. The plan was that we were going to spend an hour a day reading to early readers and then do some shared reading. This project was going to take place at the local community center. The center had an after-school program through their Parks and Recreation program for younger children. We selected students who were interested in working on their reading skills during this time. The young men read to the children one-on-one, helped them write and draw in journals about what they read, and then they did some shared reading.

We took a trip to the library to pick out children's literature. We learned about interactive software and how to look up books and where to find them. Most of the young men had never been to the huge downtown public library. As Julius, one of the boys, said, "watch your back for DTTs." I asked who DTTs were and he said, "Down Town Thugs," a gang whose territory was in the area of the library's location. Quite pointedly, as we walked to and from the building, the young men with me were looking around watching their backs. The boys carried themselves differently on the street—bouncing and acting like they were ready and willing to fight at the slightest provocation.

The young men were to keep a journal of their experiences working with the young children. The idea was that they would have an opportunity to reflect on the experience every day and think about how they could make it better. Furthermore, an additional goal was that in the process of teaching literacy skills, their own poor reading skills would improve.

Not everything went according to plan. The WANTS students were reluctant to keep a journal, and I did not pressure them. In the beginning, I could not even get Paul to come down off the window ledge, where he studied people on the street below, to come read to the children. I was unable to get them off the basketball court to read.

I started to play basketball with them—sometimes in a skirt and pantyhose and my bare feet. They would tease me and dribble the ball past me. However, they would let me shoot. Some days, when my three-point shot was on, they were impressed. After we played, we would go up to the center and work. The WANTS students began to build friendships with the younger children. They began to work on homework with them and read with them if they did not have homework of their own. Most importantly, they would talk about issues that were difficult for them. One of the younger girls was getting beaten up on the bus. Instead of reacting violently, Dwayne said, "I'm playing mediator." He was trying to sort out the situation between a young girl and a boy at the community center who kept hitting her on the bus. One day Jarrelia was crying so hard that she was unable to tell anyone what was the matter. Dwayne, one of the WANTS students, took her by the hand and brought her to the snack bar to buy her some candy. By the end of the tutoring session, she was actually smiling. These moments meant more to these young people than the reading or the homework help. These were moments of caring that were few and far between at school and in the neighborhood—especially between the WANTS students and younger children.

During the first year of my project, I relied mostly on observations and discussions with students to gain a better understanding of the young people experiencing the WANTS school culture. Because of the literacy project, though, I was able to build trust and rapport with at least a handful of the students.

Dwayne. Dwayne was a dark-skinned, very tall African American ninth grader, who was also very strong. He was a leader among his peers, and he had a wonderful sense of humor, which occasionally got him into trouble in the classroom. Because he had been caught with a knife at his former school, he was sent to WANTS. He said that a group of kids "jumped" him, and to defend himself, he held the knife to one of the kid's throat. He said, "I should've killed him." Someone asked him, "Do you know what would have happened if you did?" "Yeah," he said, "I'd go to jail." "Have you ever been to jail?" The other person asked.

Dwayne replied, "yeah, sure." The other person who had done programming in prisons said, "jail, maybe, but I doubt you know what it's really like in *prison*." Killing was justified if someone jumped you and it was seen as self-defense—even if it meant going to jail. Most of these young people professed that they were not afraid of going to jail, but this, most likely, was part of the "frontin'" or "thuggin' it" they had to do routinely in their neighborhoods.

Quite by accident, I met Dwayne's first-grade teacher, who told me that he had been trouble since then and also had difficulty with academic work. I knew from listening to him read to younger kids that he had difficulty reading even elementary texts at the beginning. He made great progress by the end, but it made me think about how some students are labeled early on as troublemakers and never get a second chance. Dwayne represented this group of youngsters well. He had never been tested for any kind of disability because it was assumed that his problems were just "behavioral."

James. James was in the same grade and a member of the same gang as Dwayne, and he was also African American. I knew through April, which was later confirmed through his own admission, that he was actively involved in the gang scene and that his major rivals claimed the territory right outside the school building. We had to be careful driving to and from the Community Center because of this fact. He and Dwayne were close, and they hung out at SWCC. This was their home turf. James was very polite and considerate, and he worked well with the young children at SWCC—many of whom he knew before the project started. He was from a middle-class family with older brothers and sisters (his sister dropped him off and picked him up every day from school), although they continued to live in one of the poorest and most violent sections of the city. His mother was a well-known, respected, and well-liked, first-grade teacher in the same school district—embarrassed that her son James had been caught with a BB gun in school. When I spoke with her on a few occasions, she described her frustration with her son—that he would not go to school despite her pleading with him to go, that he would go out and not come home when she asked him. It was clear that she feared for his safety—she knew that he had a gang after him. In other words, she was a scared mother who felt powerless over her son's actions.

Julius. Julius, an African American, was new to WANTS when I was starting the literacy project. Like Dwayne, he was a ninth grader and a class clown—but he was a bit goofier and less mature than Dwayne. He said he had been caught with a knife and hence was sent to WANTS. He summarized what many other students felt about being at WANTS in a single phrase, "The district kicked us out . . . they don't care what happens to us." Not that Julius was angry about this situation; he said it quite matter-of-factly. He was a member of one of the toughest gangs in the neighborhood—the one whose territory surrounded the school. Because he had been shot at several times and thus was evidently in danger, he felt he needed to be a part of this gang. Conversely, he was constantly in trouble at school. In fact, before the end of the school year, Julius was sent to jail for threatening a teacher with a large pipe.

Julius had been involved with a multitude of social service agencies for at-risk youths. He had been in several programs that were designed to steer him away from violence and trouble, yet he still ended up on this path. He told me during one of our many conversations that his sister was "a good kid—like she gets straight As and is like a peer mediator or something." He knew what it meant to be a "good kid," and he realized that his mother feared for his life and that he was a disappointment to her. She had become a religious woman after quitting her drug abuse and would go to prayer sessions regularly to pray for her son.

Paul. Paul was a white tenth grader who did not seem, at least on the surface, to have any gang affiliation. He was from the Valley (a mostly white section of the city), and didn't seem to express the same concerns about going certain places as the others did. He talked a lot about fighting and said that he had been caught with a "sword" in school, although I had never actually heard of him fighting. Interestingly, he was very patient with the young children at SWCC. I was often second-guessing him, though, because I had caught him in several lies early on in the literacy project. Retrospectively, it seems he was going through a period of testing me to see how gullible I was. However, once he and I had a traditional-style interview (sat quietly in a room together with the tape recorder), he seemed to trust me more. I realized after the interview that the reason he lied was for his own protection. He needed to always be "frontin'" or at least joking so that others "wouldn't mess" with him. The stories he shared with me were not overly dramatized versions of the truth that he told the others in the literacy project. Instead he told me heartfelt stories about his father's abuse (although he never called it that—he loved his father and knew he was doing the best he could to raise his son to be a "good kid"). He talked about his relationship with his girlfriend and finding religion (he and Dwayne regularly attended Bible study together). These stories were just below the surface of this young man, who tried to act like such a "thug" in front of the others. This behavior was not atypical for these young men, however.

Donise. Donise was an African American ninth grader who came into the literacy project late because she had been out of school for several weeks. In fact, she had run away from home, the home she shared on and off with her mother and her grandmother. She ended up leaving the program because, as she told me, she would need to go into hiding because her mother was pressing charges against her because Donise had hit her. Her side of the story was that she hit her mother because her mother hit her first, and if her probation officer found her, they would send her to the juvenile detention facility because she "had a record." During the time she was hiding from the authorities and not attending school, her grandmother (the person she was closest to in the world) died. I suspect her grandmother's death forced her out of hiding, and she was placed in the local juvenile detention facility.

Amani. Amani was a ninth grader of Arabic descent, who talked openly about being Muslim. When he first arrived at WANTS, he was attacked several times by groups of boys. One time, Julius and another boy had been suspended for five days for assaulting Amani and stealing from him. Amani had been in his share of fights at school, too. Like Donise, he joined the literacy project late. His community service assignment was to clean up at the community center, where I conducted the literacy project. I would see him down at the center sitting around playing cards or playing basketball. He asked if he could help with the project, and thus I invited him to participate and read with one of the young boys. He was really good with the children and seemed to enjoy it. Even so, he only came a few times, but on these few occasions he shared quite a bit with us about his life experiences.

A Look at the Numbers:
The Fall 1998 Survey

In the fall of 1998, I gave students at WANTS a survey about their violent behaviors and drug use. The survey instrument was developed by the Hamilton Fish National Institute on School and Community Violence and was entitled the National School Crime and Safety Survey. We conducted observations of students as they took the survey to see their responses to the questions and the survey that guaranteed them anonymity and confidentiality—two concepts they did not understand or believe. These students' lives were under such scrutiny that they did not believe that anything they said or wrote would be confidential. Most were on probation and thought that anything could be used against them in court, to get them in further trouble with the law. They had been betrayed by adults and learned to trust no one.

In every group I saw, someone would say something like, "We ain't gonna tell you that." One of the students said, "Have you brought any weapons to school in the past 30 days? Yes, ha, on the 3rd day of school," with a smile on her face. One of the boys interrupted, "Why we gonna tell you that?" One boy said the same thing about the drug questions, "Ain't nobody gonna tell you the truth about drugs." I believe they did not. In this school where students would talk openly about smoking marijuana before school and during school, and being high in the classes I observed, most of the students answered "never" to the question about whether or not they smoked marijuana.

In one of the classes, students demonstrated resistance to the survey by making up answers. In others, students would refuse to complete the survey. In one class, a girl, who finished her survey early, got up and started to fill out another boy's survey for him. When the teacher said, "You're not supposed to fill out his," she replied, "He bein' stupid." The teacher escalated this hostile situation by telling students who were whining that they wanted to go home, "you gonna go home all right . . . in the pattywagon."

Students would often ask the teacher or other adults in the room questions from the survey such as, "Miss, have you ever been in a gang?" Students struggled with sitting and answering the questions—they wanted to talk about the questions and their answers—real or fictitious. It seemed they had a hard time understanding the survey questions. Many of them had very low literacy rates, and some, who may have been illiterate, doodled on the survey. Some made comments ranging from, "man, this sucks" and "we gotta do this WHOLE packet?" to "why you wanna know this stuff?" Two of the boys thought it was funny to say their answers aloud—joking about how many fights they had been in, and how many times they had hurt someone at school. Despite the resistance, the survey revealed some interesting findings.

At the beginning of the second year of my observations at WANTS, students responded in the following ways to the survey: 24.3% of students had reported having been hit, punched, or slapped in the past 30 days (8.1% reported this happened to them 10 or more times); 27% of students admitted they had hit, punched, or slapped another student in the past 30 days at school; 43.2% of students admitted to having seen someone else attacked with a weapon at school; 16.2% had witnessed a robbery with a weapon; 18.9% had seen a robbery without a weapon; 56.8% reported they had seen a severe beating at school; 27% said they had seen a sexual assault; 61.1% had seen a knife in school; 48.6% had seen a gun at school; 21.6% had witnessed a shooting at school.

Only 25% admitted to being in a "gang," yet most students talked about being a part of the known gangs in the city. Of those who admitted gang membership, 47.1% conceded having violent initiations; 31.3% indicated their gang was using drugs; 46.7% revealed that their gangs were selling drugs; 62.5% admitted their gang fought with other gangs; 68.8% that they beat people up; 31.3% participated in drive-by shootings; 41.2% revealed their gangs were stealing cars.

In addition to the survey questions in the National School Crime and Safety Survey, I created a set of questions about students' families and their own drug use. First, 32.3% of students had a parent who had been incarcerated; 77.4% reported having a "good relationship with their parent/guardian"; 48.4% told their parent or guardian what they were doing after school and on the weekends; 64.5% "usually had dinner with their family"; and 27.8% were physically punished.

Students' reports of their drug use seemed inconsistent with what I heard in observations and interviews. Students talked frequently about daily marijuana use and drinking alcohol, yet the percentages did not reflect this. Only 30.6% reported they "rarely" drank alcohol and 25% reported "sometimes to very often" drinking alcohol. For marijuana use, 48.6% wrote that they had never used marijuana, 20% rarely (fewer than once per month), 11.4% sometimes (1–3 times per month), 5.7% often (1–2 times per week), and 11.4% very often (more than twice per week). Only one student admitted to sometimes using any other kind of illegal drug. The only other illegal drug I heard mentioned was crack.

For parental alcohol and other drug use, 22.2% of students reported having seen their father drunk, and one student admitted that his or her father used illegal drugs. Similar figures were reported for mothers: 27.8% had seen their mothers drunk (8.4% on a regular basis); and 10.2% knew their mothers used illegal drugs (two students reported that their mothers used illegal drugs more than twice per week). The highest figures were reported for children having seen other adults in their home drunk (38.9%), but only 2.8% reported other adults using illicit substances.

Students were also asked about their attitudes about school. To the question "I like coming to school at WANTS" 38.7% reported yes. The rest answered no. However, when asked if they enjoyed most of their classes, 74.2% said yes, and 25.8 said no, and 70% felt they were learning from their teachers. Nevertheless, the overwhelming majority responded "yes" (71%) when asked "I would like to become a better student." Most of the students at WANTS had received the message loud and clear that they were less than adequate students academically. The overwhelming majority of students performed far below their grade level on standardized tests in reading and mathematics. In fact, most students told me that they were "used to failing."

In Marked Contrast:
A Brief Introduction to the Suburban Middle School

In the preface, I discussed the dramatic differences between Lorenzo Hill (the affluent suburban school) and WANTS in terms of physical environment. My introduction to Lorenzo Hill resembled the one to WANTS. I was working on a grant designed to assess the effectiveness of a program designed to reduce violence. In the case of Lorenzo Hill school, it was the "No Putdowns" program designed to teach students alternative ways of dealing with conflict to prevent violence. I observed students learning about the program and asked them and teachers what they thought about the program's effectiveness. One of my first observations was of a sixth-grade classroom discussing what it meant to be "popular." This shed light on the minds of middle school students in affluent suburban schools about what it meant to be accepted and what it meant not to be accepted.

First Student Observation at Lorenzo Hill

When I arrived, students were returning from the library where they had been working on a research project. The room was carpeted and filled with bright posters and decorations for Halloween. There were homework assignments posted on the board and students' desks were set up in collaborative work stations. Students talked quietly among themselves—a few students asked me if I was a student teacher. I told them that I taught student teachers and that I was just there to observe their class.

Students sat quietly as Ms. Holloway wrote the word "popular" on the board with a circle around it and told students they were going to make a Web. She asked students what it meant to be popular, and students raised their hands (they did not shout out answers), and she had them go up one by one and draw a line and write what they thought on the board after they said it aloud to the class. For the most part everyone participated—with the notable exception of the two students who sat alone on the margins and who contributed very little. The responses to the question, "what makes you popular?" were as follows:

Boy: Having lots of friends

Girl: Have the right clothes

Girl: Be perfect

Boy: Smartest

Girl: Having the right friends

Boy: Athletic

Girl: Boyfriends and girlfriends

Girl: The way you look

Boy: The music you like

Boy: You hafta be "all that"

Girl: You hafta be involved in all kinds of activities so that when your friends call to ask you to do something and you're always busy, so they think you're really important.

Boy: You hafta be a perfect person who does all the enrichment activities or extra credit—does lots of extra work.

Girl: Kendra said, "big money."

Ms. Holloway: Can't Kendra talk for herself?

Kendra shyly says "big money." And she goes up to put it on the board.

Boy: Who you hang out with—and the right places—like with older people at the [local coffee house] and the mall or [at the local] deli.

Ms. Holloway: Are you allowed to go to these places by yourselves?

Students: Yeah.

Girl: Normally don't hang out with your parents

Ms. Holloway: You're popular if you don't hang out with your parents?

Girl: Yeah

Boy: If you have boy-girl parties

Girl from the margins: When you're older, smoking and swearing

Girl: Having the coolest car

Boy from the margins: Going to R-rated movies

Ms. Holloway: Okay, let's look at what we have—if a boy or girl had all these qualities would he or she be really popular?

The majority of students said no, and students agreed that smoking and swearing should not be on the list. Thus, the teacher discredited overriding the one contribution of one of the girls who sat alone in the margins. One of the boys who clearly seemed to be popular himself said that being nice to people made you popular. Some disagreed and one girl said, "Being nice to the *right* people makes you popular."

Students said where you shopped—the Gap, Old Navy, Abercrombie and Fitch—were indicators of popularity. Ms. Holloway pointed out the importance of money for the popular person to be able to afford clothes from these places.

One boy said kids were popular if they agreed with people instead of saying what they really thought. Ms. Holloway asked how many people had ever done this—most agreed that they had at some point. Students said that smoking and swearing decreased one's popularity and gave examples of the older kids who hung out on the green before school smoking cigarettes—that they were not popular or cool.

Most students agreed that being athletic was the most important trait of a popular person. There was one boy who sat alone and was squirmy throughout the discussion and only contributed R-rated movies. Ms. Holloway reprimanded him a few times, but he seemed to have trouble engaging in the discussion.

Ms. Holloway asked what kinds of qualities they liked in a friend. They responded that they appreciated a good personality, a good sense of humor, the ability to keep a secret, loyalty, honesty, and a person who was not a braggart. When peer pressure was discussed, students were familiar with the concept and said it was pressure put on a person by people one's own age, maybe siblings, or friends to avoid embarrassment in front of them. Students then broke into small groups that they selected to talk about "What's hot and what's not." There was one group of all girls, one group of all boys, a large mixed group of boys and girls, and one small group that seemed to be comprised of the misfits—the boy who was in trouble and two others who did not speak at all during the discussion. Interestingly, the children did not make the connection between their own behavior in selecting groups and what it meant to be popular and what they had just discussed in class.

In their groups they talked about songs, movies, books, television shows, what time they had to go to bed, and so on. The particularly interesting thing was how these little groups were sites for determining popularity, and I was wondering whether others were aware and doing the things they had just discussed. The groups seemed to reinforce notions of popularity. There was no debriefing about the nature of how these labels get created and can be used to leave certain people out and hurt others. It seemed to reinforce stereotypical notions of popularity and how these notions get constructed and reified.

The what's hot and what's not categories were interesting, too. In this grade, at this point, students were still subject to fads such as the Pokemon cards and

Halloween costumes, and so on. They all listed the Harry Potter books because they were really popular in their grade. Other hot items included Cargo pants, the Gap, and other fashionable stores, gelled hair for boys, highlighting hair for girls, MTV, boys, girls, certain shows, and movies. What was not hot were things that had been really popular but were no longer such as Furby, Giga pets, Doug's first movie, and one group even mentioned Bill Clinton.

When the period ended, students gathered their belongings and went to lunch. In our conversation following the class Ms. Holloway said she had done two other "No Putdowns" lessons. She thought students related to this form of lesson structure and she built it into the lesson plan. It was clear that she went through the curriculum and only selected what she considered relevant to what she was already teaching and material to which she thought her students would respond favorably. She said the block schedule for language arts really lent itself well to doing activities like this one. I found it particularly interesting that language arts was the only class scheduled every day for 84 minutes.

I asked Ms. Holloway when students discovered that certain things were no longer cool and when they started taking notice of the opposite sex. She said that there was an amazing transformation that seemed to happen between Christmas break and the break in February. More specifically, when students returned from February break, they seemed to be changed—so much more sophisticated about relationships with the opposite sex and about their schoolwork. She said that, even though they were so often treated as babies, they really have a certain level of sophistication about them and were aware of a lot of things.

Another story was about a student who had three unprepared marks from the previous week and whom the teachers were trying to get on homebound instruction because of his destructive and disruptive behavior. He had made a mess of the boys' bathroom on three separate occasions—including smearing feces on the walls. He would "get in her face" about things. Ms. Holloway said he was really a problem. Apparently he had been an only child until this year when his parents (one of whom was a teacher in the district) adopted five children from Texas (of the same family of Hispanic descent). She said that since then he had had trouble and they were recommending home schooling. She also said that one of the other boys in the study hall was one of his adopted "brothers." He was the first student of color I had seen all day at the school. She said that the adopted children worked really hard and seemed to be doing well in school.

There were no narratives that involved physical violence of any kind. I realized how I had become so used to hearing and seeing outward physical violence at WANTS and the other urban schools that I was amazed that the most important issues centered around popularity and verbal assaults and cruelty as a result of one's status. Clearly the nature of the problems in these two schools regarding violence seemed to be dramatically different after my first visits—but were they? And if so, how?

The Organization of This Book

It is the goal of this volume to assess the lessons learned about personal and structural violence in two particular school districts. The experiences of the students and staff at the WANTS school provide the primary examples and are the focus of this book because it was this site where violence was most prevalent. However, to gain a better understanding of the nature of suburban school violence and its roots, information about Lorenzo Hill Central School is interwoven throughout the discussions of personal and structural violence. It is important to remember that these events were observed and translated through my lens. The preface and introduction of this book describe my personal experiences entering into this project and the ways that social location influences how we interpret the meaning of violence. One important part of one's social location is socioeconomic status—themes around poverty and affluence will weave throughout this book.

The first part of this book describes personal violence: the experiences of the students around issues of family violence, bullying, gangs, relationship and sexual violence, and others. The second part of the book discusses structural violence (using Smith's, 1990, qualitative strategy of examining how social organizations influence the lives of individuals involved in the violence): the setup of the WANTS school (funding arrangements, staffing, structure of the day, policies of the district), the teacher and administrator concerns raised, and the implications for students. Structural forms of violence at Lorenzo Hill will also be addressed (special education, poverty, and separation). The final section discusses the implications, conclusions, and strategies for reducing violence at WANTS as a result of the findings of the present ethnographic research. Furthermore promising practices and components that were used to reduce violence at WANTS will be highlighted. The programs in place at Lorenzo Hill will also be featured and implications for promising practices at suburban schools discussed.

PART I

Personal Violence

CHAPTER 1

The Important Role of Personal Violence at WANTS

Defining Personal Violence

There is no single definition of personal violence. In fact, notions of personal violence are socially constructed. Thus, personal violence is understood differently by different people, and the interpretation of the concept is affected by social location. For some, personal violence includes harassment, physical, emotional, and sexual abuse, fighting, hitting, and threats. For others, personal violence is any behavior that triggers fear in another person.

The city school district in which WANTS was located had so-called "levels" of violations for actions that could be considered personal violence. Level one violations included cutting class, being disrespectful or uncooperative, failing to follow the reasonable request of a staff member, smoking, and other disruptive behavior. Level two violations comprised behaviors often considered under the umbrella of personal violence such as fighting, reckless endangerment, using vulgar and/or abusive language, destruction of personal or school property, striking a staff member, striking a student, threatening a staff member or student, and theft. Level three violations (some of which resulted in students being assigned to WANTS) were as follows: arson, assault of a staff member or student (physical or sexual), extortion, possession/use/sale of alcohol, possession/use/sale of illegal drugs or any other mood-altering chemical, possession/use of a weapon or dangerous object, and vandalism.

Loeber and Farrington (1998) defined violent offenders as those individuals who had committed one or more of the following crimes: homicide, aggravated assault (e.g., weapons offenses and attempted murder), robbery, kidnapping, voluntary manslaughter, rape or attempted rape, and arson of an occupied building.

They left out "simple assault and juvenile fist fights" agreeing that "it is often difficult to agree on the threshold between what is and what is not legally violent" (p.
14).

At Lorenzo Hill teachers and students did not feel that "violence" was a problem in their school. Perhaps because they did not include in their personal
definitions of violence behaviors such as: bullying, cruel treatment, ostracizing,
hitting, and verbal fighting. Most considered physical fighting "violence," but felt
that these behaviors happened so rarely that they were not considered problematic. I also struggled with developing a personal definition of what was violent and
what was not; that is, I tried to determine my personal "threshold" of acceptable
violent behavior. For me, the threshold seemed to depend on the context and the
perception of the individuals involved. I found my personal threshold at Lorenzo
Hill was different from my threshold at WANTS. At Lorenzo Hill, I was more
likely to notice behaviors such as pushing, teasing, and ostracizing that would have
gone unrecognized or would have fallen below my radar screen at WANTS.

Researchers, educators, instructional designers, and others often try to create
uniform definitions of personal violence when they design research projects and
interventions around this issue. All too often, we, the researchers, educators, and
instructional designers, impose our social construction of reality onto those we are
trying to study or educate instead of trying to find out how individuals interpret
their own reality. We operationalize personal violence by stating, for example, that
"personal violence is _____ (fill in the blank)." However, I found that many individuals identified levels of personal violence by using terms such as "soft" violence
versus more "hard-core" violence. Furthermore, individuals often ranked violent
actions similarly to how they ranked drugs (see Williams, 1998). These rankings
were socially constructed and based on a person's social location. Generally such
behaviors that did not involve physical touching, such as putting down or ostracizing others, verbal sexual harassment, verbal taunts or cruelty, were often not seen
as forms of "violence," and, in some cases, hitting and slapping were not considered violent (usually in settings were physical violence was more pervasive).

Individuals considered the subsequently listed behaviors as physical, violent
actions: slapping, hitting, punching, fighting without a weapon, girl fights (using
nails and pulling another person's hair), raping, fighting with a weapon, shooting,
killing. These rankings were fairly consistent, but social location was the determining factor as to what level of violence individuals would tolerate from others or
engage in themselves.

Many of the boys at WANTS with whom I spoke privately acknowledged that
they would shoot to kill if necessary. Students at WANTS also had quite complex
definitions of violence and what was acceptable and what was unacceptable behav-

ior. For WANTS students, acceptability of an action depended not necessarily on the act itself, but rather on why the act was committed in the first place. Thus, killing might be acceptable if done for the right reason (e.g., to protect another person or to project oneself). For the students at Lorenzo Hill, where personal violence was much less frequent, certain acts were simply unacceptable under any circumstance.

Definitions and rankings of acceptable forms of violence vary dramatically based on a person's social location (i.e., gender, race, social class, geographic location, age, religious affiliation, and so on). As Delpit (1995) has argued, "we all carry worlds in our heads, and those worlds are decidedly different. We educators set out to teach, but how can we reach the worlds of others when we don't even know they exist? Indeed, many of us don't even realize that our own worlds exist only in our heads and in the cultural institutions we have built to support them" (p. xiv). We must begin the research and design process by looking inward to examine our own standpoints or worlds. Then we must engage in qualitative inquiry to better understand the worlds of others from varied social locations if we want to improve our understanding of violence and our attempts to reduce it. The worlds of children at WANTS are decidedly different from those at Lorenzo Hill.

We cannot address the issue of violence using the same strategy for each of these worlds. We need to understand each world first before designing and implementing violence-reduction strategies. Then, if we find that the primary problems are related to verbal cruelty and not to physical violence, we implement programs such as the "No Putdowns" program that deal with the latter. If we are dealing with gang violence and street warfare, we need individually tailored programs that address the issues young people face surviving on the street. First, we need to understand how young people perceive and rank violence and where they draw the line of acceptable versus unacceptable violence before we can create effective programs.

Although not specifically labeled as a qualitative research project, Geoffrey Canada (1995) describes growing up as an African American male. In the environment in which he grew up, violence was pervasive, and carrying weapons was viewed as an essential part of survival. In his book *Fist, Stick, Knife, Gun* he chronicles his early life experiences around violence, and how these experiences influenced his perceptions of violence and his later work with youths in inner New York City neighborhoods. He talks about the need to fight, and what he felt he needed to do as a young person to stay safe. He writes, "The year was 1964 and I was in sixth grade at P.S. 99. I had learned my lessons well both in school and on the streets. I found school, though, to be the lesser challenge" (p. 70). Canada describes finding his first knife (a K55) in the gutter and how carrying it allowed him to "bop" through rival gang territory. He states, "with my K55 in my pocket I would bop right through groups of boys whose challenging looks questioned my right to travel through their block. The knife was my passport. As I approached a group, my hand would slide into my right pocket to position my knife so that it could be immediately opened, then I would set my eyes straight ahead and wait for a challenge" (p. 71). Canada's definition of personal violence changed as he matured and had experiences outside his neighborhood. Individuals' definitions of personal violence, such as Canada's, are shifting based on their experiences. As an adult, he observed, "There are children all over this country who are hiding weapons in their closets, in sneaker boxes under their beds, under their sweaters in their dresser drawers. They are certain that they need their guns or knives for their own safety, sure that their very lives depend on having those weapons" (p. 72). This statement applies to many of the students at WANTS, although these young people have been caught by school personnel with their weapons.

I set out to find out how the students and staff at WANTS and Lorenzo Hill made sense of personal violence in their lives. Students described specifically what it meant to be violent or whom they termed a "thug" and how they learned to "thug it" (behave like "thugs" to survive). Many of the students experienced great personal loss because of personal violence in their lives. Some turned grief and pain into anger and retaliation. Some experienced feelings of excitement or rush with the drama of personal violence. Students mentioned the role of gangs and families as sites where they learned personal violence strategies and could enact them and were often rewarded for their behavior. Young people seemed to be creating shifting views of violence. In most cases, the more violent the culture in which one lived the more acceptable various types of violence were or the higher one's "threshold" between what one considered violent. In addition, the young people who lived in more violent cultures were more likely to have more complex definitions about acceptable forms of violence than those who did not.

Student Acceptance of Personal Violence as "The Way It Is"

Students have repeatedly told me that this culture (the neighborhood around WANTS where knifings, stabbings, shootings, jumpings, gang involvement, and other criminal behavior were common) was not going to change. Thus, many had adopted an outward complacent acceptance about the culture as was so eloquently summarized by a seventh grader, "it's just the way it is. There ain't nothing I can do about it, so why should I sit around and worry about it, we all gotta die sometime." Both of the seventh-grade girls in this particular interview at WANTS agreed that it "don't matter when you die—we all gotta go sometime." There is such a dehumanizing quality—death is seen as not a big deal. Tamika had just been to her cousin's funeral the day before. One of the girls who was supposed to be at one of my focus groups was absent because she was at a wake for a family member. Not only was tremendous loss a regular occurrence in the lives of these young people, but the way how many of them would deal with loss was to accept that dying young was simply a fact of life. Sometimes, perhaps to avoid being hurt when someone close died, some young people would avoid intimate relationships. Personal violence and its consequences were simply parts of daily life for WANTS students.

Staff Experiences at WANTS as Victims and Perpetrators

Teachers experienced violence as both victims and perpetrators. As the new special education teacher said during the second year of my work at WANTS, "you hafta have pretty thick skin to work here. Like today, I just got called a fat pig by one of the students. You hafta let that roll off your back—you can't be quick to anger here." I had heard that from many of the teachers—comments about having to keep their emotions out of the classroom, and not letting students see any weakness. In a way, teachers learned to "front it" as did the students. Teachers, who showed weakness or vulnerability such as Jerry, were tormented by students and ostracized by colleagues. He ended up quitting before the start of my second year there. Jerry displayed his anger with students by getting frustrated and yelling and kicking students out of the room. Students were defiant outwardly and re-fused to do what he asked. Other students then lost respect for him and saw him as an easy target.

Teachers were not always the victims, though. Tom bullied students occasion-ally in and out of the classroom. Because students respected and liked Tom—they thought he was a good teacher and he did things with them outside of class—they generally wanted to please him, although sometimes Tom would bully and threaten students. In fact, I noticed teachers threaten and bully students on a regular basis—some more than others. Ken was large and could intimidate stu-dents with his loud booming voice and physical presence. He tended not to get angry with students, but occasionally he would threaten or bully students as well. Teachers, much like the students, never saw themselves as perpetrators, but often as the victims using whatever skills they could to protect themselves within this environment.

Student Definitions of "Thug": Not Me

Students had different definitions of what constituted a violent person or "thug." These definitions did not include the young people in the project despite the fact that many others considered them among the school district's most violent students because they had brought weapons to school—it was always about people who were "worse" than they saw themselves. In keeping with the notion of an unarticulated acceptability ranking of what constituted personal violence, students at WANTS tended to view their violent behavior as acceptable, but the behavior of those who were worse as unacceptable.

Amani, for example, said, "[A thug is] a bad kid that likes to cause trouble . . . don't care about nobody . . . like to start shit . . . a thug . . . A thug claims to be 'bout it. They drink 40s [40 ounces of malt liquor], smoke weed, sell dope, beef all day [fight and talk about fighting], talk shit all day, blame stuff on the white man, harass women . . . Man, in the ghetto, ya know what I'm sayin' that's just the way it is. It's in the family. No father. Don't have a lot. Got mad [many] relatives in lock up [prison]. What I'm sayin' is, shit, people get hard. They got to." Amani did not see himself as a violent thug, even though he met some of these criteria he set for himself because as he said, "I got heart." Having "heart" or some caring feelings for others was what separated the real "thugs" from those who played the game for their own protection. For Amani and others, what made an act of personal violence less acceptable than another was not the act specifically, but whether or not someone had "heart." Thus, a cold-blooded killer was unacceptable, but a killer with heart—perhaps protecting a fellow gang member or family member was acceptable.

Another student, Ronald, said that a thug was "someone who thinks violence is fun. They love to do stuff that ain't right like carrying guns even though they know they will get caught, get arrested." Again, like Amani, acceptable violence was not necessarily based on one's actions but if one did it for fun or without remorse or heart. Ronald also did not see himself as a violent thug because he could choose when to be violent. Being able to control oneself and decide when to be violent or not was part of what separated the real thugs from the pseudo-thugs. Discourses of self-control were common among young people in this setting when trying to differentiate themselves from those who were thought to be truly violent individuals. He said, "I made it 10 weeks of being good so I can stay here [at regular school]. My probation is up. Some faggot teachers try to get me in trouble by writing referrals, though." Ronald's comment here about "faggot teachers" was common among students who did not see themselves as violent or as thugs. They were victims (in their minds) of teachers who "had it in for them" or being in the wrong place at the wrong time.

Young people who did not have intact and supportive families themselves recognized the importance of family in preventing youths from behaving violently. Youths who did act violently because of poor families were seen as more acceptable. Talika said, "Basically it's misunderstood. Some people act bad 'cause of their homes. They get beat and yelled at all the time. They ain't bad seeds. There are a few bad seeds out there but most aren't. Basically most people just got problems. They aren't born bad. Bad seeds are born bad. Bad seeds shoot people, don't listen to their moms, being ignorant." Talika speculated that young people were bad seeds because "they don't feel love. They want to be loved, but they don't know how to get it." Talika, like Amani, mentioned the importance of family in shaping violent youths. Also, here Talika supports the notion of certain people and acts as being unacceptable. Shooting people is unacceptable violence and this is what bad seeds do. In her mind truly "bad" or violent people are born that way, but there are those who are not that bad—they just have tough home lives and do not feel love—like Amani's description of having "heart." In these instances, violence and violent behavior are acceptable, but not when someone is "born bad" or does not feel "love" or have "heart."

Paul said that thugs or those who were violent kids were those who "hang out in crews [gangs], have guns, do graffiti, smoke pot. They feel more love on the corner than at home. WANTS had kids who were real delinquents and kids who weren't . . . about 50/50." Separating the "real delinquents" from those who were not seemed important to nearly every young person who was asked about what violence was or what made young people violent or "thugs." It seemed important to create a dichotomy in which they constructed themselves as not real delinquents or thugs when they spoke with me or other adults. However, when they spoke among themselves, it was important to let other young people think they were thugs or willing to be as violent as possible.

Thuggin' It:
The Important Role of Personal Violence in the Status Quo

After each workshop that tried to teach alternatives to violence (before these were embedded into the school day), I observed that students demonstrated their resistance and the importance of maintaining personal violence in the status quo by acting violently. Fights immediately followed such programs in an effort to demonstrate who was really in charge and what behavior was really acceptable. Fighting served to keep gang members united and to establish a pecking order at

WANTS. Perhaps part of why students at WANTS did not consider themselves violent or thugs is that violence was a part of daily life both in and out of school. Some learned to expect violence and learned to take it—these children were known by the adults in the school as the victims. Some learned how to cause other students to fear their wrath—these were the bullies. Some learned to strategically avoid violence—the avoiders. In addition, there were some who reacted violently to nearly every situation without remorse—these were the predators. There were those who pretended to be tough and willing to behave violently—these were the front-ers.

While I am resistant to creating labels and categories, these were the more typical student reactions to the violence around them. Students were not always only one of these. Sometimes they would shift from one to another. Although these labels were somewhat dynamic, usually once one was determined to be one of these, it was difficult to change the public's perception. Generally students were forced into one of these groups.

If students showed any sign of weakness in this environment, they would become the target of seemingly endless torment. Some students were easier targets than others though, because of how they carried themselves or how they looked or dressed. Children with thin skin in this environment typically did not last long. If the constant verbal abuse was difficult to take, some students did not return and would drop out. If they violated the terms of their parole (attending school regularly), they would end up at the juvenile detention facility. Some of the wealthier families would send their children to a Catholic or another private school.

Perhaps the most important trait to surviving in the violent atmosphere of this school and its surrounding neighborhood was to never show *any* vulnerability. Demonstrating that one deeply cared about another person, such as a romantic partner, family member, or a close friend, was sometimes viewed as a weakness. Walking, talking, dressing, and acting were all very important when "thuggin' it out" in the 'hood. *Thuggin'* it out was an overall description for acting, walking, talking as if one was willing and ready to fight at the slightest provocation—and not showing "heart" or "love" as Amani and Talika described earlier. I remember watching a young man "thuggin' it" in a blinding rainstorm. He had no coat, no umbrella, and stood straight up, face into the wind and rain and walked with no emotion, as though it were a perfectly lovely day. The young people who were bullied in this culture were those who were unable to "thug it." They were quiet, shy, and did not carry themselves as though they were on their way to a fight. They were the ones, who, according to one administrator at the weapons school, "have *victim* written across their forehead."

"Thuggin' it" did not necessarily make one a "thug." Thugs were hardened and cold and were violent without "heart." Thuggin' it was just seen as what one needed to do in order to survive in this culture. Thuggin' it was the act—the front, the façade. However, one could not let on that this was only a front. Those suspected of "frontin'" (pretending to be hard or bad, but unable or unwilling to back it up) were often challenged. It was possible for students to "mind their business." These students were ostracized and isolated as well. They were often white or middle-class students who had shorter sentences and simply wanted to "do their time" peacefully at WANTS and get out.

Home and Street Families:
Sites for Learning, Practicing, and Rewarding Violence

In a survey of WANTS students administered in the fall of 1998, it became apparent how many children lived in female-headed, single-parent homes. Seventy-nine percent of students reported living with their mother or stepmother. Eighteen percent reported living with their father or stepfather. Five percent reported living with foster parents. Fifty-two percent of respondents indicated that they usually ate dinner with their family, whereas only 40% reported telling their parents about their after-school and weekend activities. About two thirds responded that they had generally a good relationship with their parents (see Corvo & Williams, 2001, for more information on these statistics).

The data supported my original concerns about physical abuse, substance abuse, and other illegal behavior in the home. Twenty-six percent of students reported being physically punished by their parents or guardians. Twenty-two percent reported having seen their father or stepfather drunk. Twenty-eight percent reported having seen their mothers or stepmothers drunk. Thirty-nine percent reported having seen other adults in their home drunk. Eleven percent had seen their mothers or stepmothers use illegal drugs. Three percent reported seeing their fathers or stepfathers use illegal drugs. Twenty-six percent of respondents reported that they had a parent or guardian who had been in jail. These numbers are just what was reported. As I witnessed during the administration of these surveys, students would often say, "we ain't gonna really tell you this stuff."

The quantitative data bore out my original theory that students adjusted their perceptions of violence as necessary and as they were supported by their families. Eighty-four percent of respondents expressed a measure of agreement that their family would defend them if they got into a fight. Only 31% indicated some measure of agreement that they did not fight because their parents would not like it. When asked if they knew if their parents or guardians thought they should get into trouble if they behaved violently at school, only 34% said "yes"; only 19% said "no"; the largest response category was "don't know" with 44%. Nearly half of the students did not know if their families thought they should get in trouble for behaving violently in school—these young people did not receive clear messages about what types of violence were acceptable from their families, at least in part, because acceptable violence was complicated by the reasons for violent behavior.

Findings from the Home Visits:
Relationships with Family Members

As a part of the research project at WANTS, we conducted home visits with families who agreed to participate. The home visits resulted in abundant information frequently unavailable to those working in schools. Parents (most often mothers or grandmothers) cared for their children but expressed frustration and an inability to protect them or control them. They feared for their children. This was the case for Peety whose grandmother described two neighborhood gangs "jumping" her granddaughter and assaulting her with a hammer when she got off the bus. She tried to fight off her attackers with a knife, but when she was caught under the zero tolerance policy, she was sent to WANTS. Her grandmother defended her during her hearing with the school. She described her fear for her granddaughter's safety because the girl gangs "walked up and down past my house threatening. They are the baddest girls I ever laid eyes on and with such terrible language. They get dressed in their best clothes and walk up and down yelling and cursing, and they fight, fight like boys used to do—but girls? They never behaved this way, and it's unbelievable how mean and bold they are." As a result, her granddaughter was never allowed to leave the house by herself, at least according to her grandmother.

Most parents justified their child's weapon-carrying behavior because they all felt that weapons were needed for protection. They tended to blame the dangerous schools and neighborhoods. Eleven-year-old Billy's parents, for example, had three children who had never been in trouble in school. They were very religious and his father (who lived in the home) was a Christian minister, and his mother worked full time outside the home. Billy, like many students at WANTS, described to them the violence in his school and because of his relatively small size, he was threatened physically and verbally. He was caught with a knife that he brought to protect himself. His parents expressed concern with the school's response rather than their son's behavior.

Some parents had given up hope for their children as was the case for Mimi. Her mother said that life was easier when her daughter was either in juvenile detention or in a group home. Mimi's mother said that despite her daughter being on medication to control her anger—she was unable to keep her daughter in line—she was a bad influence on her younger children because she taught them to smoke cigarettes and use foul language. Mimi's mother admitted during the home visit that the mother's live-in boyfriend sexually assaulted Mimi. However, her mother said that Mimi blamed her mother saying that she "didn't give him any [sex]." Therefore, it was her mother's fault. The two younger children in the home were also placed in alternative schools.

As in Mimi's family, there were other parents with more than one child in trouble with the legal or the school system. Many had more than one on probation. Andrew's mother said that he and his brother (also on probation and at another alternative school) were incorrigible. "No matter what anybody does, they just don't care. Even his [Andrew's] law guardian said he is out of control, and no one can do anything to change him." His probation officers had given up hope, and his mother was unable to make him go to school despite his problems with truancy and his probation. She was "tired of " both of her sons' behaviors.

Some parents seemed to be more understanding than others of their son's or daughter's weapon-carrying behavior, but just about all parents found it impossible to set limits because the children appeared unmanageable. They felt powerless to control their children's illegal behavior both in and out of school, although they feared for their children's safety. Some parents were angry and had given up hope of being able to protect their children. As a result, some sought help from the probation system or other forms of the juvenile justice system. Some parents focused on their own personal problems associated with poverty and unemployment during the home visits. Others had several children (including grandchildren, nieces, and nephews) and had difficulty making ends meet, often working multiple jobs. Still other parents were grateful that their children were at WANTS so they could get more individualized attention because they had been doing poorly in school before.

Learning and Practicing Violence at Home

Many WANTS children grew up in homes where physical fighting was seen as the only way to resolve conflicts. In focus groups and interviews with WANTS students, they were asked how their parents dealt with conflict. They all said fight (physically), one said "call the cops," and another one indicated that her father would leave her mother for a few days at a time. There was constant talk about fighting, jumping, or attacking. Some, but not all, of this talk translated into violent action.

So many of the children at WANTS learned coping strategies for living in violent worlds from the time they were very young. Many of the students at WANTS were victims of physical, emotional, and sexual abuse in the home. April confided many stories of rape and incest in the homes of many of the children, and how these students had difficulties in relationships as a result. Marisa was a 13-year-old girl who looked much older. She had been removed from her home because her father was sexually molesting her. She had a 27-year-old boyfriend with whom she used various drugs, and she would sneak out of her foster home to see him. She was in trouble with the law and had been to the juvenile detention facility. Her situation was far too common at WANTS. Nearly all the girls there had some history of sexual abuse in the home—most often at the hands of their mothers' boyfriends. Sam's father had been found guilty of several counts of child molestation—including molesting Sam. Donise and Paul each described physical abuse by their parents, although they did not call it abuse.

No matter how abusive their parents were, many young people in this project wanted their parents or adult caregivers to be proud of them. It struck me when Paul, who described years of abuse by his father, said that when he took up boxing and was "good at it" that his "father was proud" of him. Once he experienced the feeling of making his father proud, he wanted to continue to do things that made his father proud, so he "got a job and got a girl—like a boyfriend-girlfriend-like situation. . . ." Eventually the job and girlfriend took time away from his boxing, and a pregnancy scare made his father less proud and in fact resulted in more abuse.

Donise also tried to gain her mother's respect, but just when their relationship seemed to be improving, something would cause a physical fight. The last one Donise described to me was when her mother "shook her" and Donise hit her back. It was difficult for young people to gain the respect of their parents—particularly in abusive families, but they still tried.

The majority of students at WANTS experienced abuse in the home: verbal, physical, sexual, or a combination of each. Students tended not to talk as much about this kind of violence except to normalize the experience somewhat by saying things in class such as, "everyone's parents whomps 'em." Abuse was so normalized that consistently in response to Annie's question, "when is hitting positive?" students would say things such as, "when your mom hits you because you have no business doin' somethin' you're doin'." Several students would nod in agreement. Students did not view this abuse as "violence," and parents felt hitting was necessary to "toughen up" their children for the reality of life on the street.

For parents and caregivers in WANTS neighborhoods, what constituted violence was complicated. For many, definitions of violence were mediated by circumstance; that is, certain circumstances required certain behaviors—these behaviors were not necessarily violent. For example, many parents did not see their child's weapon-carrying behavior as problematic because they acknowledged the importance of weapons for self-protection. Some parents admitted to being physically harsh with their children as a critical part of "toughening them up," so they could survive in the world in which they lived. Many parents justified their own violence against their children because this kind of violence was to teach them important lessons, and ultimately to keep their children safe—therefore, caregivers (and often their children as well) did not view this kind of behavior as violent, but rather as a necessary part of survival.

Learning Violence with Street Families: Gangs and Personal Violence

The perception among the young people was that the adults in the school culture—at least the ones making the rules—did not understand or care about what students needed to do to protect themselves. Conversely, many of the influential adults in the students' home lives believed that the students needed to fight and sometimes carry weapons to protect themselves. If weapon-carrying and the behaviors with it are expected by students' families, then it is not surprising that young people carried weapons, fought, and belonged to gangs. This dynamic certainly was true for many of the young people at WANTS. Adults who did not live in this culture made decisions that there was "zero tolerance" for fighting and carrying weapons. Policy makers and other adults considered violence similarly to how they treated drugs. More specifically, we adults have no tolerance, and we teach children to just say no. Users are treated as criminals. However, young people see drugs as a part of life. Some people use drugs; some don't. Some people abuse drugs; some die from using drugs too much. Youths see violence in the same fashion. Some people fight; others don't. Some people fight too much, some go to jail, and some die. The same sense of invulnerability surrounding youths and drug use envelops young people's sense of violence. However, in the concrete WANTS situation, there were some gang-involved youths who realized the danger they were in and who were aware that they could be shot if caught at the wrong place at the wrong time by the wrong people. They did not expect to live very long—or at least very long outside the prison system. They were not naive enough to think that they could escape from being the next fatality, but fear of death or the possibility of incarceration were insufficient to get them out of the gang lifestyle. The fear of death would be greater, many thought, if they did not have others to protect them.

Gangs played a major role in the conflicts and resulting personal violence at WANTS. I first found out that there were gangs in the city when I started this project. In fact, I saw a list of the 19 known gangs in the city in the proposal of a neighborhood agency for federal funding. The gangs were primarily identified by their geographic location: Avenue Boys, 5th Avenue Boys, King Boys or Freestyle, 1500 Block, B-Block/110th, Bruce's Block, Boot Camp, Fussin' (female counterpart to Bootcamp), Brighton Brigade, Brick Avenue Boys, Colvin Street Boys, FBIC (subgroup of Latin Queens and R2), Gracetown, Latin Kings, Uptown or Midland (Graystone), Bricktown, PRP, K-Block, and Backyard. I was shocked. I discovered a few more on my own—DTT (Down Town Thugs), 8-Ball, 911/Quickness (the female gang that was the largest and most feared), the Walkers (another female gang), and MFG (Midland's Finest Gambinos). I had known nothing of these gangs and had never made the connection from what I saw on the news or read in the newspaper about the shootings on the south side that these shootings were gang related. Gangs. Those living around the city did not like to call them "gangs." Youth workers called them "street crews." In November 1997, due to an increase in the number of fights in the high schools in the city district, the superintendent wrote to parents that gang-related violence did not occur in the schools, and he wanted to prevent that from happening. Before I worked on this project, I would have easily believed the superintendent. However, I witnessed firsthand gang-related violence at WANTS. In fact, many of the simple brawls were somehow connected to gang conflicts.

Boys and girls alike described the rituals that were required to belong to gangs. Girls had sex with multiple partners (usually older men)—often violently in the form of gang rape. Boys described being beaten severely—sometimes with weapons for a few solid minutes. They described having to demonstrate loyalty and toughness by robbing or hurting others in front of their gang members. Violence was taught and reinforced within the gang families. It was a significant part of what young people did within their groups. Violence was a way of demonstrating that one was loyal—that one cared.

Personal violence is difficult to define—even in the school setting. Teachers and students are victims and perpetrators and define personal violence differently. Children who experienced physical, emotional, and sexual abuse in the home from the time they were very young, and who were assigned to WANTS, did not label most acts that adults considered "violent" as such. To many young people growing up in environments where personal violence was pervasive, it was considered normal or "just the way it was," and was very complicated. Young people within this culture had complex ways of defining acceptable violence, including the reasons for behaving violently such as protecting others or "having heart." Violent behavior (as constructed through my lens) was learned and practiced at home and on the street. The tools they learned to use to keep themselves safe—fighting, carrying weapons, and gang membership—were the same behaviors for which their schools had no tolerance. Even though, these contradictory perceptions caused great conflict for the students.

CHAPTER 2

Social Location and Perceptions of Personal Violence

Notions of personal violence at the two schools depended on one's social location—one's race, class, gender, age, geographic location, and so on. Race and social class were intertwined at the WANTS school, although the situation was different at the Lorenzo Hill School because there were only a few students of color (no African American students), but there were poor students. At Lorenzo Hill the less affluent students tended to be ostracized and be the victims and the perpetrators of violence more often than wealthier students.

At WANTS, nearly all students qualified for free or reduced lunches—indicating that they lived in poverty and, although the overwhelming majority were African American, there were some other students of color as well as white students who received their lunches at less or no cost. Poverty at WANTS where nearly all students were poor was typically not used as a reason to ostracize or oppress a person, but racial minority (in the case of WANTS, white students) students were ostracized and often oppressed by other students. Gender played a significant role in the ways that personal violence was interpreted and practiced within relationships. The role of gender was different at WANTS and at Lorenzo Hill. Age, usually whether one was considered an "adult" or a "child," also affected the way violence was understood. There was a less obvious difference between WANTS and Lorenzo Hill. At both sites, however, adults and children had entirely different perspectives about violence and consequently had difficulty understanding one another's conceptions of violence and issues related to it. At both sites adults seemed to underestimate the personal violence that the children experienced. At Lorenzo Hill the children's experiences included physical and verbal abuse on the buses and at school, ostracizing, and other forms of cruelty, but these forms of violence occurred often unnoticed by the adults. Conversely, at

WANTS adults tended to underestimate the importance of the gangs and the presence of physical violence within relationships.

Race and Class

The role of race was complex in these settings. I found that despite difficulties talking about race, adults and young people did recognize race as important in a variety of ways. The majority of students at WANTS were African American, and most students lived in poverty. Thus, students who were either African American or poor were likely to be members of the dominant groups. Being obviously wealthy or white would mean that a student would be persecuted verbally and sometimes physically. At Lorenzo Hill, most students came from fairly affluent homes and were white. In this site, the majority ruled and the more popular students were likely to be wealthier and always white.

When new students or new staff first arrived at WANTS, students tended to ignore and ostracize these new members of the school community regardless of race—even though many students knew one another because they were cousins (sometimes distant) and grew up in the same neighborhoods. Outside speakers from the neighborhood centers were also greeted more warmly—particularly if they knew the more popular students. Strangers, regardless of race, took some time to be accepted. Teachers were not considered as worthy of respect until they earned it.

I noticed as a researcher that students shunned me when I first walked in the door. I felt like a ghost. Students would look right past me, as though I was not even there. I would sit in discussion groups with students, and my presence would be ignored. It took months before any of the students even acknowledged me, and it was not until I started the literacy project when some of the students began talking to me. Gaining acceptance, particularly as a white woman from a different neighborhood, without a clearly defined role or title in this culture, was particularly difficult.

Racial similarity and neighborhood identification played a role in the speed of student acceptance of other students and adults. In my case, as a white adult from a different community, it took a long time to gain acceptance (if I ever did), as it did other white staff from outside the city. However, the few African American staff gained acceptance from students more rapidly. For example, Sherry talked about an almost automatic acceptance and enthusiasm she felt from students of color when they found out that she was racially "mixed," despite her social class (living in a wealthy suburb of the city). Sherry told me:

[Students would say things like] 'All right! Black teacher.' They would say it like that . . . Yeah and sometimes they would say, 'are you from Africa or something? Are you Indian? Are you Hawaiian?' And I'd say, 'I'm all of those.' And so one day somebody said, 'are you African or are you Hawaiian?' I think it was something to that effect. She doesn't know what she is . . . I'm all of those. I'm Indian, I'm Hawaiian, I'm black. I'm . . . Cause I do looked mixed. Yeah. And Jamie said that to me. I knew when she first came that she could relate to me. Because right away when Jamie said to me, 'where are you from? Are you mixed or something like that.' I knew that she was. I knew it. Because why would she ask me that? Because she felt that she could relate to me, right? And I could tell by her hair texture and looking at her that I said, OK, she's mixed. And when her mother came I knew. I knew when her mother came down . . . her mother looks like she's Hispanic white. When she came down . . . she didn't tell me. I knew with her. And I think that that made Jamie feel more secure. So they don't . . . so things like that, yeah. [There was an automatic trust] with some, yeah, I'm not sure about Christy cause Christy's white. But yeah, I think so, yeah.

The intersection of race and class was particularly interesting in Sherry's case because Sherry lived in a wealthy suburb of the city and her children went to a middle- to upper middle-class public school. Despite the socioeconomic difference from most of the WANTS students who were typically poor, she was accepted because of her color. Nancy, by contrast, was white, but she lived in the same neighborhoods that many of the children from the school called home. The students accepted her too. She described the impact of geographic location and the importance of seeing students outside of class in their own neighborhoods to build trust. In other words, ethnic background became less of a factor if a teacher's home turf was the same as that of the students. Tom built trust with students by eating lunch with them in the cafeteria and by bringing students to his rugby games on Saturdays. Nancy talked about what she did:

I live in the city and I've always lived in the city, and I truly believe that living in the city is a commitment to my job. I know other people don't believe that, but I've worked with a lot of teachers who are terrific teachers but live in the suburbs and when it comes down to the nitty gritty level . . . going into a kid's house for dinner, or going and doing a home visit, they draw the line. And so they don't have that same view of things. I like living in the city. I like going to the same grocery stores that some of these kids go to. I like them to see me in a regular, every day living context. I like being involved in basketball league. There's an organization called Valuable Junior Athletic Association that my husband and I have been involved in for years and we've been officers and stuff. And our children are grown now, but I still have contacts there, and I like being able to come in and say, Ricky, talk to me Ricky . . . he loves basketball . . . Nobody in Ricky's household is going to connect him with a basketball league. But I can connect him with a basketball league and get the fee waived and get Ricky involved in something. Living in the city, I know those kinds of things and I can do those kinds of things. You don't know that living in the suburbs. But I got married at this church next door. My husband's whole family is from this area. He went to school here. My mother-in-law graduated from here. She taught school here. So it's kind of like this full circle that I've come to.

Because Nancy knew these children outside the school, as well as inside, she was able to earn their trust and build caring relationships with them. She was not afraid of these children of whom others, she thought, believed they were "axe murderers." She said:

> I'm not fearful down here. Actually, not. There's some kids that I'm cautious about, and I'm not a fool. And there's some kids I wouldn't be in a room alone with, but I'm not fearful overall of coming to work. My son is in the police academy right now, training to be a police officer and already I'm starting to see some things in him that I thought, 'oh no, they're brain washing you.' But he said, 'Mom, I want you to carry mace.' And I said, 'no.' Yes, so we've had this little battle back and forth. He said, 'you know you're there right in the afternoon, you come out in that parking lot by yourself.' He said, 'you've just got to be smart, Mom'. Well we're still debating it. But I almost feel if I carried the mace I'm giving in to this.

Nancy fought "giving in to" the stereotypes and the misconceptions that these students posed a threat to her. These stereotypes and misconceptions seemed to be pervasive not only within the mostly white police department, where her son was training, but among others in the white community. I noticed that many of my white friends and family members were concerned for my safety until I explained to them that the students were the ones at risk of being hurt far more than I was. Students had no "beef" with me. Some students though had "beef" with Nancy, though, because she was a disciplinarian, and for some, she was responsible for sending them to WANTS. Despite this background, she was not afraid. Adults often failed to see the connection between the pressures they felt from their families and friends to carry weapons, such as mace, to stay safe, and the pressures the students felt to stay safe too.

Many of the teachers were not able to describe race and class. When I tried to ask specific questions about race, class, and gender, most white teachers changed the subject. One such example was Jerry's response when I asked him what role race and class played in the classroom and the behavior of his students. He said:

> It's a tough issue. Some teachers think it does play in. I don't know. I don't really know. If this was say, 80% white population, I don't know if we would have a VCR/TV in each room or down the hall I can pick it up and show something. I don't know if there'd be supplies . . . if there was say 90% white if there'd be a full time teacher for just the middle school students and a full time teacher for the high school students. It seems like it makes more sense cause these students all need more help, but I don't know. Like you say it can be interpreted in any way. If you want to believe that then I'm sure that's how you feel. But if you don't want to believe that that's how

you feel too. It's all just somebody's opinion I don't know. Unless you can prove it. . . somebody has a document saying, you know let's see, o.k.

Perhaps Jerry's difficulty articulating his own personal views about the role of race and social class may have been the lack of discourses to talk about race and class. There was a certain degree of paranoia about being labeled "racist" for saying the wrong thing. Therefore, in many cases it was easier to dodge the question or to try to stumble through a politically correct answer as Jerry did. Moreover, Jerry, like most of the teachers at WANTS, was in the racial minority compared to the total number of people at the school, but he was among the majority of those in power (administrators and teachers). Race in his case was further complicated by his position of power as a teacher within this environment.

For the most part, student groups segregated themselves by race and geographic location: The gangs were structured by city blocks, and students tended to "hang with" students from the same block. In the literacy project, Paul, who was white, and Dwayne, who was black, were very close friends. Most of Paul's friends were black, even though he lived in the "Valley," which was a mostly white section of town. Paul had white friends, too, but when he was at WANTS, he "hung with" Dwayne and other black students. Paul and Dwayne's friendship broke the unspoken rule that one needed to hang out with members of their neighborhood (same socioeconomic background) and race. Paul said that students and the black hall monitors would accuse him of trying to "act ghetto" or "act black," but as Paul said, "I just try to be myself," although he admitted that he acted differently with his white friends from how he acted with his black friends. He was very matter of fact about there being clearly a black way and a white way of acting. He learned how to navigate both worlds, but when one world found out about the other, he had trouble explaining. For example, he told me that he was on the news when a reporter was doing a story on WANTS and his white friends saw him on television with black students, hanging on the corner. He said that they asked him why he was hanging out with such "thugs." He responded, they were the other students at WANTS and that he was just sitting on the corner waiting for the bus. For students like Paul, who straddled both the white world and black world of friendship, it was necessary to keep the two completely separate.

Amani, the only student who was openly Muslim and whose parents were from the Middle East, made an interesting observation about social class when he described doing community service in one of the local private high schools, comparing it to his own public school experiences. He said: "Those kids get real dishes. That's what I had to do was wash up dishes after those faggot kids ate. I hate private school kids. My mom wants me to go to [a local private Catholic school], fuck that shit . . . after that shit, my mom brought me to Palestine for eight months." Amani, like other students, observed the difference between the have and the have-nots. Students commented about the disrepair of the school and that they were not getting the same level of education as other students. Amani said after leaving WANTS, "I hated WANTS . . . it was all right, but it's not the right education. It's mad easy . . . I don't know how to explain it. They don't teach you nothin'." Many students recognized that they were being short-changed as far as their educational pursuits, but were unable to articulate this feeling. Some did not mind the watered-down education, because they had always been poor students, and some of the teachers taught to the lowest level of under-standing.

Students struggled with issues of race and social class, and social groups were segregated by race and gender. Social class was difficult to determine, although those who were unkempt and smelled bad generally were outcasts. Below is the description of one of the first white girls to come to WANTS during the second year of my observations. There is obvious tension around race and gender:

> When the girl walked into the classroom, Steven, one of the other students said, "what's your name girl?" She did not respond. He asked, "hey girl, do you play an instrument?" Annie, the teacher, told him he was being disrespectful. Then Steven asked her, "hey, do you speak another language?" She said, "yes." He asked her to say something and she said something in a foreign language. Tarissa, the only other girl in the room (who was African American) was disgusted with the boys' behavior (one of the other African American boys, James, had been harassing her quietly). Tarissa said she had to go to the bathroom and stormed out of the room.

> The lesson went on, and when there was a break in the action, Darryl, the African American young man next to Steven (who was also African American) pronounced, "You know what? White people are not stupid, just dumb. I don't trust them at all."

> Steven responded, "I have a friend who is white."

> Darryl added, "They's sneaky."

> When Tarissa returned from the bathroom, the boys continued to harass her. Darryl said, "Tarissa, I smoke eyebrows for breakfast (she has very thick eyebrows)."

In this exchange, there were more boys than girls. This occurrence was rare though at WANTS because the girls' attendance was higher than the boys'. In these instances, male harassment of females was common, regardless of race, and teachers had a difficult time getting students to stop. Occasionally, when the behavior got out of control, teachers would write "referrals" for in-school suspensions. However, too often this behavior was considered "harmless flirting," even when it was clear that the girls wanted it to stop but felt powerless to make it stop. More often, the girls outnumbered the boys, and boys in these situations tended to be silent.

In the setting at WANTS, where whites are the minority, the racist comments I heard were typically more like Darryl's. There would be comments about a general mistrust of whites, but more often there were stereotypical assumptions made about music preferences. Paul said that when black students first met him when he was hanging out with Dwayne, they did not trust him and were curious as to why a white boy from the "Valley" would be hanging out with one of the boys from the 'hood.

Race and Class at Lorenzo Hill: The Issue of Difference

At Lorenzo Hill there was virtually no racial diversity, but there was great socioeconomic diversity in that there were very wealthy and very poor children at the school. Students tended to be in cliques based on their socioeconomic status. The popular students were typically wealthier and healthier. As a result, students identified popularity with athleticism (e.g., being a fast runner), attractiveness, thinness (obesity was unacceptable), where one lived (the trailer park or on the lake), and expensive clothes (name brand). In this culture conformity was important. Any visible sign of difference resulted in exclusion, but these more important aspects of difference were those often linked to socioeconomic class.

It was not that students who were different for whatever reason were obviously treated poorly or called names, but it was evident that these students were not accepted because they would not interact closely with other students during games, class activities, or in the hallways. Some would try to talk to other students in line or in class and be ignored. They would try to get attention by acting out or not participating. These students also tended to cling on to the teachers and try to be near them. The girls would hug the big physical education teacher, and the boys would just be close, looking for supportive words. They were clearly not a part of the group. They were on the margins, and they knew it.

In some cases, those on the margins, but especially boys, acted out in physically aggressive ways. These few boys tended to make up the majority of the chronic discipline referrals and were outcast by teachers, bus drivers, administrators, and students alike. They had reputations as troublemakers and seemed to get into more trouble because people were waiting for them to do something wrong, a self-fulfilling prophecy. Conversely, girls only rarely acted aggressively. There was one girl at Lorenzo Hill Elementary who had a reputation among staff for being aggressive and had been in trouble a couple of times for her behavior. She lived in the poorer section of the district and was on the "toughest" bus route.

Violence and Gender at WANTS

When I told people who were not from the city school district that there were an equal number of girls and boys at WANTS, and often more girls than boys attending school, they were usually shocked to learn that so many girls were bringing weapons to school. It was expected that girls did not fight or behave aggressively, and girls at Lorenzo Hill generally lived up to this expectation. Boys overwhelmingly comprised the list of discipline referrals for aggressive behavior, but in the urban district where WANTS was located, girls were reported as being violent just as often as boys. When girls behaved aggressively or violently, adults seemed to notice this behavior more readily than when boys engaged in the same behavior (hitting, slapping, and so forth). Girls, then, seemed to pay the price for violent behavior at higher rates than boys. Often the old adage "boys will be boys" meant that boys involved in fights were not as likely to be severely punished (e.g., being removed from school) as girls were who were caught fighting with one another.

Teacher and Administrator Reactions to "Violent Girls": "Girl Fights Are Worse"

Nearly every teacher in the WANTS district, when I asked about girls fighting in school said, "girl fights are worse." Many of their reactions were almost identical to the ones of a retired veteran teacher from the school district who said:

> We were told not to interrupt fights. We were told that the administration would do that and that teachers should not do it. We were told by our union not to touch students. Many teachers still do to this day, yet they're not so much admonished or reprimanded, they're just told to stay out of it. 'Press your little buzzer if it should happen in your room. Get the administration. Get the cop up to try to rectify what's going on, but don't touch the students for your own safety and also for any harassment charges or even sexual harassment charges if you should touch a female. [When speaking of a fight in his classroom between two girls] I just let the fight happen. By that time, the students had stopped it within the class. They were aghast that I wasn't doing anything except staying out of the way. I was physically concerned about what would happen to me. I did my duty in the sense of trying to get someone up there that could take charge. But there was no way I was going to stop that fight. They were pulling hair, scratching. No weapons were involved.

I heard very tough male teachers claim that they would break up fights between boys but stay away from girl fights because they were seen as "more dangerous," that there were "no rules," and if you got in the way, you could be seriously hurt.

Girl fights were visibly more emotionally charged with screaming, crying, and yelling. Strong emotion had no place in school. Most adults did not know what to do in these instances and were afraid. In addition, because girls were not supposed to fight, adults tended to pay more attention to them. These fights seemed quite different from the boys' fistfights, and the perception of adults and other students was that girl fights had no rules and as a result were more dangerous. Even so, there were some rules: scratching, kicking, biting, and hair-pulling were allowed. In addition, there were important reasons for fighting. The most important reason—boys.

When students, particularly boys, talked about girl fights they said they were "cool," but many girls agreed that most often these fights were "stupid" and "over boys." I began to wonder if girl fights were a setup where boys would talk about girls' boyfriends and love interests in such a way that girls would fight each other simply because girl fights were "cool." Furthermore, I wondered whether part of the reason boys perceived girl fighting as cool was because there was some element of sexual fantasy that boys had about two women being together passionately—even if the passion that brought them close together was rage or jealousy. In fact, James admitted that young men liked it when girls fought over them.

One boy said, "I saw these two girls going at it. Girls are nastier fighters than boys. They'll scratch at each other's eyes and rip out each other's hair." Another boy explained why he thought girl fights were worse, "when girls start going at it they are more violent than the guys . . . guys will throw punches, but girls will go at it. Cat fights. The nails come out and all this other stuff . . . most girls I know if they throw a punch it really doesn't hurt that much, but if they dig their nails into your face it hurts a lot." The object in a fight was to win—and if you could not win, then it was viewed as important to hurt the other person as much as possible. Because girls were not taught how to punch and did not typically practice or engage in physical activities that strengthened the arms, they were not as likely as boys to be good punchers, so they used what hurt—nails, teeth, hair pulling, or weapons such as mace and pepper spray. Interestingly, these two weapons did not require getting close to the target, or being strong, as a knife or box cutter would. Some girls, though, could fight like the boys. They had well-developed and strong arms and legs that they used. Some girls at WANTS were described as punching like men, and they were the ones who would get suspended because of fights.

Girls' and Boys' Hierarchies of Femininity and Masculinity

Stereotypical notions of masculinity and femininity were important both in the WANTS and in the Lorenzo Hill school cultures. However, I witnessed the more "traditional" forms of femininity at Lorenzo Hill: being attractive to boys, being soft spoken, and being demure. At WANTS greater importance was placed on toughness and the ability to "thug it." Girls would tell me that the boys liked it when girls would fight over them, so girls would need to be willing to demonstrate that they would fight at the slightest provocation or threat to their relationship with their men. Most of the girls felt a need to not only be tough, but also to be attractive to boys—spending what little money they had on their hair and nails, although some girls learned how to do their elaborate hairstyles and nails themselves or with the help of friends or family. However, many girls seemed to find negotiating the turf between toughness and tenderness difficult. There were many examples of the lines blurring, but perhaps the most obvious was girls constantly hitting the boys they liked—giving new definition to "hitting on" boys.

For boys, masculinity seemed to be consistent with Frank's (1996) analysis. Frank identified three "pillars" or arenas that were critical for hegemonic masculinity: the body, athletics, and sexuality. These three areas were key for boys who were doing "masculinity." First, the body was important in Frank's analysis. At WANTS and Lorenzo Hill, being physically big and strong and considered sexually attractive were essential in gaining status and avoiding victimization. Second, Frank found athletics to be an important component of masculinity. At WANTS in physical education classes and at the community center, I observed the basketball court was a critical site for establishing a pecking order and dominance among boys. Boys at WANTS spent hours in sport-related activities. They would study the sports page and talk about their athletic prowess. Boys would come from gym class hot and sweaty and engage in lengthy discussions about playing. Not surprisingly, the better players were more popular. Girls at WANTS though rarely engaged in gym class. Sometimes they would stretch, but mostly they sat and talked and watched the boys play.

Female masculinity? Girls who were bigger and stronger in the WANTS school culture tended to be among the more popular students. They were rarely victimized, and they were leaders. They were outspoken and rarely challenged by other girls in discussions. A big, strong body tended to improve a girl's status in this environment, too—as long as she had demonstrated that she was not afraid to use her body to physically fight. Sometimes really strong girls would take on the boys to demonstrate their strength. This seems counter to much of the feminist literature that describes girls (mostly white) starving themselves to reach a cultural ideal of thinness. There was no such ideal within this environment. There was no discussion of dieting or exercising to lose weight. Girls at this site were not necessarily expected to be good at sports or compete with the boys, although some physical education classes combined girls and boys, but they needed to be tough. I remember playing basketball with Donise, who could not shoot the ball high enough to make it to the hoop. She just laughed and sat down. The boys took no notice of her unsuccessful attempts and continued to play the game. It was not important. It was not a part of her sexuality. However, Donise did need to be tough. She openly admitted punching her mother when her mother hit her. This kind of public description of one's willingness to fight was important for girls as it was for boys.

At Lorenzo Hill, having a strong athletic body was important for boys and girls. In focus groups with sixth graders both boys and girls agreed that being athletic was a relevant attribute in establishing their popularity. Clearly the lines between traditional masculinity and femininity were becoming blurred at both WANTS and Lorenzo Hill, but in slightly different ways.

Sexuality was extremely important in the school space where masculinity and femininity were being negotiated. Middle school boys at WANTS were often talking about sex when they were in groups with one another—who was "gettin' some" and who was not. Being a seventh grade virgin was clearly a terrible thing to be. One would be called "faggot" or "gay." These kinds of discussions took place frequently in the human sexuality and sexually transmitted disease (STD) workshops I observed, as well as in the cafeteria, classrooms, and hallways. The more popular boys could convincingly describe multiple conquests, and despite knowing the lingo about protecting themselves against STDs, they never described using condoms.

I do not mean to suggest that all boys were sexually active in the same ways, but that the discourse on sexuality focused on masculinity, and the boys were proving their masculinity by demonstrating that they were having sex regularly. The whole notion of "gettin' some" suggested the focus on male pleasure. Girls at WANTS did not use the same words when they talked about sex, although it was a very important topic for them. Their conversations revolved around their boyfriends or older men with whom they were involved and were more about relationships, although sometimes girls discussed sex with these men. It was important for girls to be experienced sexual partners—available to boys (or older men) once they had developed breasts and physically looked like young women. Having a boyfriend was essential, just as it was to demonstrate one's loyalty to one's man—which sometimes meant fighting other girls and young women, even if it meant causing bloodshed.

In contrast, the boys and girls at Lorenzo Hill were just beginning to become romantically interested in the opposite sex toward the end of sixth grade. Boys and girls still would play together outside of school and would work together in groups within school. "Having boy-girl parties" was a sign of popularity. Children at Lorenzo Hill did not talk about sex openly or even boyfriend-girlfriend relationships. This dynamic was markedly different from their counterparts at WANTS, who were a year older and talking openly about having sex on a regular basis. However, it was consistently clear at both schools—heterosexuality was the only option. Any suspicion of homosexuality was dangerous and had the potential to result in victimization.

Girls and Gangs. After meeting with Tarika and Talera, two WANTS middle school students, and two women from the local newspaper, who were doing a story on girls and gangs, I realized the size of the chasm between how much of white, suburban, middle-class America, including the media, framed violence and how the young people at WANTS, who indeed lived in violent urban neighborhoods, did. The reporters were genuinely shocked at the girls' stories and descriptions and tried to get the girls to change their perspectives on gangs and violence. However, they failed to understand what the girls were saying—that they were trying to do the best they could to keep themselves safe, and fighting, the carrying of weapons, and gang membership were the best strategies they knew.

I was not shocked by any of the comments the two girls made because I had been conducting my ethnographic research for over a year by then. I had heard the attitudes and perceptions before. However, I could tell that the other two white, middle-aged, middle-class professional women working for the paper were shocked and dismayed. It made me reflect again on how easy it was for adults—even adults who lived in the same city—to remain unaware of the violence and criminal behavior that was a part of some girls' daily lives. Prior to her discussion with Annie, the reporter did not know that there were girl gangs in the city. She had done some investigation on her own after that discussion and learned more about the largest girl gang in the city "911-Quickness" that had close to 100 members. In so doing, she found out more information about other girl gangs—mostly those located on the east side (the part of town where professionals lived and where the university was located). There was a new girl gang that I had not heard of before that called themselves "the Walkers."

Tarika, the more vocal of the two, said of girls in gangs that "all the girls were pregnant from the same guy or same group of guys" because they had to have sex with whomever the girls in the gang said they had to in order to become a member. These encounters, of course, were unprotected, which then resulted in so many of the young women becoming pregnant. Sex, though, was capital for young women, for they could trade having sex for protection. As women talked about why they joined gangs, they all gave similar reasons: to belong, to be social, and to be protected. The desire to belong was tantamount to many young women. Being a social outcast was difficult and made one a target of victimization. These young women wanted to be social, and, most importantly, social behavior revolved around finding a boyfriend. Gangs offered protection, but girls were scared of other groups of girls. If they were alone, they would be targets. However, they rarely realized that they were also targets even as members of a gang. Tarika talked about being suspected of *being down* with a gang that she claimed she was not and she was jumped by a rival gang as a result.

The reporters' comments made me realize that the language and desires of adults do not make sense to young people. They want to remove violence from the lives of young people, yet most adults fail to recognize the violence that surrounds them. Adults are bombarded daily by violent images in the media, bullies in the workplace, wars, abuse, assault, and harassment. This logic is similar to adults wanting youths to be drug free, yet the overwhelming majority of adults use psychoactive drugs, including alcohol, prescription medication, cigarettes, and others. We fail to recognize that young people are social animals as well and the same drug use and violence that accompanies adult relationships also accompanies the relationships of young people. I understand the reporters' comments about being afraid and wanting youths not to carry weapons and hurt each other; however, to the young people who have grown up where this behavior is the norm and not the exception, the perception is that there is no other way—there is no alternative. Thus, girls, just as boys, need to belong to gangs, carry weapons, and engage in violent behavior ironically to keep themselves safe, or so they believe.

Doing Gender at Lorenzo Hill School

At Lorenzo Hill Elementary School, I was struck by how early gender differences in behavior became apparent when trying to understand violence and its precursors in school. There were expectations among teachers and administrators that boys would behave more aggressively, less maturely, and were in trouble more often. Boys were expected to be more interested and more involved in athletics, although by the time students reached the middle school, the expectation among students was that girls needed to be athletic too.

As girls' bodies were developing in middle school, athleticism became increasingly important. Wealthier girls tended to participate in healthy lifestyles involving sports. Furthermore, the ideal female body was not just one that was thin, but also strong and athletic.

I asked the principal at Lorenzo Hill Elementary several questions about the kinds of discipline referrals she received. As I looked at the list and the reasons she compiled, I noticed that the overwhelming majority were boys. I mentioned this to her. She hadn't noticed. She said that girls in general were better behaved and better prepared for school. They became mature more quickly and seemed to have better social skills. The few girls who received recess detentions were never in trouble again. Only nine of the 50 referrals were girls, and one seemed to be a chronic offender with three referrals.

During my first student observation at Lorenzo Hill Elementary during free play in physical education class, I saw a group of very obedient children who sat quietly when they were asked to, although in every group a few boys sat in the back and moved around. The gender segregation was surprising, although some of it the teachers intended, and the other part happened naturally.

When I first walked in, there was a fourth-grade class already in session. All of the boys were playing a kind of modified football game while the girls sat on the bleachers and cheered for each team. The teacher was the football coach at the high school. In the last five minutes of class the boys and girls switched and girls got to play. Because they needed one more boy to make even teams, the teacher chose one of the smallest boys in the class. I expected there to be some teasing about this selection, but there was not. There was little interaction between the genders when students were asked to line up to pass to their next class. However, these children had clearly learned how to obey orders, how to play by the rules, and what the rules were for boys and girls. When they were told to line up quietly, they did so.

I conducted a focus group with the principal and three fourth-grade girls. The principal had students sign up to have lunch with her every day. Usually she said it tended to be the girls, but not always. In each of the groups I observed, there was one obvious leader. In one of the fourth-grade girls' groups, I was particularly struck by one girl, Jaimie, who was clearly the leader in the group, and the other girls watched and did not speak until it was clear that she was finished. The principal asked her about recess and some problems she'd heard about the girls' kickball game that Jaimie and another girl, Emmie, were responsible for organizing. Jaimie had the list and showed the principal who was on each team explaining, "we change it every week." The logic was fascinating. The focus was on collaboration not about competition. She said, "we used to fight when we'd pick teams using captains; so now we just do this, and people don't fight—Emmie and I just pick the teams every week on paper and tell people what team they're on." Nicky piped in that it worked better this way. When they talked about how they structured the game, they asserted that it was not about competition but about everyone getting a turn or having equal time for every team. She said, "we don't go by three outs and you switch; each team gets five minutes to kick and then we switch . . . if we forget our watches we just wait until everyone on the team has had a chance to kick, and then we switch." It was interesting to me how they elected to resolve the conflicts that arose around choosing teams, and that it was up to the most dominant two girls to decide and to write the teams on a piece of paper, and the others would go along. The once competitive game of kickball had transformed into a collaborative effort. They played on the field next to where the more popular and athletic boys competed in an aggressive football match. Girls within this site of free play were practicing the skills of collaboration right next to the site where the boys were practicing the skills of competition.

The genders rarely mixed. In fact, the girls claimed that the boys wanted to play their kickball game, and they told them they could only play if the boys would allow them to play in their football game. The boys replied that girls could not play football, and so the girls told them they could not play kickball. Sometimes the boys would take the girls' ball if it went into their space, and sometimes they would take the boys' ball if it came into their space, but usually the two groups did not intermingle. I asked if girls would tease those who were not as good at kickball and they said "no," that it was not really about being good or scoring but about having fun and getting a turn.

Observing Recess: What About Disability? The 30-minute recess followed the half-hour lunch for students in the elementary school, and students went outside nearly everyday for active play. They had a perfectly manicured and well-equipped playground. Monitors usually stood and watched quietly, but there were no reasons for intervention.

In addition to the kickball and football games (which comprised only about one third of the students on the playground), other students played on the many playground toys. Some girls sat quietly in groups and talked. A teacher pushed the only obviously disabled student on a swing. I thought about inclusion and realized that the playground was not a place where inclusion seemed to happen—at least not voluntarily.

Disabled students, despite the movement toward classroom inclusion were ostracized in sites where students had more control over their personal actions (playground, buses, gym, and lunch). It was not that students were ever obviously cruel toward students with disabilities, but they clearly did not include them in their games and fun activities on the playground.

"Doing gender" began early and was reinforced in school as young children learned that boys play rough and girls cheer them on—at least these were the messages reinforced at Lorenzo Hill. The messages seemed somewhat different from the WANTS environment, although girls were still expected to be weaker than boys and not be as good at sports as the boys. The fundamental difference was that girls at WANTS expected girls to be able to fight and be tough.

Age and Personal Violence:
It Was Different "Back in the Day"

The generation gap and difficulty communicating between generations are not new phenomena. The inability to communicate and take seriously what the "other" (adult or child) was saying had significant implications for adults and youths in both WANTS and Lorenzo Hill—often resulting in sarcasm, frustration, put-downs, and other forms of resistance and personal violence from both groups. Watching adult-teenager interactions was similar to watching two people from different cultures speaking different languages—nodding, sometimes politely (although more often showing great exasperation), not really understanding what the other person was saying. Usually, because adults were in positions of power over youths, the burden of responsibility rested on the teens' shoulders to learn the adult language, or else they risked grave consequences. Failure to abide by the rules set forth and enforced by adult culture could result in students being placed in school suspension or removal from the culture altogether. Lorenzo Hill students seemed to take these adult threats more seriously than the WANTS students did. Perhaps this was because the Lorenzo Hill students were younger, or because WANTS students had learned that adults did not understand their worlds. WANTS students accepted that they were "bad kids" in the eyes of adults, and there was little they could do to change this perception—not that they necessarily wanted to.

Some of the WANTS teachers were still in their twenties and thought of themselves as young and able to relate to the teenagers. However, the teenagers, although they may have thought some of these teachers (particularly Tom) "were pretty cool for a teacher," still considered them to be "adults" and out of touch with their teenage reality. Adults did not seem to make much of an effort to understand teenagers' perspectives on their own behavior and behaviors of others. Sometimes they would listen as students tried to explain their side of a story, but generally adults thought of students as "hormone cases" who were overly fixated on sexuality and their own bodily changes. Most adults acknowledged that the time in middle school and early high school was the period when children were going through a great deal of change physically and emotionally, but adults did not meet them on their terms. Teens were expected to obey adult-made rules blindly. Those who challenged the rules were charged with "failure to obey request of staff member."

People defined violence differently based on their age. What adults considered violent was often not considered problematic or violent to students at WANTS. This difference in definition was further complicated by race and socioeconomic class. As mentioned, teachers were mostly white and middle class, and students were mostly African American and poor. At Lorenzo Hill, where conformity to adult standards was more widely accepted by children, adults and children had similar definitions of violence. Although teachers did not think there was a violence problem at Lorenzo Hill, many students reported being victims of violence either in school or on the buses. Adults were still out of touch with the students' realities.

Race, social class, gender, geographic location, and age played a major role in how one framed personal violence in this project. Young people who grew up in the WANTS neighborhood (who were often poor, African American, or racially "mixed") tended not to consider certain acts of physical violence, gang membership, and weapon-carrying as problematic in contrast to adults living outside the community who were usually white and middle class. These adults seemed completely unaware of the violence these children experienced. Adults within the community also saw the aforementioned behaviors as problematic and were beginning to realize that their efforts to reduce them had been ineffective and that they needed new strategies. Unfortunately, the communication between adults and children in this environment was limited and in conflict because both sides had different ideas of what needed to happen for young people to be safe.

Interestingly, a similar although less dangerous pattern was evident at Lorenzo Hill as at WANTS—children did not believe that adults understood them, and adults in the school believed that children in their school did not need anti-violence programs, even though the overwhelming majority acknowledged on a survey that they had experienced violence and verbal abuse in school and on the school bus.

Different Levels of Acceptable Personal Violence

There appeared to be a fundamental difference between WANTS and Lorenzo Hill in terms of the levels of acceptable violence. It was as though certain forms of physical violence fell beneath the radar screen of those working at WANTS. Typically verbal taunting, teasing, assaults (unless there was a fear that these assaults would lead to a physical altercation), sexual harassment (particularly if verbal in nature), pushing, shoving, slapping, and other forms of "less danger-ous" physical violence school personnel saw on a regular basis without responding.

There were forms of personal violence that I thought went unnoticed or had no response in both Lorenzo Hill and WANTS. This was the fairly obvious ostra-cizing of certain students who were "different." Consequently, these students ate meals alone, sat alone, and sometimes did group projects alone (or at least sat si-lently and did not contribute).

We seem to have developed a hierarchy of acceptable violence in America that is different for different groups based on race, social class, gender, and other aspects of social location. If we are to successfully reduce and ultimately create safe schools, we need to address the "lower levels" of violence such as teasing, ostraciz-ing, slapping, and so on. Programs such as the "No Putdowns" curriculum (described in the final chapter) address these lower levels of violence while recog-nizing cultural differences. We need to understand how individuals in schools from various social locations make sense of violence and make decisions about acceptability of certain forms of violence before we can identify strategies to re-duce school violence problems.

CHAPTER 3

Personal Violence and Feelings: Pain, Fear, Passion, Love, Anger, and Revenge

Along with developmental changes, young people at WANTS were struggling with intense emotions, some as a result of tragic losses: anger, attraction, sadness, loneliness, happiness, and so on. Most of the adults sent a message loud and clear (a message consistent with most schools)—emotion, especially strong emotions, had no place in schools. Emotions were to be controlled at all times. The young children at Lorenzo Hill also learned that strong emotions and personal issues had no place in the classroom. The nurses' office was where young people in physical pain were sent at both WANTS and Lorenzo Hill and, if severe enough, children were sent home. Young people were not allowed opportunities, particularly within the school setting, to display their emotional pain outwardly. As a result, young people learned to deny their emotions or cover them with anger and aggression. Some students found supportive people within the school with whom they could share their inner turmoil (caused by passion, loss, and grief), but many did not. Many students, whether at Lorenzo Hill or at WANTS, had a difficult time in school and struggled with their emotions and how to behave in adult-deemed "appropriate" ways. However, there were significantly more students at WANTS with more emotional strife because of their stress-filled life from living near or below the poverty line, living with violence at home or in their neighborhoods, or dealing with regular loss. Moreover, at WANTS, many students just chose to avoid school altogether.

Pain, Grief, and Violence:
What Do Schools Teach Us About Handling Pain?

In many cases, WANTS students had experienced great pain—some in the forms of physical, sexual, and psychological abuse and others in the forms of loss, loneliness, and despair over the loss of loved ones to prison, drugs, or death. I heard so much about the pain and loss that young people at WANTS felt on a daily basis, not from the students themselves, but from the staff who had built trusting relationships with students. Perhaps because they did not show their grief the same way I would, outwardly—they did not cry, or at least not what I saw, or sit around with sad faces—I did not think their pain was that severe. I began to think differently as I struggled to deal with my own loss during the first year of this pro- ject—the death of a young girl I had known. I began to open my eyes to the ways that pain, grief, and loss were demonstrated. Frequently, grief was demonstrated by violence—often in the form of retaliation.

I had my first emotional kick in the stomach while I was at WANTS; not a real kick, but it hurt like one. I couldn't cry. I could only respond in my grown-up way, asking more questions than there were answers. The bottom line was that one of the most horrendous acts of human violence that I had ever heard of had happened to a young woman, a former student of mine, who had grown up in the same neighborhood—only a couple of blocks from WANTS. I was her counselor when she started at the local university—the first in her family to attend college. I had talked with her about her goals—her future, her plans—but it was all over now.

The long search for her began in June 1996 when she disappeared. She did not show up for work, a job that she and I had talked about because I had worked for McDonald's too when I was a teenager saving money for college. She was too. She had grown up in a very poor section of town—near the WANTS school. She was black. She was obese. She was extremely shy. These are personal attributes that our dominant culture condemns. As a result, she was painfully insecure. However, she had a boyfriend. This fact made her feel a bit better about herself— more attractive, safer, and protected. I remember asking her about walking to McDonald's in the early morning hours in the dark. She told me that her boy- friend walked with her, to protect her.

After nearly two years of searching, it was announced at a press conference that her body parts had been stuffed in the walls of her next-door neighbor's, her boyfriend's home, where he continued to reside with his parents. With her rotting flesh in his walls, he continued to deny any involvement in her disappearance, although he had been questioned by the police for months. He confessed to knocking her down. She hit her head and was unconscious. He did not call for help. When he realized she was dead, he tried to get rid of any evidence. He must have cleaned up well, for his parents claimed they knew and suspected nothing. What parents would suspect such a thing of their son?

I am including this story because I heard the news when I was at WANTS, and it made me realize the important expectation that one will not show pain or vulnerability openly in school. I was a block away from where the police were going through the boyfriend's parents' home—next door to her parents' home. I had just finished one interview with a teacher and was about to begin another interview. Life must go on, right? It was beyond what my mind could really fathom. The horror movies that I never watch might depict such a plot, but I still could not manage to really deal with this story. It is somewhat strange that I heard it from the woman who had told me so many horrible stories about the pain and abuse that the students at WANTS suffered. It was almost as though she was the best person to tell me. I had learned how to hear painful things from her and lock them away.

Life went on. I did what I was scheduled to do for the rest of the day, feeling a sense of despair, depression, and detachment. I did not stop. I began to think about the pain that these students at WANTS feel every day—the pain of having an incarcerated parent, the pain of having an abusing parent, the pain of having a drug-abusing parent, the pain of having a friend shot and killed, or the pain of abandonment. So many of their lives were filled with unexpressed pain. However, the feeling that really hit me hard was that, "this world sucks!" to put it in the terms of these kids. I thought about how I could protect myself in this world that I was researching—a world where a young girl's body parts could be found in the walls of her neighbor's house. The feeling I had was that I never wanted to go back again. I wanted to stop doing this research. I had collected enough "data," I said to myself. It's time to stop. I wanted to escape. At times, I'm sure these children did too. They could not drive out to sleep in the suburbs—they would escape any way they could, frequently with drugs. I was thinking about one of my best friends who died from leukemia. He was in the hospital for the last time from May until almost September experiencing terrible pain from open lung surgery. They gave him Demerol—self-administered. Living in a hospital room, worrying about whether today will be his last, in pain, was horrible for him. His shots of Demerol gave him some pleasure. Some escape. His situation was not that different from the situation of these children. They lived in atrocious conditions. They worried if each day was going to be their last. They were in great pain from abuse and loss. Drugs helped numb the pain and introduced pleasure into an otherwise pleasure-free life. Drugs were easy—easy to buy and easy to use.

Amani was depressed and entertained suicidal thoughts upon his return to regular school. He was using drugs as a way to deal with the pain. He said in an interview:

> I'm thinking about how everyone dies someday. A lot of my family is dead. You get used to it. But my moms man, I don't even want to think about my moms dying. My moms she's old fashioned. She did not know I would get in trouble for the box cutter. She hated WANTS. She is not going to like my report card. I can't really tell her my feelings. We only talk about regular things like food—she'll ask, 'what do you want to eat tonight?' That's how it is in my house—just me and her. I need somebody to talk to . . . I'm getting to wanting to shoot myself. I don't know what's wrong with me. It's hard for me here. I'm smoking too much weed right now. I'd tell everyone, 'don't smoke, don't start. It's messing me up right now.' I'd like to know about weed— other people's weed problems . . . I am skipping [class] right now because I can't handle being in class, even though I should be in there . . . I'm depressed, and it ain't the weather. People keep telling me, it's the weather and don't worry. I got track practice. I don't feel like going. I feel a little violent. Shit. I don't know how to explain my feelings. I don't.

Students like Amani medicated themselves to deal with their grief, pain, loss, and depression. The drug of choice for many was marijuana—as Amani described. Young girls who were pregnant continued to self-medicate with alcohol and marijuana. As one young girl told the assistant principal one day about her daily marijuana smoking throughout her pregnancy, "trust me, you'd rather that I use it than not—it keeps me out of trouble in school, so I can sit still and listen."

I began to think about less harmful ways students dealt with grief and stress. For some young people and their families in this environment, one way was through religion. Religion and regular church attendance came up frequently in discussions about death from violence. Some students would accept that it was "God's will" if it was time for you to die. Paul told me that becoming a part of a Bible study group and having a Christian life helped him get his life together after he was sent to WANTS.

Others used other strategies to cope, for example, basketball or other forms of exercise. Exercise is my drug to help the pain go away. I thought to myself, "Why not get these children more involved in exercise?" Where can they run, bike, play without fear of being jumped, beaten, or shot? Gym class every fourth day for about 15 minutes of play time is not enough. Some of the boys played basketball at local youth centers, but I noticed that the girls frequently had no such outlet. Perhaps fighting provided the necessary stress release. Similarly to competing in a sport, the buildup of anxiety, the surge of adrenaline, the competition, and the relaxing come down. Could fighting be a stress release? Both Paul and Dwayne described fighting as a stress reducer. They fought for sport—boxing at a local gym.

When my friend died of leukemia, I buried myself in work and used my body's own natural opiates through exercise to deal with the pain. I realized that "successful" students, like myself, learned to leave pain and suffering at the school or work doors, go in, do their job, work really hard, and don't outwardly show the pain. Many of the students at WANTS, labeled "unsuccessful" students, brought their pain into the building. They showed it by disruption in class, by questioning the direct relevance of what they were learning, by acting aggressively toward others. As a culture we have learned that emotions, often in relation to important interpersonal relationships, are personal and should be separated from the professional. Schools teach this norm early. However, children who have been overburdened with grief and can no longer conceal it, are removed from sight through alternative schools, suspension, or expulsion. Adults are hospitalized or imprisoned.

After about two months of observing at WANTS and hearing about my former student who had been dismembered, I wanted to do what so many people do about the problems with poverty, violence, and pain. I wanted to close my eyes and hope it would go away. If it did not go away from me, standing there in this school in the center of the violence, then I could go away from it. White flight. However, I could not. I wanted to figure out a way to make things better—even if it was just for a handful of students. What could I do as a researcher? I thought about including students in the writing of this book and not just of me as the researcher interviewing and observing them, but allowing students to determine what they would want to write about. Feeling powerless and deeply saddened by the events I encountered during this research project, I took many breaks from this project.

I talked to a colleague and friend who was a white woman doing research with teenage mothers—all of whom were black or Latina. We discussed how difficult it was to get these young people to see us as allies, as people who could be trusted as confidants. We felt invisible in these sites as researchers because the young people did not understand our role, and it was a struggle to explain our role to them. It was our goal to improve these young people's situations with our research and our writing. We thought about writing to other white privileged folks to try to make them understand the lives of these young people, so they would stop searching for simple solutions such as building more prisons, putting more cops on the streets, and removing young pregnant women from their schools to give them a watered-down version of their high school curriculum.

The day after I heard the news about Angel, the young woman who was murdered by her boyfriend, I had a meeting with a woman who was virtually a stranger at the university. She came to ask me about the doctoral program. We talked about violence, racism, and my project. We cried about what we had seen and experienced. As a white woman who was the mother of two black sons, she said she didn't have the option to run away from racism. She was confronted with it every day. She told me about co-counseling, a strategy that she said many social activists used to get through the difficulty of seeing this kind of pain daily. As she left, she said to me, "The Quakers have a saying—the Way will open." I held on to that throughout this project. When she left, I remembered that I was not fighting to change things all by myself. There were others committed to improving the lives of young people.

Shortly after this encounter, I had a meeting with my colleague and mentor who had just returned from Germany. Having grown up in London as a Jewish girl during World War II, she thought about the Nazis torturing and brutally killing the Jews in concentration camps as she flew over where the camps had been. Her relatives had been subjected to horrors that defy imagination. She said that the Germans seemed to have a different approach to violence. They seem to start with the assumption that anyone is capable of horribly violent acts against another person in a given situation. They saw this happen not too long ago. In the United States, though, we have a notion that there are "good guys" and "bad guys." "Bad guys" choose to be bad. "Good guys" choose to be good. Because it seems to be based somehow on conscious choice, this perception allows us to treat "bad guys" with contempt. In fact, we can justify locking up or even killing really "bad guys." Video games and other childhood games teach us from the time we are very young that we need to protect ourselves from bad guys, even if it means killing them. Video games are often based on this idea.

Grieving: The Profound Loss

Many of the WANTS students had experienced profound loss in their lives— parents who had been incarcerated; friends, cousins, siblings, and other family members who had been shot, some killed. Most students were separated from their closest friends when they were sent to WANTS. They had to get to know new teachers and new students. There was no desire to build much of a bond because students knew their relationship was temporary—like most of the relationships in their lives. As one girl said during her intake to WANTS when asked if she knew other students at the school, "I ain't gonna talk to nobody, so it won't be a problem."

When I sat in on a group of seventh- and eighth-grade girls who were learning about AIDS and transmission of HIV, there was an announcement made about a support group for daughters of incarcerated parents. The woman who ran the program said, "they don't still have to be incarcerated, maybe they were and they aren't anymore, you can still join." All of the girls in the group filled out the form to be involved. Each of them had experienced the incarceration of a parental figure.

Many of these students were not given time or space to experience grief over the losses in their lives. By failing to allow students time and space to experience loss, we dehumanize it. When the death or loss of a loved one is not experienced with grief, pain, or suffering, we learn not to feel compassion over any loss or death—including our own or that of somebody else. Students at WANTS will laugh at videos of disabled shooting victims or at a movie clip of a grieving mother who has lost her child to gunfire. They have learned not to show or feel pain in response to loss. Instead they have learned to return the hurt or respond with a retaliatory killing. When these young people experience a profound loss in their lives, instead of sadness, they more typically describe rage or the desire for revenge or retaliation. Sometimes the response is to make light of the situation, or to develop an "it's just the way it is" attitude. Some use religion as a way to make sense of the death that surrounds so many of the young people. As Adolphi said when talking in class about getting shot to protect his "ace": "We get to make it to heaven. That what was meant to be. God meant it. I die or not. Someone has a gun on me, I'm shot, that's God. If not, take the gun off me, I will kill you . . . It can happen any time! In a mall. It don't matter."

Adolphi responded emotionally, "This is reality. It's not like that. It's not nice and all that stuff! I'm not going to say, 'woops, I'm sorry I bumped you!' I ain't cryin', but if it comes down to it, I gotta do what I gotta do. That's me—ya know what I'm sayin'? It's my life. It's between him and me. It comes down to me. So I feel for him, but I say 'you choose!'"

Retaliation is such a part of shooting that Steven responded to this exchange by saying, "The dude is stupid. He knows if he kills one, the other will retaliate." However, Adolphi was quick to say, "Exactly, you don't get yourself in that situation. You say, 'chill, chill, chill,' but it happens so fast!"

Students talked graphically and without visible sadness or fear about violence they witnessed. Steven said in class, "I know someone who was shot in the brain and is still alive! They was just in the wrong place at the wrong time . . . brain was gushing down his nose . . . I remember one night I heard a shot. I was inside. . . ." He described this with great animation but with a smile on his face, as though he was a stand-up comedian trying to elicit laughter and the attention of others.

The gang-related shootings in the city for the previous two years were nearly all retaliation shootings. The students at WANTS who were most afraid of being shot were those who were somehow connected with the last gang shooting and knew that retaliation would come. Sometimes going to jail was a strategy to stay alive to eclipse retaliation shootings, as was the case for Julius, who had a week where he was shot at three separate times, although he never admitted to me that jail was a saving alternative. Julius threatened to attack a teacher, and he knew this behavior would get him arrested, although he showed no fear of being shot. Similarly, he displayed no sadness over the loss of his friend who had been killed and went through his day doing what he thought he needed to do to live through it.

Grief and Loss of Infants. Caseworkers working with teens and even preteen girls who lost babies have said that these girls often show no visible signs of grief or loss. However, individuals who have worked within criminal justice systems have indicated that women trace back their careers in crime to feelings of such profound loss and despair over the death of a baby or child that they felt there was nothing else to lose so they turned to drugs and associated criminal activities.

It is important not to make judgments about young girls and women based on their outward demeanor regarding grief and loss. Young women need support to cope with the loss of their babies just as other young people need help addressing their grief from loss of loved ones.

Aggression and Addiction

Violence was not only seen as a way of life for children at WANTS, but some detected similarities between how children at WANTS used violence and how individuals generally engaged in any kind of addictive behavior. Goldstein and McGinnis (1997) outlined the similarities between aggression and addiction:

> A long-term, stable behavior, repetitively enacted; subjective compulsion to use it; reduced ability to control or reduce it, in frequency or intensity; frequent relapses associated with negative emotional states, interpersonal conflicts, situations where used before; initiated and sustained by both person and environment; yields short-term pleasure despite long-term negative effects; used in response to, and to relieve, stress, negative mood, general arousal; often encouraged and rewarded by (peer, family) "enablers"; often experienced with a "rush" of pleasure/excitement; frequently accompanied by denial (e.g., attribution of blame); preoccupation with others' use of behavior (e.g., excessive viewing of violence on television); high rate of health risk, injury, death; taught, encouraged, rewarded by society." (p. 11)

Students at WANTS demonstrated many of these notions that Goldstein and McGinnis espoused. For example, students with whom I spoke described the feelings of an adrenaline rush from fighting, a preoccupation with aggression, high rates of injury from violent acts, and rewards from family and friends for behaving violently. Aggression within this environment closely resembled addiction in the ways Goldstein and McGinnis depicted it.

Paul and Dwayne provided perfect examples of the parallels between aggression and addiction. They were both trained boxers. For them, fighting was a rush. As Paul explained to me one day, "it's like I start punching and I can't stop. All these teachers tried to break it [a fight he was in during school] up, and I just hit whatever was in my way. It's like I don't think, I just want to keep hitting." He described it like an uncontrollable rush of emotion. These young people had little physical outlet for their aggression other than basketball. I observed many pick-up basketball games down at the center. These games were very serious, but rarely violent. The exception was when Julius was in a fight that started as a result of gang turf issues long before the basketball game. Tempers flared on the court, and he got into a fight outside the center. The fight did not happen on the court. However, the basketball court at the center had been identified as a safe space that young people respected. When the fight broke out outside the center, there was an adrenaline rush not only for the two fighting but for all of the bystanders. James, Dwayne, and Paul were also pumped up and wanted to fight. They could not seem to settle down and do the literacy training work with the younger children afterwards. Their conversations indicated their preoccupation with the altercation and what it meant for them. In fact, the drama lasted long after the actual aggression had ended, and there was much speculation about where Julius had gone—if he had gone to get some of his "boys" or whether he had gone home to get a gun as he said he would. This postfight drama happened at WANTS too. Students would be distracted and would talk about the most recent fight in class and build the suspense by speculating what might happen next to escalate the situation. No formal learning could take place in the classrooms after fights at WANTS because students would be too preoccupied.

Life Goes On: Dealing with Fear and the Desire for Revenge

A few days after I heard about Angel's murder, I was back at WANTS. I had another interview with the business teacher. After the interview, I passed by to say hello to April. She was sitting in the principal's office. Bruce, the principal, had returned the previous week after his recuperation from back problems that had been brought on by severe stress. He and Nancy were having a rather serious conversation, and April looked exhausted. She and I went to her office, and we started to talk as a young man was putting away newspapers and tidying up a bit. She introduced us. This was when I first met James, who was very polite when he greeted me. James was doing his community service for the school, which apparently involved cleaning. As he was leaving, April asked who was coming to pick him up. He answered, "my sister." She returned, "you be good to your sister— please take care of yourself."

After James left, April asked me if I had heard about the latest shooting. I hadn't heard about it. She told me that just outside the school building at about 9:30 the previous night one of her student's brothers who had just gotten out af- ter a year in jail (he was 17, and I did not know what he was in jail for) was critically wounded by a gunshot. She said there was a retaliation shooting at 3 a.m. of someone else. These two shootings were believed to be in retaliation for a mur- der/shooting that happened a few months earlier. The murder victim had been best friends with James. April was very worried about James being caught in the series of retaliation shootings. Instantly, I was scared too. I was scared for James. I was scared to go out to the parking lot. Selfishly I was scared of being caught in the cross-fire myself. I was scared for these kids.

April said that there would be another shooting, and it would likely involve one of the students at WANTS. She was afraid because they did not have a police officer at the school at that time. The district had approved funding for a police officer, she said, but apparently the mayor was holding up the process.

Nancy came in at some point during our conversation and said there was quite a crew forming outside. In fact there were eight African American males in front of the building, who seemed to be high school age or slightly above. It sounded as if they were worried about James, the young man who had just left. But they were clearly worried in general. There was quite a posse organizing out front, but then again, nearly every time I've driven by that corner, there were young people "hanging out."

When April left she said that she had called the school to which Ron had been transferred to see if he was okay, but she had not heard back yet. Ron's brother had always been in trouble. His mother did not want Ron to follow that same path. Therefore, she made sure he got involved with activities at the Com- munity Center. "If you want to know about a place that makes a difference, it's the Community Center. They have made an incredible difference in Ron's life. And James's too." She had said something to James about the people at the center making such a difference for Ron, and James said it had for him too. The coun- selors at the Community Center work with young people on how to act, and they do not tolerate swearing. Generally they do not put up with many kinds of behav- iors, but they work with those who are willing. When I worked on the literacy project at the Community Center, I experienced it as somewhat chaotic, but kids seemed to like being there. In addition to offering recreation, they had a variety of programs that taught young people about sex, diseases, job training, drugs, and so on. The center was a community agency comparable to many in areas of poverty—operating on a shoestring budget. They had more children who needed supervision and programs than they could possibly serve, and they tried to work closely with the young people under their tutelage. Their goal was to provide a safe haven where children could learn life skills to help them survive and to show them another way of life—one that did not revolve around violence.

I left when this day's events were reaching their climax—when the people inside the school walls stood waiting for someone to get killed. The police were starting to gather. I felt very nervous about what was going on outside. As I walked down the stairs, there were the two hall monitors looking out the doorway that faced the corner where the group was forming. They heard me come down the stairs and looked to see who it was. They were obviously very concerned.

I made it to my car. I saw two women from the day care center downstairs coming out, and I felt a bit safer with others around. I was on the opposite side of the building from the action, which was also reassuring. When I got into my car, I realized that I was not at any risk. These kids, though, were at great risk. They had to pass through territory that was not their own to catch the bus—without any weapons to protect themselves when everyone else out on the street had weapons.

It was a very cold day, but nevertheless there were many young people out on the street corners, approximately three to eight African American young men at just about each one as I was driving back from WANTS to the university. The way they were hunched and the fact that nearly all had sweatshirt hoods over their heads indicated that they were quite cold. They seemed just to be standing there. A police car and a police officer were on one of the corners. There seemed to be a group on one corner and another across the street.

What were they doing out there in the freezing cold? Were they socializing, perhaps with drugs? They were not welcome at bars where many people socialize around two of our socially acceptable and popular drugs. Some of them might not have been welcome at the community centers, schools, libraries, stores, or malls. The corner they could call their own. The corner they would fight for. The corner they might die for. This street. This block. They had nothing else. Their standing there reminded me of the pioneers fighting for land. It was not theirs, but they fought battles to defend these corners as theirs because they had nothing else. They felt they deserved it—they had earned it.

I wrote this account in the safety of my office—located on the hill—the ivory tower less than a mile away from where I was reminded of the approaching holiday season. Nobody I saw on campus had any idea that this kind of fight for survival was happening a few short blocks away. In fact, even I could put it out of my mind for a while when I got back to the safety of my home, waiting for the holidays to come to see my family and other loved ones—to shower them with gifts, food, and love. For some of these children, the holidays were just days where their poverty was rubbed in their face. They saw others with so much, and they had so little. They feared for their safety—at home and at school. They feared for those they loved, but only few feared for them.

I woke up the next morning and saw in the morning paper there had been a shooting a block away from WANTS at 4:30 P.M.—shortly after I had left. An 18-year-old boy, someone's son and brother, was shot and killed. He had many cousins at WANTS. It probably had been a retaliatory shooting. The folks at WANTS knew that someone was going to get shot and would probably die. They were usually right about such matters.

When I went back to WANTS that day, it was "business as usual." Life went on. There was some discussion of the shooting, and the students most affected were absent, but generally the school continued with students sitting in classrooms and teachers trying to teach. There were no visible signs of emotion. April confided to me that she feared there would be a retaliation shooting soon and that one of the students would be involved.

Fighting for Passion:
Heterosexual and Familial Love as Underlying Most Conflicts

The least common denominator of nearly every fight was some form of intimate, caring relationship, such as boyfriend-girlfriend or biological or gang family relationship. I realize that the first part of this statement is focused on heterosexuality, but in high school—at least the ones I observed—this was the only kind of acceptable sexuality. Any time homosexuality came up in a conversation or a talk, it was viewed with outward disgust and horrible name-calling. Homosexuality in these environments was simply not tolerated. In fact, the most violent acts were against those suspected of being homosexual.

A group of students at WANTS were talking about their friends. The boys said that they did not have a "best friend" as the girls did. They had an "ace" or someone they trusted more than most, but they would not even trust their ace in their home because he would probably steal from them. They would not trust him with anything important either. Although, as Steven said in class, "the ace will do anything for you. Ace dies for you." Adolphi said, "yeah, there was this fight on the south side. Gettin' it. We die for others." To this Steven replied, "yeah, when we fight, we go down, all together." They would die for their ace, even though they did not necessarily trust him.

The boys admitted that if they had anything serious to talk about, they would talk to a girl. Also, they would not "hang" with the same boy very often because they would be thought of as gay. If two boys went to the movies together, they would leave a space between them. There were many conscious acts boys engaged in to avoid being considered homosexual. Girls did not seem to feel the same need. In fact, the girls in the group were shocked about the boys' behaviors and said they thought it was "sad" that peer pressures forced them to act the way they did.

Heterosexual coupling (having a boyfriend or a girlfriend) though was viewed as a very important goal in these adolescents' lives. For boys this meant having regular sex with one or multiple partners. For girls, however, this meant having a serious boyfriend. Because being in a heterosexual, sexual relationship was viewed as so important, it was not surprising that most conflicts arose out of jealousy, fear of losing a sexual partner to another, flirting, hearsay, or standing up for a romantic partner.

Given this emphasis on sexual coupling among young people, it was not surprising that many young women were pregnant. Birth control was viewed as a sign that a girl did not trust or love her partner. Another sign of true love was to not use a condom during sex. In fact, among the middle school students at WANTS, despite knowing how HIV and other STDs were spread—the use of a condom was not seen as an option. The students instead talked about how to convince their partner to get tested for HIV before they had sex. The students quickly became silly during this discussion because they knew they would not ask their potential sexual partner to get tested—this would shake the signs of their trust.

Feeling Disrespected by Students, Staff, and the District

Disrespect was a popular term within the WANTS community and the surrounding neighborhoods. A lot of importance was attached to being respected—and the perception that one was not getting the respect one deserved could be used as an excuse for physical violence. Feeling disrespected was something that was mentioned to varying degrees by nearly all of the staff I interviewed at WANTS. In addition, respect, or lack of, seemed to be at the root of many of the conflicts that arose among students and between teachers and students. I witnessed the lack of respect on a daily basis. At times it was really difficult to take. Sherry captured this well:

> Basically I feel disrespected . . . not respecting me as an adult and as a teacher? Yes, because in the hallways, they're talking. They're saying everything. They're saying profanities. They're yelling. They're harsh playing. They're jumping on each other.

Whether they mean it or not I think that they're not respecting themselves nor are
they respecting the staff mainly in the halls and cafeteria. I don't know what they're
doing in the other classrooms but that's how I feel, yes. There's no respect.

I felt disrespected at times myself, for example, when students pretended as
though I was not in a room. On one occasion, a young man deliberately wrote on
my leather planner case. Another time, when I was interviewing Tom, a group of
seventh- and eighth-grade boys came to the door and made obnoxious noises, suggesting we had engaged in a sexual escapade. Tom made the students come in,
and he screamed at them to apologize to me, but none of them would look at me
when they did, and they continued to make a big joke of Tom and me talking to
each other in a classroom alone. The staff also hinted that they felt disrespected by
the district. This show of disrespect took the forms of lack of support (including
financial and administrative), little guidance, and an unwillingness to change the
structure of the school.

Lack of respect was also a common rationale for violence among students.
Feeling disrespected was enough of an excuse for students to get into a fight. In
fact, when I conducted a pre-test, 64% of students agreed or strongly agreed with
the statement, "I would fight if someone disrespected me." One's self-respect was
worth fighting for according to most students, although assembling a group of
other students for support was usually part of these fights.

Summary

The culture for many of the WANTS students with whom I spoke and observed seemed to revolve around violence. This was not the case at Lorenzo Hill
where violence in any form, physical or verbal, was almost never discussed. At
WANTS there was a great deal of talk about violence when students talked to
each other in the cafeteria and before the start of class. These conversations were
highly animated, and students who could tell very dramatic and violent stories
captured the attention of their peers. When students told violent stories to each
other—the response was not horror or fear, but rather excitement or thrill—as one
would describe a drama or thriller seen on television or in the movies.

The experience of personal violence as both a victim and a perpetrator was
common for WANTS students and sometimes, although to a lesser degree, staff.
The nature and type of this personal violence, harassment, abuse, beatings, and so
on, depended on one's social location. For example, girls' fights tended to be noticed more often and treated more harshly. Topics such as sexual harassment were
rarely mentioned. Furthermore, there was a great deal of importance placed on

heterosexual sexual relationships. These relationships were important for boys to be seen as heterosexual (because suspicion of homosexuality would result in violent victimization). Race and class affected one's perception of personal violence in a variety of ways—the violence one witnessed in one's neighborhoods and at home, where one lived and, therefore, what gang one could belong to. Many of the students who lived in the 'hood experienced violence as a regular part of life. This common occurrence meant that students experienced loss frequently. Students struggled with emotions around violence—particularly grief and sadness, passion, anger, and obsession with respect and revenge.

At Lorenzo Hill, there was not the same widespread loss that students at WANTS experienced regularly. The most extreme case of violent behavior at Lorenzo Hill was marked by loss of family, suggesting that the experience of loss with no outlet for the grief places children at risk of acting out in school. One of the ways children acted out was through personal violence against themselves, property, or others. Clearly, where loss was more frequent, acting out was too. Therefore, it is necessary that educators examine how students experience loss in their lives. This kind of research should not only involve obvious loss through death of loved ones or divorce, but also loss of friends through moving, loss of friends and family to prison, loss of a home, or loss of a pet. Loss seemed to be a common denominator that had the potential to lead to violence in both the urban and suburban schools. Therefore, school personnel need to be sensitive to the kinds of loss students in their school experience and the ways children handle these losses.

PART II

Structural Violence

CHAPTER 4

Power and Structural Violence: Controlling Resources

Structural violence often goes unnoticed. Structural violence is the result of processes that perpetuate violence in institutions, and for the purposes of this study, within our schools. This section will focus on structural violence by identifying how structures and processes affected the lives of those at WANTS and Lorenzo Hill in ways that were not always evident to those living within them.

Structural violence is strongly influenced by power. Those in power make decisions for those who are not, and those in power also determine how resources are allocated. This principle is applicable to education and the ways that structural violence gets played out with the denial of sufficient personnel, time, money, teacher preparation, literacy training, protection, attention, academic support, and so on. This chapter focuses on the role of power and particularly resource allocation and the impact on structural violence against youths labeled as "violent."

In the United States, we have adopted a quasi-medical approach to "treating" violent or potentially violent school-aged youths. We seek to find causes and cures. We speak about prevention and intervention. We throw temporary, short-term money at schools to prevent and intervene. We talk about risk factors. We see violence among youths that appears to be spreading like forest fires out of control partly because of the media bombardment of images of violent young people. The images we see are dominated by white suburban youths: Littleton, Springfield, Paducah. When the children killed look like those in power, there is often action and an urgent cry to "stop school violence!"

The strategies to reduce school violence become analogous to chemotherapy. We often try to remove instead of repair the cancerous cells (or in this case "violent" youths). In the process we realize that the cure may permanently damage or even kill healthy cells that surround the cancerous cells. However, if we do nothing, the cancerous cells will certainly kill the healthy cells. The other fast-growing cells (e.g., hair and nails) die with the treatment, and we tell ourselves that it is a small price to pay for the overall health of the body. After all hair and nails are not essential to the functioning of the human body. In this country do we think there are groups of children who are not essential to the overall functioning of society? Are we willing to sacrifice certain groups of children for the overall health of our society? Do we systematically remove instead of repair violent youths? Do we then damage those around the youths (families, peers, and so on) labeled violent by removing them rather than helping them? It would seem so when the most popular strategy for those who bring weapons to school because of our "zero tolerance" policies is expulsion.

The world has struggled throughout its history with the question of what to do with those whom the dominant group considers unfit, problem-causing, "bad seeds." This question has plagued societies through the ages. For example, the science of eugenics has existed and been practiced in the American education system. Eugenics is a "science concerned with improving a breed or species, esp. the human species, by such means as influencing or encouraging reproduction by persons presumed to have desirable genetic traits" (*Random House Webster's College Dictionary*, 1992, quoted in Martineau, 1996, p. 27). Martineau wrote that "the Protestant mission of the eugenicists was to protect the public health and improve the 'master race' by controlling the immigrant masses. In this context, poor and immigrant children were the objects of an inquisition imposed by eugenicists through the compulsory educational system" (1992, p. 27). She continues to describe an educational system that was designed for the poor and immigrant children but that did not allow or include the voices of these children and their families in the planning and administration. Children experienced corporal punishment and fell victim to what she labeled "symbolic power and symbolic violence." She described the former as "the power to name, to constitute or construct knowledge—which manifests itself in symbolic violence—the power to impose arbitrary, and arbitrarily impose, expressions of social reality through the 'instruments of knowledge.'" (Harker, 1990, quoted in Marineau, 1996, p. 28). We have developed an educational system where groups of young people have not been afforded symbolic power and therefore fall victim to symbolic violence. The dominant group has made decisions about how best to educate those without power.

Symbolic violence then leads to systemic violence, which Epp and Watkinson defined as "any institutional practice or procedure that adversely impacts on individuals or groups by burdening them psychologically, mentally, culturally, spiritually, economically or physically. Applied to education, it means practices and procedures that prevent students from learning, thus harming them" (1996, p. 1). This harm is not intentional. Often the intent is to design strategies to help children. However, dogmas such as "zero tolerance" policies that are designed to protect, often have the result of becoming systematically violent for students. As Epp and Watkinson observed:

> But our school systems have not been successful for all students. There are students who do not benefit from public education. Many of them plod quietly on, not recognizing their own failure to thrive. Others silently drop out, unable to cope with the exclusion they experience. A few express their alienation through acts of violence. When this happens, school authorities focus attention on individual rule breakers rather than on the reasons for the outbursts. All of these responses are connected with what we have called educational systemic violence (1996, p. ix).

WANTS offers a very clear example of systemic or structural violence, and hence this section will focus primarily on the WANTS school. However, there was structural violence at Lorenzo Hill too. Some students at Lorenzo Hill who were thought to be troublemakers were often labeled as "Special Ed kids" and tended to live in poverty. There was an alternative high school for students who were aggressive, drug abusing, or just did not fit in. These students experienced the same kind of structural violence that WANTS students did; that is, they were removed from their high schools physically and emotionally. Students were told (some in more obvious ways than others) that they were not wanted and they did not belong in mainstream society. However, I am reluctant to draw any other parallels because WANTS served as the primary focus for this research, and the alternative high school at Lorenzo Hill did not. I also do not want to seem as though I am suggesting that alternative schools or education processes are inherently examples of structural violence. This is not necessarily the case. However, alternative education has tended to receive less resources, be housed in less adequate buildings, have less experienced teachers, and be considered less important. Alternative education could be a great way to work with students who do not respond well to the mainstream educational structures, but not if it is seen as less important and less worthy of resources.

WANTS students suffered because of structural violence. They were victims of policies, procedures, and lack of resources. Students at the urban district that controlled WANTS were mostly urban, many lived in poverty, and many of them were African American. Violence seemed to be a primary concern to administrators, teachers, and students. WANTS came into existence because the cost to hire a private tutor for all the students suspended (a state mandate) for weapon carrying became too costly for the poor, urban school district. An alternative program serving all the students caught with weapons at the same time was thought to be less financially draining.

In contrast, Lorenzo Hill students lived primarily in suburban or rural environments, came from wealthy families, thus a district with many resources, and were almost all white. However, students did experience structural violence because of their socioeconomic background. The few poorer students, though, were far more likely to be excluded from regular classrooms and placed in special education classrooms. Teachers and administrators alike frequently expected students from poor homes to be problem students and to need special education. In the district, it was rare to hear of a child from a wealthy family being suspended from school, but it was quite frequent to hear about a poorer student being suspended for drinking, fighting, or drug use. No student had been expelled for bringing weapons to school during the year I worked there. The primary problems were thought to be drug use and abuse. Students caught drinking or using or possessing other drugs would be suspended with a private tutor (a state law) for alcohol and other drug use.

The students at WANTS were all victims of the "zero tolerance" policies for weapons in schools. This mandate required that students caught with anything that could be construed as a weapon (with the exception of guns)—most often box cutters or blades of some type—were removed from regular city schools for one calendar year and sent to WANTS. School administrators focused on rule infractions (thou shall not carry weapons to school) instead of examining why these rules were broken. Many students assigned to WANTS failed to make it there. Although estimates vary, approximately 30% of students (16 years or older) opted to drop out of school instead of attending WANTS. Once they dropped out, they were no longer of concern to the school district. They often became the concern of law enforcement officials and the judicial system.

Although WANTS did provide teachers in the academic core areas of mathematics, science, English, and social studies, students only received 30 minutes of instruction in each subject area per day. Students were often in classes with multiple subjects being taught at once because the teachers were expected to teach multiple subjects—sometimes outside their areas of certification and expertise. This section describes how teachers and students experienced and described structural or systematic violence, and how they struggled to make sense of the experience of education within the setting of the WANTS school. Teachers and administrators at the school had different views from the administrators in the central office, and the students had different views altogether.

The District Policy at WANTS

The city school district policy for possession of dangerous weapons/objects was not unlike many others. It read:

Based on a disciplinary hearing, any student found guilty of possessing a weapon other than a rifle, pistol, revolver, or firearm may be excluded from attending a City School District's regular program for a period up to one year. Students excluded who are under the compulsory attendance age will be required to attend the District's Alternative Program for Weapons Expulsion unless deemed inappropriate because of safety issues.

The policy specifically identified the following items: dagger, dangerous knife, razor, stiletto, box cutter, any explosive, incendiary or poison gas, dangerous chemicals, noxious sprays or any object that is used inappropriately in the same manner as a weapon with intent to do bodily harm. As a general rule, students caught with firearms were arrested. If they were younger than 16 years of age, they went to the local juvenile detention facility. If they were 16 years or older, they went to jail.

During the first year I was at WANTS, there were 94 students assigned to WANTS. The average daily attendance rate was 60%. Roughly one third of the students were "dropped from the roster," meaning, they dropped out, moved out of the area, went to juvenile detention facilities or jail. Not only were these young people expelled from their schools, they were removed from the educational process. Many felt there was ultimately only one door open to them—the door that many of their family members had taken—imprisonment, formal removal from society.

Victims of Zero Tolerance:
How Students Ended Up at WANTS

I noticed in my participant observations in the field both at WANTS and during the literacy project with WANTS students that all the students had their own stories about how they ended up at the school. Perhaps because what they all had in common was that they had been caught with a weapon at school. Every time someone new came to the school they had to "tell their story" of how they got there. All the stories I heard were very dramatic. They involved a big fight and a big weapon. Paul, for example, said that he was caught with a "sword" when he was in a huge fight. James said he had a gun. Dwayne said he brought a big knife and held it to a kid's throat; the kid had "jumped" him and threatened to cut his throat.

In their interviews with me and in conversations I overheard between students and adults in the school, students downplayed their weapon of choice and gave the "adult" version. They offered this version after they knew I had overheard their stories to one another. Paul told me a story of having a fishing knife in his pocket that he had put there the day before to keep his little brother from playing with it and hurting himself. In his words, "it wasn't very big . . . it wasn't a very big knife." His "sword" had been reduced to a small knife when talking to me. When his brother got into a fight in school, Paul jumped in, and the knife fell out of his pocket. Paul's brother was sentenced to "afternoon school"—an alternative education program located in his high school. Paul was sentenced to the weapons school because he had the knife. Several students at WANTS denied knowledge of the "weapon" in their possession until a teacher or administrator found it.

Other students claimed (of those who admitted they purposefully brought a weapon to school) to adults that they had brought the weapon to protect themselves. One young boy, who had been the victim of horrendous sexual abuse from his stepfather for years, was bullied mercilessly. He was caught with a huge butcher knife. Never did I hear him boast about this the way the others would boast about the weapon they had. He was silent. At WANTS he was tormented (he was white, overweight, insecure, quiet, unkempt, and wore glasses). He felt he had no way to protect himself, so he quietly took his beatings. Occasionally he would come into the guidance office when I was there, just to sit quietly by himself. He did not come in to snitch on his abusers; he simply wanted a place to escape. He was learning the role of victim very well in this setting.

Many of the students at WANTS were victims of some form of abuse. They were victimized by family members, other adults in the home, other young people, rival gang members, boyfriends, and girlfriends. Many lived with substance-abusing relatives or abused substances themselves. Others had parents who were in and out of the criminal justice system, and most had "done time."

In an effort to protect themselves, students often carried weapons to school. They thought this strategy would work for them. They did not think that adults could protect them all the time. They did not believe that anyone else could protect them. Tarissa told the story of how she ended up at WANTS. This story was similar to others I heard from girls who carried weapons to school:

> This girl wanted to fight me. The next day she came with her older sister. They talked junk, dropped their stuff. I got into a car and went home. My brother told me to watch out—to have others with me. They [the girl and her sister] came again at me. I told the principal. This time I came with a knife. I stepped back. I said, 'you're not gonna fight me.' The knife fell. It was over. I kept the knife. I told all the staff and principal about this girl. They said nothing. I was so upset. Someone ratted on me on the knife. I think it was the sister's friend . . . I knew if I had a knife I would have to protect myself—you know most of the gangs walk down the streets with weapons.

Tarissa, like many of the young people, felt threatened, went to adults, felt the adults were unresponsive, took matters into her own hands, and brought a knife to school. She said later that she had no intention of using it; she just wanted the girls to leave her alone. Some young people will admit that they were willing to use the weapon if provoked. Tarissa said, "I just had to stop her from harassing me. I wouldn't have cut her. She's nothing but little white trash. I'm a good person, but I have to defend myself."

Many students turned to adults to help them appeal their cases. April had several examples of students who wanted to appeal because they had been sent to WANTS for using a paring knife to slice an apple, or because they had borrowed a family member's jacket and were unaware of the weapon in the pocket. One such example was an eighth grader who claimed she borrowed her mother's jacket. Her mother carried a knife because her ex-boyfriend was threatening her. She had an order of protection against him, but she still carried the knife when she went out. The daughter was caught with the knife during a random locker search and sent to WANTS. At the hearing, her mother came in and swore that the knife was hers and that her daughter had no knowledge of it, but the school district had zero tolerance for such things, and she was sent to WANTS. Another boy who worked in a grocery store told me that he had a box cutter in his pocket from work the night before. When he realized the knife was in his pocket, he took it in to the principal's office. He claimed that they said they would hold it for him until the end of the day. According to his story, before he knew it, he had a letter home saying that he needed to attend a hearing for bringing a weapon to school. He was also sent to WANTS.

Students knew the policy was hurtful. They did not want to go to WANTS and tried to appeal, but the zero tolerance policy rarely let appeals be granted. Sherry told me that her daughter had been caught with a paring knife, and nothing happened to her because she worked in the school district. She felt guilty, she told me, because one of her students who was miserable at WANTS had also been caught with a paring knife, but she had nobody to support her appeal. Having a parent who worked in the school district did not guarantee that a student would be pardoned. Although James's mother was a teacher and Brandy's mother was a teaching assistant, these young people were still sent to WANTS.

As the number of students attending WANTS increased, so did the number of random searches for weapons, and still more students were sent to WANTS. Zero tolerance was a serious matter that resulted in a major disruption of a student's academic and social pursuits if a weapon was found on him or her. As WANTS students quickly realized, academics were easier and taken less seriously. Many students saw this as a good aspect of WANTS. However, they expressed concern over the low number of students, which meant fewer potential friends or romantic partners. Students would say that the school district did not care what happened to them—they just wanted them out of the regular school. This was clearly evident when students made the transition back to their regular schools. Teachers shared many of these same concerns.

Students' Perceptions of Zero Tolerance

When asked directly what zero tolerance meant, students did some theorizing because only a few students knew the policy's actual meaning. Interestingly, some students offered harsher punishments as necessary for "thugs." They said things such as "when they don't take shit from anyone . . . when they ain't tolerating no cursing, fighting, bad things." Once these policies were explained as being part of the dynamic responsible for sending them to WANTS, students expressed opinions similar to Tamika, who said, "basically, they don't understand how it is today. What they [school personnel] really need to do is to give them [bad students] mental help . . . counseling, psychiatrists, help them feel good and they won't act so bad anymore." Tamika's belief that "they [adults] don't understand how it is today" was common. There was a frustration among teenagers that adults were from another planet—a place where they spoke a different language and had completely different (and often opposing) views of their worlds. The reaction of many adults when youths carried weapons was one of horror and that the carrier was somehow more violent and aggressive and dangerous than the other students in the school. Young people did not necessarily view carrying weapons in the same light. Some students saw it as perfectly normal and understandable. Carrying weapons, they thought, worked to keep themselves and those they loved safe.

Some students did acknowledge that zero tolerance was a sensible strategy. For example, Amani said that maybe zero tolerance made sense because "too much youths dying . . . and they need to clean up youths' acts . . . too much fighting, beefin' over bitches, bitches start shit." However, he observed that zero tolerance was not a good way to get kids to stop acting bad "it helps in a way but not really. I guess they gotta do something . . . I don't know, someday you might just be havin' a bad day and damn, they get you on something stupid. You ain't really a thug. You know what I'm sayin'?" Even in Amani's example, there was a need to be flexible because sometimes young people just had "a bad day" and would be treated like a "thug," even if they were not *really* a thug.

Paul summed up one of the basic problems with zero tolerance policies:

> You got to understand a person's situation. For me, I had to stand my ground. A kid got in my face and we got into it, over a water fight. It was the last day of school . . . I had stashed a knife in the bushes that morning. It was a coincidence. It was a big knife—my little brother had it and it was in my tackle box. He had cut himself with it.

I had taken it away from him. I forgot it was in my pocket until I was on the bus that morning, so when I got off the bus I knew I had to get rid of it before going in school. That's when I hid it in the bushes . . . During the fight it was me, one of my brothers, a whole mess of people were trying to break it up. During the fight, I hit an administrator. Somebody told me later that they saw me hide a knife in the bushes earlier that day . . . It was my first fight, and I had to go to summer school at WANTS and go there for a whole year.

The teenagers wanted adults to understand their situations—their lives. Similar to Paul, they wanted adults to be reasonable and flexible. There was so much frustration as students tried to make their case for adults who seemed to be speaking a different language from the young people. Often they just gave up. They learned to accept from policies such as the one on zero tolerance that adults would never understand, thus reaffirming that it was necessary to take matters into one's own hands and carry a weapon for self-protection.

Determining What's at Stake

Structures beyond the control of the children at WANTS dictated the lives that the children could have. Students felt that getting a good education might help them escape poverty, but many of these children were never good in traditional school classrooms. They were poor students, and they did not see education as a vehicle for getting them out of poverty. Thus, they needed to be successful within their current environments. They needed to learn how to succeed within their neighborhoods more than they needed to learn how to succeed in school. They had learned the former but could not (try as they might) figure out the latter.

Students who engaged in violent behavior in school and ended up at WANTS most often felt that they had nothing to lose and a great deal to gain by fighting (with or without weapons). Those students at other urban schools within the district with whom I spoke who did not fight or engage in violent behavior did not do so because, as nearly all of them said, they were "good students" and "wanted to graduate" and some "wanted to go to college." In nearly every case for those students for whom fighting was not viewed as an option, there was a lot at stake if they did engage in this kind of behavior. They would be sent to another school, possibly miss school and get behind, not graduate, or not go on to college. These students seemed to be on a path that they thought was leading them out of poverty (to a good job or college) and felt that being a "good student" was an essential part of staying on that path.

Students who engaged in what the school district defined as violent behavior (assaults, fighting, using weapons) felt that they had a lot more at stake if they did not fight. They would be "punked." They might be jumped, hurt, or shot in the back if they walked away. Walking away from a fight was not seen as an option for these students. Because these young people often did not see school as offering them much because they were not usually well invested in school, as demonstrated by their failing grades, lack of participation in extracurricular activities, and poor attendance, they felt they had less to lose by fighting than by not fighting. Fighting successfully made them achievers in the arena in which they knew they needed to be most successful because they would not be getting out of their current situations. The value of receiving passing grades by teachers was less important for young people who saw their future on the street—or saw no future at all. Understanding what young people view as important, or what is at stake, is critical to predicting students' violent behavior. If they see a future for themselves, with themselves playing a role in that future, then they will be less likely to behave violently.

The WANTS middle school students were asked in a variety of settings by different adults, "what are your goals for the future" or some variation of the question "what do you want to be when you grow up?" The answers remained consistent for students—almost as though they had to have some answer for this question they were asked so often—without any thought given to what they would need to do to accomplish this goal. Shaun's answer best illustrates this lack of understanding on the students' part. African American and about four feet tall, the shortest and smallest in his class, he wanted to be a professional basketball or football player. Did he even play these sports in school? Not usually. However, this was his goal. The boys often said some kind of professional sport, and the girls would say things like "singer, dancer, have kids . . ." Some were "go to college—get a good job—own a business." I had a conversation with a group of middle school boys. Some said they wanted to go to college. I told them about some programs and how they could go to college, but that they needed to do well in school. Their eyes became dazed when I talked about the reality of actually getting into college—filling out an application, having good grades, and taking standardized tests. So I asked them what they thought college was like. The response was overwhelming—it was all about partying—drinking, smoking weed, hanging out. Never did they mention that they might have to attend classes or do homework—college was all about partying. In fact, the partying aspect was why they wanted to go. They thought college would help them to get a job where they could make more money. They did not describe what kind of a job they would actually be doing to make money, but just that they would make more money if they went to college. This attitude explained to me why it was that students who claimed to "hate school" would elect to go to college.

James really wanted to go to college. He was the only one. However, he wanted to go to play Division I football. I heard that he was a very talented player who could possibly make it to Division I, but academically he was far behind. I heard from a varsity football coach in the district that he was being recruited until coaches saw his grades and that he had been sent to WANTS. Despite the reduction in enthusiasm coaches had about recruiting him, he was still determined. He spoke about his academics more than the others—what courses he would take and how he was worried about some of them. He knew the NCAA regulations to get into a Division I school and play ball. College was still not about more schooling for James. It was about playing football. However, after he was removed to the weapons school, he was no longer as hot a commodity for football either.

Student Concerns:
"Weapons School Fucks You Up"

Students received the messages of structural violence loud and clear—that they were not worth the resources needed to provide them an adequate education. They viewed themselves as academic failures, and they saw the WANTS experience as just another way of telling them this message. I heard many comments from students about WANTS being a negative experience—particularly from students who were there during the first year of my research. Amani said, "you don't get as many good teachers and classes . . . I feel like I missed a lot of things. I lost a lot of opportunities. It's hard for you. It's stupid. People ask you what school you go to and you gotta say (head down) 'weapons school.' Stupid man . . . It [being at WANTS] made me feel bad. It still don't feel right. It made me feel bad to have to say that I went there."

Not every student experienced the shame that Amani described as "some kids acted proud, like it was cool to be there. I wasn't proud. Kids would be bringing their babies up into there fighting with the momma or daddy over the kid. It was real ghetto." Some students told me that they did not mind being at WANTS because many of their friends and family were there.

After Paul returned to regular school, he said of WANTS, "I hated it there. People treated you real bad, like you were a criminal. There were cool teachers, but other people looked at us like we were all bad asses. There were nerd kids there and everything. Smart kids couldn't get a good education . . . A lot of times there were problems because of [where WANTS was located]. Uptown people [a gang from the other side of town] had to keep their mouths shut. It was a problem at times. Not for me but for others." Paul described further the problem of the location being in the territory of one of the most notorious gangs in the city, "kids would come into the building from the block looking to get somebody." He said, like others who were able to avoid trouble, "I got no problems with people, I mind my own business."

Students who attended WANTS received the message that they were not worth the resources to educate. They recognized that they were on the margins of the academic structure, and most realized that they would never be welcome again in the mainstream. Some of the younger students believed that they might have a chance to reenter the academic mainstream. Generally, though, students and also many teachers with whom I spoke (both at WANTS and in other schools within the district) did not expect that students could succeed academically after having been to WANTS.

Teacher and Administrator Concerns: A Situation Set Up to Fail

During the first year of my observations and interviews at WANTS most of the teachers spent quite a bit of time complaining about factors that they considered beyond their control; that is, the systems and structures in place that kept them from being as effective as they wanted to be. These factors included, but were not limited to, the structure of the school day, the lack of resources, staffing decisions (particularly the number of and demands on the part-time teachers), and "the district's" (central school district's administration) lack of support in general to the school. The staff felt as though they were isolated victims of a poorly planned and inadequately funded program where they were supposed to hold students in a punitive way until they had "done their time" and could return to their "regular school."

Ken, the business and computer teacher, summed up his feeling about the district which was consistent with many of the other teachers:

> The district has decided that this is basically a prison and they are not going to finance it. If they are not going to finance it, how can you stay? And [the principal] has an up-hill battle . . . he's working hard to convince them otherwise, but he's not, it's so obvious. They're asking . . . first of all they can't decide what it is they want to do . . . then they make it almost impossible for him. They take somebody [a student] who needs twice as much time to learn and they give them half as much time. And then they're really loading you up [with courses and students] . . . the real purpose of this school is to cut down on the homebound costs not to help students.

Ken's perception was consistent among most of the teachers—that they had been given an impossible task with insufficient resources, no mission, and an impossible structure.

Bruce described his perceptions of how the administration above him viewed the weapons program they were developing:

> I would rather deal with a hundred and fifteen students at times than deal with all the administrators I have to deal with. And when I say administrators I'm talking, everybody from coordinator all the way up to the superintendent because I have kept the rules and I know what the parameters are and I know how to play the game. I know what the students are supposed to do. The students know what I will do. We know one another. Four years into the ball game the administrators from my level all the way up to the Board of Education don't really know one another. No one really knows what I'm doing here or what's happening here . . . we're into year four, which I know is extremely important, and anybody who would listen to it or read it perhaps would say, you get four years into something, and people still don't know what your doing. No, they don't. And the rationale for that is something as important as an alternative school should be fairly understood by every administrator. When I say that I'm talking from your coordinators in schools all the way up. They should know that there is a place over here where kids are being taken in. Run through some special programs and released back into the system. And it should be a very well defined system for doing that. There was no very well defined system for doing that. Myself and the staff had to . . . cause I was told, go and adjust. That's it just go and adjust.

Bruce was frustrated dealing with his administrative equals and superiors. He struggled with the fact that the people creating the policy that ran the school, after four years of being in operation still did not know what was happening there. He was angry that he was not given any guidance but was told to "go and adjust." He felt powerless and unsupported. Teachers expressed similar lack of support. They talked about how the district office staff people did not know what was really happening at the school and how needy they were. They felt that the structure of the school day needed to be changed, but when they raised their concerns, they went unheard.

How the School Started

Paul, the math teacher, Raji, the science teacher, Tom, the English teacher, Bruce, the administrator, and April, the counselor, had been with the program since the beginning—four years before I started my observations. Each of them recounted generally the same events when the school opened its doors. I quote Raji here because she was one who actually described the beginnings in our interview (the others had told me parts of the story during more informal observations):

The first thing we did, I interviewed [for the teaching position], and I said, "I don't want to be with any weapons." And he [the administrator interviewing her] goes, "no, no, no!" . . . They interviewed then hired me so I'm here. [When she started there were] six to eight kids in one room . . . One tiny room like [the size of the principal's] office. That size of a room [about 10 feet by 12 feet]. There was a big table for Bruce, the administrator, and there were those desks for the kids, and we had six or seven kids all cramped into one area . . . that's how we started. Then gradually we needed more space because they kept sending me more kids. We didn't have the space. So we make . . . the whole second floor was taken by the WANTS program at the Academy. That's what's tough. They started renovating because it was a huge hall and they started putting up the walls, and we were teaching them and we were doing all kinds of things. And in the beginning it was an all day program. The kids would come at 8:30, 8:45 and then stay until 3:00 because in the beginning the community service was not in place. Until they were assigned and things got worked out, they were there for the whole day, and when we opened up, suddenly we jumped from six to eight students, and we had to rent the whole floor, and it was a big huge hall. Suddenly, with no preparation, nothing, we were getting 30 kids. Okay to 35 suddenly. So there they are at 9:00 in the morning. No books, nothing. There they were. What do you do with them? So . . . we borrowed a T.V./VCR from upstairs from the Division for Youth (DFY). We showed them movies, but how many movies can you show? They were there, and gradually we got them books . . . it was a totally individualized program. I mean each student because we were still homebound instructors, so they considered us as homebound [a program that teaches students who have been suspended indefinitely from their school and provided individualized instruction at their homes]. It was individualized, and having 30 to 35 kids, it was difficult to keep it individualized. We tried, and we did keep it like that for a while.

K: But that was the expectation that even when they went up to 30 to 35 kids that it would be individualized instruction?

R: Yes. Then I guess, I was really frustrated. One day I talked to Mr. Frank . . . the person in charge of that [behavior] program. So he came over one day, and I was frustrated. I said, "why do we have to keep these kids all day?" He said, "no you don't have to. If they don't have a community service placement, they go home." I said, "why didn't anybody tell us that." That's when the split morning and afternoon started. We worked out a plan that the high school kids would come from 9:00–1:00. They would leave, even if they didn't have community service they would be gone. Then the afternoon kids would come at 11:00 and then they would have their gym and all that. That's when . . . this started I think . . . the program started in October. The new building was taken in February, and this started in April or something . . . Since then it has been much better. Then gradually they put up walls so we had classrooms. Once the classrooms were all set, then we could teach as a class. Before that it was a totally individualized program . . . I had made up a sheet and for the week I would write assignments for them and then just hand it to them . . . and then whenever they had questions, they would raise their hands and I would go around. At that time I was teaching too many classes . . . Paul was hired; he was doing math. Tom was hired, and he was doing English. I was the person teaching language, social studies. Everything was dumped on me . . . and health . . . So, then once the classrooms were set, then they gradually divided up the subjects. I still was doing all the sciences—of course that's why I was hired—and then I was doing all the languages because nobody else would teach them. I speak French and Spanish, and so I was stuck with the languages. Paul took a little bit of social studies, and I did a little bit of social studies; we kind of split. We split health gradually, too. Since we've been in this building it's more like a school, and the kids come in. But still we are teaching more than one subject at a time in each period.

Raji described the evolution of WANTS from a tutorial-like setting with more individualized instruction to an alternative school setting with classrooms and more traditional pedagogy. Teachers were forced to teach outside their area of certification and expertise as Raji described teaching nearly every subject at some point during her tenure at WANTS. She also described the "split" school day that evolved in an effort to keep the numbers manageable with so few staff—which also resulted in much less time spent on academics. Consequently, students, who were already behind academically, fell even farther behind. The program evolved quickly as the numbers grew, and the very small staff of three teachers, an administrator, and a counselor struggled to keep the school functioning. They tried to survive the best they could.

When I first entered the school, there were classroom teachers for mathematics, science, English, social studies, business/computers/occupations, and a gymnasium for physical education. Raji also described in the above passage how subjects areas were distributed—not based on experience or preparation (or even area of certification), but given to whomever had any familiarity with the topic. She was given all of the languages because she had some familiarity with a number of languages.

Bruce's perspective as the administrator in charge of the program was one of trying to do the best he could with no planning time, and being put in the position without warning and having the district change the rules from a pilot program to a fully functioning school:

In 1994 the program officially began. And I was asked in September by the superintendent to head up the program. I had no idea that it would have so many, just so many spaces, just things not in place. I knew that it would be difficult but not as extremely difficult as it has been over the past four years. In October of '94 I had hired a counselor, two teachers, and I was given one TA. So I started out with four teachers, and I was given six kids to start as a pilot. That pilot did not last as most pilots do for a year or two. It lasted several months because by February of that next year, which was just October, November, December . . . five months away, the number of six kids went from six to fifty and the number of staff went from four to twelve. And at that time that I had six kids and four staff members, I was operating out of a very small classroom. As a matter of fact, we all could not get in the classroom at one time. But as soon as the population mushroomed, I went down to the next level, which was just a large space. And I realized at that time that I had to do something that most principals had years to condition themselves for, learn for, and everything else. I had to renovate because it was just a large room, and it was not going to be mentally conducive for kids with behavior problems, and the staff was having to deal with several groups of people in an extremely large area. There would be days I'd walk in, and all fifty kids would be in there and most days I'd walk in and observe them because thirteen of those thirty-five, about fifty kids would be there plus staff. So we'd have about sixty, seventy people max one day.

All of the administrative staff and teachers tried to "make do" with the resources they had and the given structure of the school day. Bruce attempted to change the physical environment. He ended up fighting for a new school building. He was given a former parochial school on the corner of the city where the most shots were fired according to police reports. Some teachers and administrators grew tired of fighting the system to try to change it, and some just decided fighting was not worth the effort because they felt their voice would go unheard. Raji and others were just glad when their days were made shorter, the number of students fewer, and they were paid more. However, most of the teachers complained about the structure of the school day. I rarely heard complaints from students about the shorter class periods and lack of emphasis on instruction. However, the obvious result was that students were academically slipping farther behind their peers at the "regular" schools.

The Setup of the School Day

As Raji described above, the school day was split. Half the day (roughly two hours) was devoted to academic core subject areas: math, English, social studies, science, health, and physical education (every other day). Theoretically, the students spent the other half of the day doing community service.

When I first arrived at WANTS, Kelly, the school nurse, organized the community service placements. She sent students downtown to the volunteer center, where they were assigned to a community service placement. As she described the process, "The volunteer center, they have a contact person down there who interviews all the kids and then tries to match where they live, where the school is and things like that to something that would be of interest to them. Then she contacts the community site, and then I work with the kids to get them there in terms of telling them when they have to go and the requirements and all that."

The overwhelming majority of these placements, according to the students and staff, involved "sweeping floors and cleaning toilets." So the students frequently did not go to a community service site. Many of the students, once they discovered that "nothing would happen to them" if they did not get a community service placement or did not go regularly to the placement, opted not to go—especially once they heard about the type of work they would be made to do.

Despite the consistent resistance students showed regarding their community service mandate (i.e., according to Kelly, 75% were failing—meaning they either did not attend regularly or had not signed up at all), the structure of the school was such that students were scheduled to perform two hours of community service during each school day. The middle school students (grades 7 and 8) were supposed to go to their community placement sites in the morning from 9:00 A.M. to 11:00 A.M. The high school students were supposed to do their community service work from 1:00 P.M. to 3:00 P.M. This arrangement changed during my second year.

As Kelly said in our interview, "some kids go faithfully [to their community service jobs]. Some kids won't go . . . I really wonder if some of the kids who aren't going to community service are not going because they think they are not going to get out of here, and they want to stay. Some of it is I think that they have never had a punishment for not going to community service." Students would say things such as, "we don't gotta do community service." They would say that they knew that nothing would happen to them if they did not go. They knew that with or without doing community service, students were being sent back to their home schools. When I asked the administrator about this situation, she said, "it's like counseling. Legally we can recommend that a student do it [community service or counseling], but we can't require it for them to go back to their home school." The same was true of participation at WANTS. Students could elect to stay out of school for a year rather than go to WANTS and return the following year to their regular school, although most students did not realize this, and if they chose to stay out for a year, they would be a year behind their peers.

By December of my first year of observations, the overwhelming majority of the students did not attend their community service placements. When I was interviewing Ken, the business/computer teacher, in December, he asked two of the high school girls where they were doing their community service. They both said that they did not have a placement yet. He said, "aren't you supposed to?" They each shrugged as though they were unsure, but one said, "naw, I don't think so." I asked how long they had been at WANTS. They had each been at the school since the start of the school year in September.

Teachers raised relevant concerns about the community placements, and some expressed their frustrations in staff meetings because there was no connection between the community service assignment and the materials being taught. Furthermore, the community service placements took time away from their classroom time (only 30 minutes), and they wanted longer class periods to teach their lessons. They struggled with teaching material to students in such a short time span. As many lamented, it took half the period to settle them down enough for the actual teaching to begin. Additional frustration was triggered on the teachers' part because they could not meet with students after school for extra help sessions because the high school students left for their community service at noon and typically would not come back to school to receive help. The community service time also meant that there was no time for study halls or for any other help for the students. Jerry, the social studies teacher, said, "I think the problem is the way the system is set up . . . I think community service is nice. Some teachers have mentioned maybe it should be like on a Saturday. Do something meaningful, because the way it is now, there's not a chance to really work with these students if they have problems." According to Jerry and other teachers at WANTS, most of these students were doing poorly academically before coming to WANTS and were in need of extra assistance in their courses. He said that students had already learned that they would be "pushed up to the next grade" regardless of how they did academically. He said, "a lot of them know the system. That's something I found out early. I talked to several students who, I said, 'if you just put a little time in you'll get to the next grade.' They go, 'well they've got to push me ahead anyways 'cause I've already flunked it last year, and I'm due to be moved up anyways.'"

The attitude that "I'll be moved up anyways" to the next grade level regardless of performance is one that was a form of structural violence that contributed to the lack of students' motivation to attend their community service. The district policy is known as "social promotion" where students must be moved up if they reach a certain age, regardless of their academic ability. Many of these young people do not fear the failing grade they might receive—they have failed many times before—it's not like it's a real class.

Lack of Connectedness Between Community Service and Coursework

Most of the teachers thought that having students do community service was a good idea in theory, but it turned out to be a bad idea in practice. They said that there was no sense of connection between what they were doing in their community service placements and what they were learning in the classroom. Chris felt that there was a perfect connection between his course, Introduction to Occupations where students learned interview and other job-related skills, and their community service experiences. However, because so few students actually participated in their community service jobs on a regular basis, he did not talk about it in class.

Community service was poorly organized. Kelly did not even have a telephone in her office to contact placement sites. The volunteer center placed students in service sites according to their interest and where they lived. However, most of the placements involved menial tasks such as cleaning. Students viewed community service as a part of their punishment and not something that would help their community.

The subsequent conversation regarding community service at the staff meeting among Jerry, April, Chris, and Nancy sums up the differences in perspectives of teachers, counselors, and administrators, respectively:

> Jerry said, "This may be way off base, but I think it's important to know what is the primary priority here—community service? Counseling? Teaching? Integrating these? I have no idea what the priorities are of what we're supposed to be emphasizing here."
>
> Nancy responded, "We're supposed to provide educational experiences to these students because they have been caught with a weapon. They need counseling services—and community service is what they're supposed to be doing."
>
> April replied, "We need to integrate—right now it all seems like we're all loose wheels—not working together—we need to work toward a common goal."
>
> Chris said with a tone of irritation, "Maybe if we had a unified curriculum that did that."
>
> Nancy asked, "Would you like [the local conflict resolution service] to come in and help you build these skills into your class or curriculum?"
>
> Jerry said angrily, "Not if we don't know what the priorities are—academics suffer—kids are behind—is academics a priority or not, otherwise these kids are just falling farther behind and we're setting them up to fail when they go back to their regular schools."

This conversation indicates how the major players went around in a circle whenever they discussed community service and its role in the curriculum. Teachers, for the most part, seemed to resent that so much time was devoted to community service during the school day, and yet students were not held accountable for failing to go. When the school nurse left, the responsibilities for coordinating the community service were placed on the shoulders of the physical education teacher. He was a part-time teacher and spent little time talking to students about it. As a result, few students had any concept of the purpose of community service, and nearly every teacher cited community service as an example of one of the ways the school shortchanged students and was "setting kids up to fail."

Lack of Resources

It was clear to me that this program was working on a shoestring budget. Although I have never seen the actual budget figures, it was evident from discussions with the teachers and administrators that money was tight. Nearly all of the teachers mentioned their struggles obtaining teaching materials. Tom described having to make photocopies of required books for students in his English class because there was a point when they had no books at all. Now, he said, we have a few books that they share, but they're not allowed to take them home. If they do go home, he said, they never come back.

Sherry, the substitute teacher who was filling in for the language teacher who was on maternity leave, said that when she arrived there were no materials. She bought some items herself—tapes, books, posters. Others she made by hand or on her computer at home. She brought in her own camera to take photographs of her students for the bulletin board outside her room (for the most part other bulletin boards remained blank). One of the students dropped the camera on the ground (she was unsure whether the students did this accidentally or on purpose) and broke it. She was very upset when this happened.

During my first year of observations, there was no television or VCR because one had broken the previous year, and the administration didn't have the funds to buy a new one. On special occasions, the WANTS school could borrow one from the GED program that was housed in the same building one level above. This VCR was extremely old and frequently broken (although it seems that funds were available to repair it). Teachers complained about not having any instructional materials for students if they wanted to do something that might capture their attention better than lecturing. Jerry mentioned that students liked to work with their hands, a feature he discovered after weeks of sending students to the principal's office for failing to pay attention while he lectured. He was able to get some clay and have students make masks—this was viewed as a feat.

Obtaining materials, more staff, anything that was seen as vital to the school's ability to function, was viewed as a battle against the district. This is what the acting principal had to say about her constantly fighting for funds for the basics:

Instructional Media/Materials.

> There was one [TV/VCR]; it fell off the cart and broke. And what's been done about it? Now I'm asking. So those kinds of things aren't happening here. You know those kinds of support things. So if this program is going to stay somebody's got to get off the can and put their money where their mouth is. I'm prepared to do that but . . . and I'll fight and I'll push but I don't know how successful I'll be.

Staff/Personnel/Salaries.

I'm fighting now . . . my nurse tells me Monday she's leaving. But I understand part of it's personal. She has a two-year-old child . . . to spend time with her child. And part of it is frustration. She was hired, part-time nurse, part-time teacher assistant. She's done a great job with the kids . . . she's got a nice rapport with the kids. The kids are confiding in her. She's doing a great job with the community service. But the promises that were made to her by other people downtown haven't come to fruition. She didn't get paid for a month. Then they told her the salary level she was going to get paid at, all of a sudden she's not getting paid at that salary level. She's never signed a contract. Those kinds of frustrations. She's not unhappy with the kids. She's not unhappy with the staff. She's not happy with the support that she's gotten. But paying your child's day care when your not getting paid what you thought you were going to get paid is not worth it. So she's leaving.

Medical and Security Measures/Personnel.

So I don't have a nurse. I want a nurse here. I don't have a police officer. I'm still fighting to get that. That's been approved but the money's not there. The money to pay for him is frozen or whatever. But I don't want to be without a nurse. I mean I've already had three ambulances here. Rodney got hurt. Another girl got hurt and a sub-custodian one day, whose name I didn't even know, I thought she was having a heart attack out here. She came back from lunch . . . she was walking up the stairs . . . one of the kids came running and said, yo lady, you better get out here. And she's got the numb arm and chest pain and she's having trouble breathing. So I had three ambulances in three days. I don't want that liability on my head. And it's not just injury factor, these kids need medical services. Like this kid who spent two nights in the public safety building cause he punched out his mother, assaulted his mother, put his hand through plate glass, got stitched up down at the public safety building, right. So he finally gets out of jail . . . he comes in here. Yo, where's your nurse? Eight o'clock in the morning. Muddy bandage, filthy. He hadn't had any medical attention since the night they stitched him up. The first line of defense for a lot of these kids is my nurse. I'm amazed at kids who get hurt at four o'clock this afternoon and then parents tell them well go see the nurse in the morning. So I need a nurse here. I've got a severe asthmatic kid here . . . he starts having a asthma attack, I want some certified medical personnel. So I've been putting pressure on and I got a nurse for one week . . . guaranteed for one week. I don't know after that. But it's money. They're talking money to me. I said, I don't want to hear money. I want to hear what's right. And what's right is we need a nurse in this building. But there's no law that mandates based on building size, enrollment size that you have to have a nurse. So there's all those kinds of crazy things that go on. But it's valuing your programs. Putting your money where your mouth is. They talk they want to stop violence . . . they want to teach kids . . . then you have to come up with the resources and the funding. And it's just not there. I don't see it at the school district level. I don't see it at the city level as a priority.

This quote continued on with more examples of needs the school had. Her frustration is clear in this passage. She admitted that she spent a great deal of her time fighting for resources: funds for books and other materials, funds for a school nurse and a police officer, funds to adequately pay her staff. This school, located for a year in the most dangerous section of the city—where the majority of the homicides in the city occurred (or at least within a one-block radius)—did not have a police officer on duty. This school, where students were known to bring weapons to school, some of whom were regularly violent against other students, did not have anyone who was trained to deal with these types of violence. There was nobody there to protect the teachers or the students. They were the only school in the district without a police officer. The teachers and students at WANTS determined that district administrators and school board members did not think them worthy of being protected and served—after all, these kids were seen as the ones from whom other kids in the district needed to be protected.

Structural violence in the form of deprivation from basic educational needs was rampant at WANTS. Teachers complained about not having enough time to adequately teach students and having difficulty finding a balance between covering content and dealing with personal student issues. Other issues that affected the teachers' ability to teach their subject matter was the lack of books and supplies. In addition, students were not allowed to take books and other learning materials home to do homework, and there was no after-school period to study or study hall.

A Lack of Mission: The Powerless Victims

The teachers at WANTS felt helpless and powerless to improve the situation at WANTS where students were deprived of an adequate education with essential supplies and personnel during the first year I was there. They felt that they could not change the structure and function of the school. They believed the lack of resources that resulted in structural violence was not their responsibility, but the "districts," and the families of the students and the students themselves. They could not change the students or the district, increasing demands were placed on them without more time, money, or other resources. They entered the teaching profession to teach their subject area. They had not been prepared for what they found at WANTS.

Most of the teachers had just finished getting their teaching credentials. They had been substitute teaching, working for the local occupational training center, or they had not been working in their profession at all. Most of the teachers saw WANTS as their way into the district. This job, for most, was a stepping-stone—a slippery stepping-stone that they wanted to jump off of, onto a sturdier rock.

The discussion about how to handle disruptive classroom behavior was quickly derailed by Jerry's focus on the lack of mission, and he believed that "if students knew there was something they had to achieve they might do it." When Annie asked the group what the mission should look like, most of the teachers behaved like victims—powerless over the faceless "district" who, as Jerry quickly replied, "they [the district] just tell us what our mission is—they tell us what we have to do." Someone said that they did have a mission statement, but nobody knew what it was.

When I spoke to Jerry, social studies seemed as though it was the most diffi-cult subject to teach these students. After talking with Paul, I was certain it was math. After I spoke with Raji, it was science. Each teacher seemed to think that he or she had the most difficult subject matter to teach students because the students did not care about it (whatever the subject matter was). They considered it their job to teach their assigned subject matter to the students. This attitude was obvous at the first staff meeting I attended. The new teachers were confused about the focus of the program. Was it community service? Was it the subject matter? Was it to deal with students' emotional issues? Teachers struggled with this dilemma, and the overwhelming tone of the meeting from the teachers was that the subject mat-ter was most important and that they needed more time to teach this information. Half an hour a day was insufficient. Community service (where students were supposed to spend the other half of their school day) was said to be "a nice idea," but it should not detract from the teaching of the subject matter by being sched-uled during the school day. Some teachers suggested Saturday or after school would be a better time, but not during the day. Many of the teachers expressed a great deal of concern about setting students up to fail academically because when students would go back to their "regular schools" after serving their year-long sen-tence, they would be very far behind their peers who would have been in class nearly 40 minutes or more each day. Most of the schools at this point had moved to block scheduling so students were in their core courses (English, social studies, math, and science) 80 minutes every other day. Teachers were concerned about giving the impression they had failed because their students were far behind oth-ers in the district. They did not want to look bad when compared to their colleagues at other schools.

Jerry first posed the question in the staff meeting, "Is academics a priority or not? These kids are just falling farther behind and we're setting them up to fail when they go back to their regular schools." When Nancy, the acting principal said, "Hasn't this school completed or clearly articulated goals from site-based planning?" Chris replied, "No, they're making it up as they go along." They had, in fact, gone through site-based planning, but it was before Chris and Jerry were on the staff. Because of the high turnover rate and because of the part-time teacher status, most teachers were new, and few were ever told what the mission statement was that the previous group had developed. Paul, captured this situation succinctly in our interview:

> The district has to come in and say, what are we trying to accomplish here? Is it the community service? Is it the fact that we want students to be academically on task with everybody else? Because we can get them to talk about their conflicts, but if we do that, we don't do the academics. As soon as we send them back to school, within a week or two they're starting to skip here and there because they're so far behind. They can't handle the homework now. They can't handle that . . . all that a teacher might give is one ditto or two dittos a week with no homework, and this teacher is giving homework every night. And after two weeks, especially with block scheduling, they're done. So I don't want to set them up for failure.

The other issue raised was what to do in the classroom when these "other issues" came up. Jerry asked this question to which he received no reply, "When do I teach social studies and when do I deal with these other issues that come up in class?" Annie, who was facilitating the meeting, responded with a question, "Is there any way to achieve the academics and deal with the other stuff?" The physical education teacher replied, "not in the time we have and the way it is structured. We can't possibly send them back prepared teaching them only a half an hour a day—we're just giving them the bare essentials. In a lot of cases they're even further behind academically when they go back."

The Dichotomy Between Subject Matter and Other Student Issues

Teachers struggled to find a meaningful balance between teaching the subject matter they were hired to teach and dealing with the myriad of other student issues and conflicts for which they had received no training. Those in administrative, counseling, nursing, or even teaching assistant roles were very concerned about these "other issues" that frequently made it difficult for teachers to teach in their accustomed ways. Teachers learned quickly that there was no sense in trying to teach without dealing with the personal issues that students brought to class. For example, Paul, the teacher with the most training in conflict resolution, said that he had learned through trial and error that conflicts had to be dealt with in the classroom and that simply removing a student from the classroom was ineffective:

> I try to teach stuff and I have stuff on the board and I come in and if there's an obvious conflict, I'll let a little talking go by so I understand what's going on. It's so easy for a teacher just to say, oh, you're out of here . . . you're out of here. But a lot of

times I'll let a few words go back and forth so I understand something. If I don't take the time to understand what the conflict is, I'm not solving it by asking persons to leave because they were swearing in my classroom.

After a brief interlude, we eventually got back on the topic of Paul being a trained mediator. This is how he said he used his knowledge in the classroom:

> Well I'm fortunate. I'm a trained mediator. I know how to deal with students. The question is sometimes, how do you deal with students in a classroom in a bunch of other kids and save face. The best thing to do is quiet them down. Get them into their work. I've quieted a lot of conflicts down by getting them into their work. You've got to do this. You've got grades. You got report cards. Whatever works . . . [You can say] I'm going to tell your parents. So that quiets a couple down. Now there's like maybe one or two kids that don't care . . . then those are the people I send out.

The teachers had a difficult time discussing how conflicts were resolved in the classroom, but it was clear that for Paul the emphasis was on trying to "teach stuff" and that teaching students how to resolve conflicts nonviolently was not the appropriate teaching "stuff," despite the fact that he was well trained to teach conflict resolution strategies. Although he felt that it was not his job to resolve conflicts, he had learned in his four years at WANTS that these conflicts had to be managed because otherwise he would be unable to teach. However, he also had to assign grades to students, complete report cards, and basically demonstrate that he had taught at least some students *math*. Paul seemed to disapprove of the popular approach of the newer teachers to send troublesome students to the principal's office. In fact, Jerry was notorious for using this method. Jerry explained his experience with students disrupting his class this way: "They do whatever they can to disrupt the class. If it means . . . if I ask them to please stop talking, they'll make a couple sounds . . . just keep going, or a couple start keeping going. Even if you send a couple of students out to the office they'll still keep doing it. It's their way. They're here. They don't want to be here." In Jerry's explanation here, students were disruptive because they did not want to be in school—more specifically in his class. He did not think that students saw any relevance to learning history and other aspects of social studies, so they were going to be disruptive and disrespectful. In addition, Jerry had no other strategies for dealing with disruptive students except for sending them to the principal's office.

In the staff meeting, teachers generated a list of possibilities to respond to the problem behavior they saw in their classroom. They described "problem" behavior as using bad language (cursing or street language), put-downs, teasing, lack of motivation, refusal to do the assigned work, sleeping, resistance to everything the teacher does, refusing to call teachers by name (use Miss or Mister), short attention span, screaming, lack of patience to receive attention, refusal to hear the word "no," do another class's work in class, verbal assaults on teachers and other students, not coming prepared. These were the words that the teachers used to describe the specific problems they saw in class. Teachers agreed that nearly half of the class period was spent dealing with these behaviors. When they were asked to generate options for how to handle these problems they said, "Reprimand verbally, ignore, move to another place, send out of the room." Then there was some discussion about having an after-school detention and that there needed to be something "between in-school detention (which they had) and out-of-school detention."

For the most part, teachers were frustrated and unsure what to do with problematic behavior in the classroom. Experienced teachers had developed some strategy, but the newer teachers were likely to send students out of the classroom—once again removing them from their educational opportunities and once again subjecting them to systemic violence through deprivation by sending the message that disruptive students should be separated from others.

Teachers and Teaching Strategies: Trial and Error and Whatever Means Are Necessary

It struck me in my interviews with the teachers that they all had developed their own teaching strategies through a series of trials and errors—as Bruce had said they were told to just "go and adjust." Teachers and other staff tried to do the best they could with little opportunity to work with colleagues or chances to get help with classroom management and discipline. There had been no in-service training for new teachers until the second half of the year. This "training," from what I observed, turned into more of a "complaint session" than training. Teachers voiced their frustrations and the trainer listened. The teachers who had been there the longest were most confident about their ability to teach students in this context. Paul, Raji, and Tom had been at WANTS since its inception, and they had developed different strategies that involved bribery and blackmail. They did not feel they needed training. In their minds, through three years of experience, they had figured out how to work with this "population."

Bribery Using the Arts

During the first year of my observations, there were no art courses at WANTS—presumably part of the punishment was to take art and music away.

Some teachers learned that students enjoyed using their artistic talents and would bribe them with art. Raji, the science teacher, and Sherry, the temporary Spanish teacher, both bribed students with music. If they were "good" (meaning they sat quietly and listened to the teacher or did the work they were assigned in class), they could listen to the radio or tapes quietly. In the back for the room, Raji had a tape player/radio playing softly on a station that the students and she agreed was okay; however, if they turned it up too loud or misbehaved, the music was turned off. Sherry stumbled on this method as well, but she would play Spanish music. She bought the tapes herself and brought in an old tape player from home. She said that she had to put it in a place where they couldn't reach it because they would try to change it to something they wanted to listen to.

Jerry, the social studies teacher, bribed students with making things. If they were "good" by most teachers' definition, they would be allowed to work with clay or draw things related to what they were learning. Jerry summarized the notion of trial and error as follows:

> Well a lot of it is trial and error. I'm learning. I mean if you notice the classroom, you see more artistic work. We try to combine hands-on stuff with learning. And they're starting to do more of that now. So instead of just saying to take notes on this section, give a poster sheet and say let's mark in the main ideas of this section on a poster. Then you do that. But if you say take notes on a sheet of paper that's too much like work.

Trial and error was challenging for teachers because they felt that the students had very low ability. They wanted to show videos because they felt that students could relate better to television than to a standard lecture or other activities, but for the first 20 weeks, there was no television or video player available. Jerry described:

> And I'm learning too. I'm learning to see . . . like I said, in most settings the teacher tells the student what to do. In this setting I'm learning to find out what they will and won't do. And I think resources are a big problem here too. We have no TV or VCR. And for students who have such low ability for comprehending stuff sometimes it's easier to show videos.

Clearly what Jerry is learning and struggling with is the shifting of his teacher paradigm—where the teacher says what to do, and the student does it and complies quietly with anything the teacher says. This is the definition of a "good" student. Low achieving students, he is discovering, do not respond to this traditional method, and thus he is struggling to figure out how to reach the children.

Undeniably the video succeeded in capturing students' attention—even that of some of the most difficult students. In fact, I witnessed the power of the video on many occasions, but the video's impact was most dramatic in a class with a substitute teacher for the "self-contained class." (Students with labels such as emotionally disturbed who cannot be mainstreamed into the regular classrooms. These students are challenging for the regular teacher, even with an assistant, to control in a room when the student to teacher ratio is two to one.) As usual, students in this class were acting out and were disengaged before the teacher had a chance to teach. She put in a video on peer pressure. The film was low budget, lacking any special effects; its dialogue was a bit hokey, yet the instant the video started, students sat silently and watched. They did not interrupt the video performers. They did not get up and run around the room as they often did. Students at WANTS were raised by the television. They obey it and respect it. They usually do not question it. However, instruction via video was often not available, and hence teachers had to come up with other strategies.

The more experienced teachers, Paul, Raji, and Tom described going through periods to figure out what would work to teach students from different academic skill levels and with new students coming in and former students being sent back to their regular schools at different times. However, the frustration of trying to meet each student where he or she was academically became too overwhelming. Thus, as Raji pointed out, they just left it up to the student to figure out how to catch up:

> It's not individualized. We don't start when the student comes to us. What I'm doing, this is what I'm teaching; this is where you pick up. The student picks it up right there. Like in the past, suppose the student came in from F school and in F school they were on chapter 4, and I was on chapter 5 for that student [the administrator] said you have to start on chapter 4. It was becoming too difficult for us as teachers. I'm not doing it. The student has to make it up.

Paul had developed packets for students, so he could try to continue with the individualized instruction method that the program began using. He described how he used trial-and-error methods to come up with these packets, and how his teacher paradigm was shattered when he came out of college. He needed to start virtually from scratch:

> From day one they gave us no books. I mean as a teacher, when I came out of college, I'm like come on you're supposed to have books. I didn't have anything. So then I had to improvise. I came up with like these 12, 13 different packets I made up. It took me years to make them up. Some of them I got at bookstores. Some of them I made up myself. It took a lot of time. So I made up a variety of packets. Now I have the books I need. I pretty much have all the materials I need. I just need to have a little more support and the fact that it's very difficult for me to teach these kids and students when I'm teaching two or three subjects at once. I got a teacher assistant working over here. I'm working here and then there's another group just sitting there

waiting for me to get to them. And when you only have 35 minute classes it's really not being that productive.

His experience has prepared him for work with these students, but he still could not continue on the individualized instruction method with one teaching assistant and himself in a classroom with 20 to 25 students in a 30-minute period.

These kinds of frustrating experiences hardened the veteran teachers. This reality was clear in Raji's passage about making students catch up themselves. They seemed to have adjusted more to the idea of being more like wardens than teachers to the "bad kids" (those who could not catch up or catch on) while they attempted to teach those who were receptive. They did not send the disruptive students to the principal's office; they kept them and tried to work with them, or at least keep them quiet and prevent them from hurting the school property or other students. Most of the teachers celebrated small successes like these with the "problem kids" in the classroom. The nature of these successes changed day to day, but Paul captured this well in this passage:

It's very difficult. It's easier with the high school kids. It gets a lot more difficult with the 7th and 8th graders. They come and walk around the room, and it's hard trying to quiet them down. There were days where they would still talk throughout the entire period, but it's all I can do to get them to sit down this and that. It wears me out, but hey, I got them to sit down, and even though they talked, it's a big step for that kid. And for this student, not to write on the desk, and I know as a teacher someone would say, "well throw them out, send them out." Well if you send everybody to the office, how are you going to teach anyone?

Tom tried to reach most of the students, but he admitted that he was not following the state-mandated requirements. He tried to give students readings that were meaningful to them. He used their language in the classroom. He talked about street language and examined how some words came into being. But these strategies worked with the most troubled children:

See, my subject out of all the subjects [English], I think, is the easiest to connect to content and social wise because a lot of the stories relate to life experience. So that's why I chose it. So we can talk about stories and relate it to something going on. Maybe not externally in the immediate world but something they've been exposed to a lot. And usually, that's a good way to get these kids to open up about what's going on. The kids feel pretty comfortable opening up. I tried to convey some of my experiences in the class and relate them to the stories they read. And they take a key from me and they feel comfortable enough to talk. Ross has been here two weeks and he's already one of the voices. But that's one of the good things about this school. These kids need someone to listen to them . . . I let them know what's going on. I enjoy—you have to have teachers here that actually enjoy their kids. And I enjoy kids. I enjoy their stories; their stories are fascinating. I like interacting with them. I like using their language to talk to them, not my language to talk to them. I like learning and using their words all the time.

Ross was a new student who was having some problems in the school. Tom's example here demonstrates his desire to try to reach this particularly troubled student, but he, like the others, wanted to reach all the students—delighting in the small successes, and trying not to get too bogged down when they could not reach a student.

Blackmail with a Marker

"External rewards" is the phrase used in teacher training. However, at WANTS, this notion resembled blackmail because it was more like, "if you're good—I won't tell on you that I saw you smoking in the bathroom." Tom the English teacher was the most skilled blackmail artist in the group because he did it purposefully and acknowledged that it worked. Part of why it worked, he claimed, was because he developed relationships with students outside of class, and they cared about what he thought of them. The male teachers in general seemed to use more traditional methods of blackmail and bribery. If students behaved, they would not be sent to the office, they would stay out of trouble, and they could get better grades. He gave several recent examples of this dynamic. On one occasion, he caught a student smoking a cigarette in the bathroom. He did not turn him in, but he just scolded him for being stupid for getting caught. Because he never turned him in, the student knew that Tom had something on him, and Tom used this whenever the student misbehaved in class. He said that sometimes you just had to use whatever worked. Tom explained:

> I let them slide on that; so now I've got him. He owes me big time. So I use it and that's what I have to do with these kids sometimes. It's a marker. I've got markers on all these kids. And I use them. I use them all the time. And that's the big thing. The hardest thing for me is not getting the marker on a kid. Because they know I can be trusted with their marks. And how can I trade in a mark? Oh, Carnell is going to fight again. Carnell, man, this is what's going to happen. If you're going to fight this kid, you're going to be out for a week. And because I didn't turn him in before, he may listen to me just a little bit.

For Tom, his appreciation or acceptance for what his students were trying to get away with was based, at least in part, on his reflections of his own childhood. He knew that he tried to get away with things that were against the rules. For this reason, his reflections made him feel hypocritical for turning in his students for doing something against the rules:

And I try to get as much as I can on these guys just so they know that I'm not going to blow them in every few seconds. Cause a lot of these kids would get blown in. They'd be rightfully so. But I tell them from the background . . . from my experiences . . . I was pretty sneaky. So that's on what I've based all my experiences . . . I didn't smoke or anything like that, but I did a lot of stuff behind the scenes in elementary school, junior high, and I know how these things work to a large extent and these guys try to pull the same stuff I was pulling 20 to 30 years ago. So I got to where I am these guys . . . So I kind of got an idea where they're coming from, and I also appreciate it.

Tom related to students as more of a peer than any of the other teachers, so he could act in certain ways that students would not tolerate or accept from other teachers. I asked several students who their favorite teacher was, and nearly all said, "Tom."

Teaching and Mothering and Caring

Sharon Abbey (quoted in Epp & Watkinson, 1996, p. 69) conducted a study of what she termed "teacher-mothers" or "mother-teachers." She described the juggling act that mothers go through "as they struggle to fulfill commitments and expectations in the dual role of teaching and mothering." She wrote that "Mothering—that is bringing up well-behaved children—is viewed as a primary source of female identity. Society is critical of women who take on additional jobs and responsibilities outside the home" (p. 69). Most of the female teachers and administrators at WANTS equated teaching with parenting and talked about mothering their own children. They all had children of their own. There was a sense in their mothering that the women at WANTS felt a sense of responsibility to "bring up well-behaved" students.

None of the male teachers or administrators mentioned parenting, but I found out later that some of them were fathers. Sherry, Nancy, April, and Kelly talked about mothering their children and the WANTS children. These women frequently made connections to their own children in how they negotiated difficult teaching or counseling situations with students. For each of them, parenting and teaching or counseling were extremely personal.

Kelly, the nurse, quit her job two months into the start of the school year because as she said:

I'm leaving because I'm going to be home with my son and some of the kids said, "that is so great. It's so important." Based on what they are telling me and my own different experiences in my professional life, I just think that the lack of strong family in the homes is coming through loud and clear with the kids, and a lot of the kids I think feel they are the big brother, so to speak, or the protector in the family and just don't have a lot of adult support and feel like they have to make decisions and a lot of times don't make the right ones or the safe ones.

Kelly struggled with what Abbey (quoted in Epp & Watkinson, 1996) described as common for teacher-mothers—the "juggling act." She defined the juggling act as "sources of stress that women face as they struggle to fulfill commitments and expectations in the dual role of teaching and mothering: societal expectations; lack of support; the trauma associated with impersonal resignation processes; fatigue and guilt resulting from multiple demands; decisions over child care; and the relentless pressure of time constraints." Kelly learned from working with WANTS students the importance of parenting. She did not want to be a neglectful parent to her young child—she had seen the effects of neglect firsthand.

Sherry, as the only African American teacher, described the role of race in her use of parenting as a strategy for teaching the students at WANTS:

> I have a son that's the same age as Joye. Sophomore. He's a lot like Joye. Actually. He's quiet like her, very private. He has a good family support. But he's very sociable. He's so much like Joye. Joye's very talented. She likes poetry. My son is very artistic. He has an art piece at the Civic Center.

Sherry could relate the personalities and talents of her children to the children she taught at WANTS—almost regardless of race. She described her relationship with Cyndie (who was white) as being difficult at first, but that she reminded her of her child who was the same age:

> And having a daughter almost 14, I can deal with Cyndie. My daughter is quiet, though. She reminds me of Dre a lot. She's a very quiet, reserved kind of kid—very quiet, very focused, very organized. She does her work—everything. My twins—I have a boy and girl twin. They're in second grade. They're almost 8. Then two others 14 and almost 16. So I know.

This "knowing" Sherry thought helped her in the classroom. Perhaps students cast Sherry in the mothering role more often because she was the only African American woman on the staff during the first year—other than the administrator's secretary, Peggy. Peggy was sometimes cast in the mother role too. Students expected Sherry and Peggy to be more caring and compassionate than the others, and students reacted very angrily if either of these two "wrote them up" for behaving inappropriately.

Sometimes though, yelling and other strategies that one can get away with as a parent did not go over as well with the children at WANTS. April described to me once that she had yelled at a student over something that she had done, and this young woman had gotten "right in [her] face like she was going to hit [her]." She said it was the only time she was actually afraid for her own safety. Sherry described when she yelled at one of the students for dropping her son's camera:

> And like I yelled at Janet. She dropped my camera last week. It was really [her son's], and [her son] asked me about his camera and I didn't have the heart to tell him she had dropped it. And I kind of raised my voice at her. "Why did you do it?" And then I could tell that she was upset. She said, "Miss White, you know why do you talk like that? I just dropped it." I had to calm down. You see I'm like that with my kids. And then I came in and I hugged her. And she smiled. That was my way of saying, "listen, I'm not like angry to the point that I didn't like her or something." And I think that made her feel better.

Yelling was seen as inappropriate, yet hugging, which was something she would do with her own children, was seen as okay—sometimes. Any kind of touching usually resulted in students recoiling or trying to hit especially whenever teachers or administrators put their hands on students' shoulders. It was difficult to read the signs of what was appropriate for whom, but perhaps for lack of any other strategy, Sherry, like many of the other mothers, used what worked for her in the home. However, Sherry could get away with more mothering perhaps because of her racial similarity to most of the students.

Nancy talked about working with middle school students, and how these ages were difficult with her own children, and especially difficult with other people's children:

> It gets frustrating, and you do need a break from it sometimes because you are constantly in puberty and hormonal stuff. When you're raising your own children, puberty is never pleasant, but you live through it because you see the light at the end of the tunnel and you love that child dearly. When you work in middle school, it's just you're constantly in puberty and at different stages of puberty and it can really wear on you, physically and emotionally. So you do need some time to get away, summer vacations. I know most middle school teachers do not do anything else in the summer; they just chill to recharge themselves so they can come back the next year.

Nancy described the tension of raising adolescents and the challenges of working with children who were not your own. Her comments were not unlike the teacher-mothers interviewed in Abbey's (quoted in Epp, & Watkinson, 1996, p. 75) study which revealed "diffuse/specific distinctions between [teaching and mothering], especially with respect to the energy, devotion, and focus each job required, the length of bonding time, and the number of children they were expected to interact with in each role." Nancy described loving her own children intensely and struggling to have enough energy to work constantly with adolescents.

April's role as guidance counselor was very nurturing and mothering for students. The one incident I remember best was when one of the eighth-grade girls came in crying saying she had to go home because she was sweating, and it was showing through her shirt. April gave her the sweater she had been wearing so that the student could wear it to hide the stains. The girl was embarrassed and said, "what if I make it smell bad." April said, "please, just take it, I want you to stay in school; I can always wash the sweater." There were other examples of caring—teachers driving students home to keep them safe; administrators taking students to meet with counselors, probation officers, and possible employers. Nancy drove one student every night to her job because she was not getting home from work until after midnight because the bus came so late. Nancy would take the girl to work at 6:00 P.M. and pick her back up at 10:00 P.M. Nancy simply said, "the family needs her income. I want her at school—awake. It's not that far for me to drive her. It's not that big of a deal."

April knew a lot of details about the students' personal lives from their intake interview when they first arrived at WANTS. She really struggled with all the painful information she knew about her students' histories. In many ways, I became her sounding board. Stories of violence including abuse (sexual, verbal, and physical), drug addiction, incarceration, loneliness, gang involvement, and profound loss were difficult for me to emotionally handle—even hearing about them secondhand from April. She clearly was emotionally drained sometimes from hearing very painful stories from young people.

Why include a discussion of mothering and caring in a section on structural violence? Because despite these stories, there was still a need to systematically create a caring environment where students would learn to care for others in the school and let others care for them. Students felt as though some teachers cared about them, but generally they did not feel that the school cared about them. There were also no discussions about forming caring relationships with one another. In addition, they did not learn how to be cared for. The students with the "really hard shells" that did not respond to the cultural construction of mothering that the predominantly white, middle-class women were prepared to give, often ended up being suspended or dropped out of school.

Creating a caring environment in schools is essential but difficult. Simply having caring adults is insufficient to create an environment where caring is taught and rewarded. It is also essential to examine how caring is culturally constructed and how individuals from different cultural backgrounds resist attempts to mother or care.

No Outlets to Blow Off Steam

Even though physical education classes met every other day at the WANTS school, most of the students had no outlet for their aggression. I do not mean to suggest here that teaching physical aggression such as boxing and wrestling and other forms of physical violence was needed. However, physical ways to blow off steam that were healthy were simply unavailable. During gym classes, boys played basketball, and the girls typically did not play. There were no after-school sports activities, and students who had been athletes were not allowed on school grounds to even view athletic events. In some cases students' identities and what made them feel good about themselves had been shaped by their participation in athletics, and this was no longer available to them. For example, for James football and basketball were his strengths in school—what he was known for. I had talked to coaches in his home school, and they said he was capable of playing Division I football, but his career would be affected by missing a year because of the weapons program.

Most of these young people did not see the link between their aggressiveness and their lack of physical activity. For example, when I asked Paul what physical activity he did to blow off steam (because he said with a girlfriend, school, and work he no longer had time to box), he said, "I don't really have any steam to blow off because I've been getting along with my parents." I asked if there was a time recently when he needed to blow off steam and he said that he goes bowling every Friday night. This past Friday he became angry at one of his friends and threw a bowling ball at him as a "warning." He also had been in a fight that resulted in his being suspended from school for three days. Students did not understand the connection between exercising as a way to reduce stress and to increase one's ability to avoid aggression.

The Need for Individualized, Culturally Relevant Instruction, Not Outside Programming

All of the regular teachers at WANTS during my first year of observations were white except for the science teacher, who was Asian Indian, and one of the administrators, who was black. Teachers who came from social locations that were different from those of the students they taught struggled to make their material interesting and culturally relevant for them. Most teachers had a difficult time bridging the cultural and social gaps. Tom was the only one who described specifically trying to select readings for his English class that were culturally and personally relevant for his students. He described this practice:

We talk about stories and relate them to something going on. Maybe not externally in the immediate world but something they've been exposed to a lot. And usually, that's a good way to get these kids to open up about what's going on. The kids feel pretty comfortable doing this. I tried to convey some of my [personal] experiences in the class and relate them to the stories they read. And they take a key from me and they feel comfortable enough to talk. Rudy has been here two weeks and he's already one of the voices. But that's one of the good things about this school. These kids need someone to listen to them, but not just listen, but [offer] a solution. 'This is something you can try next time you get into a fight.'

Tom also talked about changing the curriculum to involve readings about and by African Americans because most of the students in his classes were African American. As an English/language teacher, he discussed the importance of using the students' words to communicate:

It's, I'll tell you Kim, you know, when they see somebody like me all of a sudden use "jiggy" or "phat" . . . My attitude with it was, it's funny when you see somebody like me saying it, so I do it for laughs. But now it's just so accepted that I can say it all the time. So I broke down the barrier [using students' own language]. . . . If you look on the walls, there are some of the more common street words, *forte* (we're using forte now) is still up there. Uh, *flounce* is to uh, to we use bounce. And flounce is sort of like when you're walking, you're kind of bouncing down the hall or something like that. The other day, I said, "you guys could bounce . . . Oh yeah you mean flounce, yeah guys, flounce, peace out, yeah, later." But you have to use their language, it like breaks down barriers.

Others tried to make courses relevant without necessarily dealing with making courses culturally relevant. For example, Ken, the Introduction to Occupations and computer teacher did mention trying to make his teaching relevant for specific students as they were going to try to find jobs (the few that there were for unskilled young people) in the community. However, most teachers struggled with trying to make their courses culturally relevant.

Low Standards and Expectations for Performance

When teachers have low expectations for student performance, this attitude often turns into a self-fulfilling prophecy. During my first year of observing at WANTS, teachers commented on students' lack of motivation and low academic ability. Little was done to assess student ability. Thus, partly because of time constraints and a constantly changing student population, most teachers would end up giving the same watered-down curriculum to all students, regardless of their ability. Some of the more experienced teachers learned to lower their expectations, but some started with low expectations and tried to raise them. Raji explained how her expectations for student performance changed after her four years of teaching in this setting:

> I am more organized, and I expect things from them. Expectations have gone higher, and they are. I don't know how to say this, but if expectations are higher, they are performing much better.
>
> K: What has caused your expectations to go higher?
>
> A: Because these kids, in the beginning the impression I had was that they were troubled kids, but they really are not. It's just that some of these kids were in the wrong place at the wrong time. They are good students; so I have to raise my expectations.

Raji described here the self-fulfilling nature of low expectations. When more was expected from students, they generally performed better than when less was expected. The business teacher explained his notions of lowering his standards most specifically, although most teachers mentioned the lowering of standards in some way. The common perception was that these students were not ever going to be scholars. They were never going to enjoy schooling, and thus teachers just had to try to do their best to teach them *something*—even if this was less than what others were learning at "regular schools":

> Social Studies can be very boring for kids because it's a huge amount of facts that they have to learn and that's really what the subject matter is. It's just a huge amount of knowledge and to give that up in the interest of compliance or lowering of standards seemed to be regrettable, but I was also sympathetic to their problems. If a kid comes in the seventh grade, we're not going to instantly turn him or her into a scholar.

More often teachers blamed the structure of the school day and that they only had half an hour to teach each day, as mentioned above, when they were expected to teach the same material as their counterparts in other schools in the district who had 80 minutes every other day. Tom summarized this well:

> The district has this traditional attitude about this program, you know, we're an alternative school in one sense, we're moved away from their students. That's the only alternative thing about this school. We have to do everything else—except in less time. I guess you can say that's alternative, but that's punitive. People get caught with knives all right, we're gonna take away two hours of school. Not that, yeah, you guys don't need the extra school . . . We're gonna knock off two hours of school and try to come up with some sort of community service so you get a diploma. We should do community service right through this school. I should do community service. Each teacher should take a group of students for one month and work on a project and then after one month, you get ten new kids. And for me, that should be everything from a neighborhood newspaper, surveys, cleaning up garbage in school, doing history on the school. But what do we do?

K: Could you propose that?

T: Well I kind of brought it up a while ago, and I believe April re-mentioned at the last meeting that she wanted to do a proposal, and central offices just denied our chances. That's the frustrating thing about this is that we could actually make this an alternative school that could better these students as citizens and also enhance their education and their future prospects but what we're doing here, is, we're just going through the motions. You can come here for half an hour, and we'll try to do our best. These teachers here try to do their best. But we're not allowed to do what we could to. I'm not talking about influx of a large amount of capital. I'm talking about utilizing the staff we have here. We have too many part-time people here.

The high rate of part-time staff was also given as a reason why teachers were unable to give students extra help. Teachers had to supplement their part-time income with other jobs, and hence they were unavailable to students after school. The part-time status of many teachers also made it difficult to build community among them. There was no teachers' room to talk. There were no opportunities for collaboration. Teachers were expected to fend for themselves and figure out how to teach these students on their own. Teachers also did not have time to get involved in the community service aspect of their students' school days because when they were not teaching, they were at another job. The teachers had ideas that they wanted to implement, but they felt that the structure of the school day made it impossible. They often felt that any attempt to raise this issue to the administrative level went unheard or was simply denied.

Lack of Parental and Community Involvement

Although some parents were involved with their children's educational pursuits at the weapons school, these vocal parents were few and far between. The more system-savvy parents tended to figure out how to prevent their child(ren) from attending the weapons school in the first place (i.e., if they had resources to send their son or daughter to a private school) or helped make sure their child received a shorter sentence at the school. The business teacher, Ken, said this of some of the parents: "They do seem to be determined in who gets out when. They intercede on their child's behalf, and you see some kids leaving sooner than others, and I think that some . . . and in large part often their parents interceding rather than their performance."

Few parents felt that they could be involved in the educational system that punished their children for protecting themselves. Often these parents had dropped out of school too. As the acting principal described the parents:

I shouldn't make that a blanket statement, but a lot of parents aren't involved. You also get to a point where as you get into middle school, I just find a lot more parents arguing with me. A lot of kids I deal with here are kids who come from parents who didn't have positive school experiences themselves. Many of them didn't complete school for whatever reason. Many of them were young mothers or young fathers. So they have a really bitter taste in their mouth about school settings and stuff and a sense of what's just and not just. And so sometimes when you try to discipline children in school you don't get cooperation from the parents. And the parent will say to you, I told him to do that. Now here I am trying to say to the child, there are other ways to solve a problem than punching someone in the face. And the parent is telling him, I told you if someone gets in your face that you hit him. So you got that dual message here. And as much as I can say, I can't control what goes on in their immediate home and on the street, but I can say in the confines of this building it will not happen because it's not acceptable. In society as a whole, it's not acceptable. But in certain communities, handling problems that way is acceptable.

Clearly, there is a conflict between some school staff and some parents in the community about what is "acceptable" and "appropriate" behavior for a child. These two parties rarely talk, and when there is a conflict, the school people hold the power in determining where (and sometimes if) a child can go to school.

Lack of Program Evaluation

There was no attempt to evaluate the effectiveness of the weapons program on students who attended. I had to hunt through the records to find out what happened to students. There were no statistics provided, no teacher observations, no evaluation of programs from outside agencies—essentially there was no accountability. The perception among staff and students was that they were an island set up to fend for themselves. If they survived, this was proof enough that the school was doing okay. Nobody talked at all about being evaluated—either the teachers' teaching or their students' academic performances. Teachers and administrators did not know what happened to students after they left the school (except in a few cases where there was a personal connection made with staff, and students would keep them updated about their progress or lack thereof).

Evaluation is difficult, and defining what is meant by "success" for a school like WANTS is even more difficult. Thus, it is not unusual that this program did not have any kind of comprehensive evaluation before my arrival. As we made plans for a formative evaluation, I quickly realized that virtually no evaluation had been done.

Fear and Protection

Learning within a climate of fear is nearly impossible, yet students are forced to try on a daily basis in schools across America. Schools' failure to provide students a safe haven to learn is a form of structural violence that many students (including those at WANTS) experience. The topic of fear came up often, but school personnel, just as the students, refused to show or admit any fear. At the staff meeting, when Annie asked if teachers were afraid to come to work, they said they weren't. When she asked if they thought the students were afraid to come to school, they also thought that they weren't. However, April explained to them that many of the students had to cross into another gang's turf, and they were afraid to do so. Sometimes this fear resulted in students not coming to school at all. April thought some of the students felt that the consequences of angering the school district were seen as less powerful than the consequences of angering a rival gang, and, therefore, students frequently did not ever attend WANTS, even when they were assigned. They simply dropped out of school entirely.

Many of the teachers claimed—in a most defensive manner—that they did not fear the students. However, some of their comments about disciplining students suggested otherwise. Teachers did not discipline harshly, and they did not want to be seen as disciplinarians. They turned such matters over to the principal. The principal also claimed he was not afraid of the students.

April, Kelly, and Nancy, who were all keenly aware of the gang activity that happened right outside of the school, were not afraid for themselves but afraid for their students. When a group of rival gang members came into the school looking for Dwayne to get him for something he had supposedly done (although he couldn't tell April what it was), this event caused fear among some staff and students. Lucky for Dwayne, he just happened to have overslept that day and arrived at school after the group had been escorted out by the police. Because there was no police officer at the school at the time, the staff had to wait until the city police responded before they were able to remove this threatening group of young people from the building. Incidents such as this made staff and students tense and more keenly aware of their vulnerability.

Many students seemed to confide in April. As a result, she knew when to be afraid for her students. During the afternoon of one of the closest shooting deaths of a teenager (peer and relative of many WANTS students) a block away from the school, April was afraid to let students leave the building. I was in the building at the time. We watched as the gangs formed outside. One of the students, James, was in with us, and April claimed he was one of the prime targets. She made sure that his sister came to pick him up at the back entrance. That day, James was not the victim, but April feared that he might not be so lucky next time.

Perhaps part of the mothering role discussed above is that the teachers, counselors, and administrators who took on this caring role were more fearful for the well-being of the students and had feelings of obligation to protect the young people at WANTS. Nancy, April, and Kelly spoke of protecting students, and what they would do to try to keep them safe—realizing, of course, that most of the time they were out of their sight. April said there were some nights when she was truly afraid to get up and read the morning paper to find out who had been shot . . . and where. So often, shootings happened right on the corner or within a one block radius of WANTS. However, both April and Nancy each said that they weren't afraid for themselves, but they were afraid for the children.

The Difficulty Building Community

Building community is an important part of creating a school where students feel safe and are ready to learn. At WANTS, there were structural impediments and other obstacles to building community. Nearly all of the teachers struggled to deal with a constantly changing student and staff population. Students were coming and leaving at different times of the year (depending on when they were caught with the respective weapon), each coming with different levels of preparedness for the subject a teacher was teaching. Raji and Paul tried to hold on to the individualized instruction model while Tom virtually gave up on it and created his own strategy.

During the first year of observations, there was no sense of community among the staff because they were coming and going at different times. The part-time teachers had no free time. They would come in, teach their classes, and then go to their second part-time job. There was no teachers' room. There was very little discussion among the teachers, although some of the teachers would talk between classes with the teacher next door to them as Paul and Raji did, who had built a relationship because they had been with the school since the beginning. In Paul's words, "I feel that I made this program along with other teachers here into what it is. The staff made it what it is. It could have easily gone down hill from day one." Then, though, he went on to explain why there is no sense of community: "That's another thing that hurts us. We have a part-time staff that keeps revolving. We get new people all the while, and when you have a staff that revolves like that, the kids take notice to it and it's . . . you're pretty much doomed in the program. You're not making it work." He, like the other teachers, blamed the district for failing to provide enough funds for more full-time teachers.

Structural violence creates an environment where some students believe they do not play a role in their own futures—where certain young people believe they have no value and therefore nothing to lose by engaging in behavior that can result in their removal from society. We need to examine the not-so-subtle ways of how young people get messages in schools that they have no positive role in society—being removed from mainstream school culture, offered part-time teachers with inadequate supplies and protection. In settings such as WANTS, where structural violence is pervasive, school personnel also feel powerless in shaping their own professional lives to have the best possible influence on students. They find themselves stretched beyond the limit of their ability to teach and are further impeded by the lack of resources, an externally imposed structure, and unclear rules and goals. Consequently, these external forces resulted in a shoddy learning environment for students who were exposed to adverse circumstances in the first place, and the school environment compounded their situation.

Using the Dorothy Smith paradigm of examining the structures outside that influence these children's daily lives, this unacceptable learning environment resulted in students falling even farther behind academically. When students returned to the "regular schools," they were so far behind that they continued to get into trouble, and many would drop out as soon as they could. Some would be chronically truant. Some would drop out of society where schools admitted they could not find them. These students often ended up on the streets trying to make money selling drugs or engaging in other illegal activities to support themselves. Ultimately, these former students were involved in the criminal justice system.

CHAPTER 5

Prep Jails:
Alternative Schools Preparing
"Delinquent Students"
for the Next Step

The ultimate impact of structural violence on the young people at WANTS was that they were preparing themselves for a life of dependence on those in power. There were clearly two paths to dependence—the welfare path (for many of the young women becoming pregnant without resources to care for their children) or the imprisonment path (for men and women who were becoming involved in the violent world of gangs and drug dealing). Students did not see that they were being prepared for any useful career. Despite having dreams of becoming professional rap artists, singers, and ball players in early adolescence, by high school, these dreams were dashed by the cold reality that the safest, most realistic place would be a jail or a home owned by the government. When the majority of students at Lorenzo Hill were being prepared for college, the majority of students at WANTS were being prepared for dependence and imprisonment.

All My Friends and Family:
Normalizing Incarceration

When I was nearing the end of high school, I took for granted that I would attend college. My parents went. My friends were planning to go. My guidance counselor did what needed to be done for me to go. My parents showed me college campuses. I visited older friends and relatives at college. When I visited, I had a fairly rosy picture painted. My visits were on weekends when students partied and slept late. I did see some schoolwork being done, but generally I saw the "hanging out" with friends—in short, I saw the fun side of college. I knew that soon I would be there.

When I observed two different classes of high school students at WANTS, I noticed that students talked about jail in ways that were strikingly similar to my ways of talking about college when I was in high school. One morning, the assistant district attorney came to speak to the social studies and English classes of high school students. When asked about what happened when you were arrested, students knew and could recite the Miranda rights. They knew that, as one black girl said, "they'll cuff you if you give 'em a hard time." They knew about arraignments. In fact, they knew far more about the intricacies of the legal system than I did. They shared notes about their judges and probation officers. Several students had older brothers and parents who had been incarcerated, and they talked openly about their situation. Most of these students were black females, but there were one silent white boy, one vocal Latino boy, one black male who laughed throughout the class, and one white girl who said nothing.

There was a lot of talk about how the "stupid cops were always arrestin' folks." Many did not think that the Latino boy's brother who was in jail for stealing his mother's car should be there. They mostly all agreed that the Latino boy should not have been charged with "assault in the third degree" for beating up another boy who, in his words, "called me a spick and punched me in my mouth." They generally agreed with the young woman who said, "I will hit back; I ain't gonna wait for the cops to show—you gonna be dead." When asked what needed to happen, a group of girls agreed that "mediation don't work—I've been to mediation 60 times—it makes the problem worse."

Then the quote that summed it up, "If I hafta go to jail, I hafta go to jail." Shrug. If you were jumped, cut, assaulted, or even insulted in any way students agreed that you could not walk away. You had to fight, and then I heard the all too familiar refrain: "If you gonna die, you gonna die."

Students were asked, "Anyone ever talk to anybody who's been in jail?" They all had—siblings, parents, aunts, uncles, and friends. One girl said, "My brother obviously likes it there—whenever he get out he ends up back in."

I heard the flood of reasons why these young people thought that jail was not bad—and in some cases better than their current situations. Some of these reasons sounded like what I thought college was going to be like when I visited: you get to hang out, play, watch TV, have your friends around, sleep late, have meals provided, and be safe and protected. They have cable, many of the girls said, and they talked about how they could sit around and watch TV. They said that they heard the food was pretty good. One girl whose brother was in jail said, "They get to sleep, eat, and play basketball—they have a library and cable." One of the boys whose brother was in jail said, "My brother told me if you like to sleep you gotta go to jail—you sleep all the time." One girl said, "It's better to be in jail—it's safer in jail—not all messed up with what's on the street." The Latino boy said, and many agreed "you can't walk down the street without worrying about someone jumping out and poppin' ya—but you in jail, you don't need to watch your back. . . you in a cage." As the teachers and the assistant district attorney attempted to change their views, saying things like "you honestly would rather be in jail—what do you like to do in your spare time?" They pretty much all agreed that sleeping and watching TV—sometimes going to the mall. With the exception of going to the mall, jail was not altogether different from their current lifestyles, but none of them mentioned the challenges of being incarcerated.

Drug Dealing: A Capitalist Response to Poverty

Drug dealing was a popular way to make money for students at WANTS. Students lived in neighborhoods where drug abuse was prevalent, and where many young people were unafraid of ending up in jail. Thus, selling drugs seemed an attractive option. Students talked about their friends being drug dealers. Girls talked about their boyfriends being drug dealers. Generally, I heard more often that boys were the primary drug dealers and that dealing drugs was a fairly typical enterprise for the gangs. The gang fights were often over turf (turf was where groups could sell drugs). The drugs of choice were alcohol (some distilled in the 'hood), marijuana, and crack.

Drugs intersected with the lives of young people at WANTS in a variety of ways. Sometimes students felt surrounded by drugs and could not escape or get help. One 14-year-old girl at WANTS described in class how drugs and violence intersected for her: "I met a drug dealer guy who gave me some drugs free [at her middle school]. I asked myself, 'why me?' I didn't know what to do with it. I took them to my brother, but I was caught with the drugs and knife." When she was asked what she could have done differently she replied, "I could have come with my brother and said, 'now fight me.' Really I should call the cops, but I live where there are hookers, there are crackheads and drug dealers. The police know this, but they won't do anything about it." The sense of hopelessness is evident here. Tarrina was being pulled into a drug culture that she could not avoid and from which she could not escape. When everyone around you is using drugs, and you are offered drugs, you take them, especially when you know that most drug dealers are armed with weapons more dangerous than the knife you hold in your pocket.

Drugs such as alcohol and marijuana were seen as completely harmless. However, some of the aspiring athletes (e.g., James) saw some connection between their drug use and their ability to play. Sometimes, athletics was an excuse to cut back. One could not quit altogether because popular young people in this culture were the ones who went to a lot of parties. Going to parties, according to the young people I asked meant "smoking weed" and drinking alcohol—usually 40s (40 ounces of malt liquor).

The Transition Back to Regular School: "Oh Dear, You Came From WANTS?"

I taught a graduate course entitled "Schooling and Violence" at the university during the fall semester of my second year of the WANTS project. One of the graduate students was a full-time teacher at one of the schools in the district. I had students conduct a qualitative research project, and she elected to do her project interviewing students who had returned back to "regular" school from WANTS and from another alternative school in the district for students with "emotional and behavioral problems." She interviewed Paul and Amani. Amani admitted to her: "I'm fucking up, skipping, failing. I'm depressed. I don't feel like doing nothing but fighting. I'm talking out my ass. There are a lot of bad days here. I'm having a bad day right now. I need a psychiatrist—some Prozac. My mom—she's on it sometimes." Paul said, "The people here [at regular school], they preach at you. They don't talk to you. At WANTS they talk to you like you're an adult. They are straight with you. You gotta do this to get this and why are you doing that? They don't play games like here." They missed the structure they condemned so much. They missed the smaller classes and how simple the work was. They did not like how they were treated and the assumptions people made.

Paul described how when he first went back to regular school, the nurse asked him where he had been before, and he told her "WANTS." He said, "She just looked at me and whispered, "Oh Dear, You're From WANTS," like I was a real bad ass.

There was no transitional support for WANTS students when they returned to their regular schools and, as a result, even some of the strongest students dropped out. Students were treated poorly, and adults and other students had certain assumptions about former WANTS students that made it difficult for them to remain in this environment. They ended up on the street, imprisoned, or like Tone, unable to be found.

What Happened to the Others?

Several students from WANTS were suspended out of school, and many, once suspended, never returned. In my first year of observing, the out-of-school suspension report showed the following numbers of students suspended for the following violations:

Insubordination	3
Fighting	11
Disruptive behavior	48
Vulgar and abusive language	37
Assault of student	2
Assault of staff	1
Striking a student	3
Striking a staff member	1
Threat of a student	2
Threat of a staff member	13
Harassment of a student	8
Harassment of a staff member	22
Possession of an illegal drug	2
Reckless endangerment	10
Disrespectful/uncooperative	30
Failure to obey staff member	47
Possession/Use of dangerous weapon/object	7

I was struck by these figures, and what was actually reported versus what I heard from the students. For example, assault of students and striking students were only two and three, respectively, yet these events happened daily, but they were such a part of the student culture, they often went unnoticed. Teachers, however, would not tolerate these behaviors against them, and they had the power to punish; thus, I have no doubt that the same two figures for staff (one for each) are accurate. The other interesting comparison is harassment and threats of students versus staff. Harassment and threats were so frequent among students that, unless the threat was particularly violent in nature, and the student was one who was known for acting out his or her threats, adults did not seem to pay attention. Harassment or threats of staff, on the other hand, were usually taken seriously and reported. These numbers reflect the power structure in the school—what is considered severe and what gets reported. Adults had more power than the students, and their protection was taken more seriously. Threats made to staff resulted in disciplinary action. However, the pervasive threats from one student to another, perhaps because threatening statements were the norm, went without reaction from adults. The kinds of events that elicited adult reaction were those that created a lot of commotion—cafeteria fights, group brawls, and several students assaulting one student (or other "unfair fights").

Structural Violence and Pregnancy

The topic of sexuality and pregnancy came up in the focus groups with middle school students, and they would become very giddy and rowdy when the topic was discussed. The more aggressive girls would express their opinions vociferously in the matter, and others would giggle along with them. Some boys and girls would chime in with derogatory comments about girls who were "'hos" (whores) and "gigs" (girls who were sexually too active for their age and let boys use them to be put "back on the shelf" when they were finished—that is, have nothing to do with them socially and would only use them sexually). Middle school girls who became pregnant were bullied and tormented. In addition, they were social outcasts and topics of discussion and rumors.

I wanted to look deeper into the issue of early teen and preteen pregnancy and the structures in place for young girls. Interviews were conducted with public health nurses and social workers working with this population. As it turned out, most cases of pre- and early-teen pregnancy were not the result of a boyfriend/girlfriend relationship or boys and girls of the same age group exploring a relationship and sexuality. More commonly, and disturbingly, it was much older men (in their middle to late thirties sometimes) impregnating very young girls. Older men with money (often drug dealers) preyed on young girls (when they were "hanging on the block" or at the mall) and used their money to promise them material goods. When asked why such older men were preying on such young girls, the answers were consistently "because they expect that they are more likely to be virgins and more likely to be disease-free." In addition, mothers would prostitute their very young middle school daughters to much older drug dealers for drugs.

There were other examples as well, such as one case where an older brother had impregnated his younger sister. However, both social workers and nurses alike stated that younger, middle school girls' stories were significantly different from the older high school girls with whom they had worked. They said that many of the younger girls could not even talk about sex without giggling and blushing. The stories of the older girls in high school were quite different. There were many more cases of pregnancies resulting from romantic relationships or similar-aged pairings.

When caseworkers (nurses and social workers) reported these cases of statutory rape to Child Protective Services, girls and their families often would no longer trust them and would no longer avail themselves of their services (mental and physical health services for the girls and their babies within their first year).

Because of the stigma facing 11- to 14-year-old pregnant and parenting girls, school was an uncomfortable place. Truancy was a huge problem for these girls. Girls also did not feel good physically because of the pregnancy, and thus they stayed home from school and fell behind academically. Once their babies were born, it was very challenging for them to catch up, cope with the stigma of too-early motherhood, and being outcast in the school community. In addition, parenting girls were dealing with the struggles of raising a baby (even though their own mothers often helped), finding appropriate care and getting to school on time. Despite the law of mandatory school attendance until age 16 years, many girls were chronically truant and had plans to drop out. There were no real structures in place to support girls' continuation in school after giving birth to their babies.

Very young girls who were successful at returning to school had a lot of support from their own mothers (in some cases mothers raising the child as their own) and were able to have a separate life at home and at school. However, even in cases where young girls had help from their own mothers, they often did not return to school because they were far behind academically and did not want to face the bullying and harassment from their peers.

The existing structures derailed pregnant girls from education and eclipsed possible opportunities for them to become self-sustaining. Thus, by default their futures involved poor-paying jobs, public assistance, repeat pregnancies, and mental and physical challenges.

Structural Violence at Lorenzo Hill

Structural violence was far more apparent and pervasive at WANTS than at Lorenzo Hill, although it was also a reality at that school, and, just as at the weapons school, tended to be linked to poverty. Poorer students were removed from the mainstream educational experience by being labeled as "special ed kids." These students were less likely to earn a high school diploma and were more likely to get low-paying jobs if any job at all. The cycle of poverty continued for many poor children at Lorenzo Hill as it did for the children at WANTS.

Special Education and Poverty at Lorenzo Hill

The Lorenzo Hill Elementary School principal explained that many students in trouble for physical fights and bullying were students who had been diagnosed as needing special education or came from poor families and were lacking in social skills. She told me that I should come in to observe at breakfast when students who qualified for free or reduced-price breakfast (those below the poverty line) arrived. She said, "I try to teach and model social skills—even as simple as saying good morning, but I can't get them to say it back. They just grumble at me. They have such limited social skills and often have learning disabilities or low self-esteem. Often these kids are quick to anger and behave aggressively." She said that she had one boy who made up six of the 50 referrals during the first half of the year. She said that he had been trouble from the start. She was not sure why—he was not labeled as a "special ed." She said that he came from the poorer part of the district—the trailer park.

The principal also described that most of the referrals happened for bad bus behavior or poor behavior during recess—the times when students were loosely supervised and free to do largely what they wanted. The rest of their time in school was closely monitored. Students ate with their teachers. They went from class to class in rows with aides. Recess and the bus were the only times when they could briefly escape adult gaze. There were certain bus routes that were notoriously problematic. So much so that bus drivers rotated so one bus driver would not deal with these groups all the time. These were the bus routes that went through the poorest sections—the one that picked up students at the largest trailer park, and the other that went through the poorest rural area.

It seemed like a chicken and egg question—which came first the poverty or the problematic behavior? Were students labeled before they had a chance? Did they earn their reputation by acting out? Did these children tend to learn violence in the home as some of the WANTS students had? I had started in the elementary school with hopes of finding some evidence either way, but it was not apparent. Some students had already been labeled as troublemakers and were watched carefully. Some of these students came from poor families, and some were considered as "special ed kids," but some were not. While the link between poverty and identification for special education seemed obvious—most of the students in greatest need of services came from poor families, the link between aggressive behavior and poverty seemed slightly blurred. What was clear was that the students who were most likely to be ostracized and teased and treated cruelly of these groups (that is, students that were most different) tended to behave most aggressively. In the suburban high school, difference was not acceptable and could result in further violent victimization—that is, via structural violence of being more likely to be labeled, ostracized, and short-changed educationally.

Summarizing Structural Violence:
What Happened to Julius?

Julius is an excellent example to highlight how institutions and processes out-side the children's control shape their lives. Many of the topics covered above, such as gangs, family violence and drug abuse, poverty, and such schooling prac-tices as zero tolerance policies, providing inadequate resources for alternative education programs, providing underqualified teachers for the neediest students, preparing certain students for life within the criminal justice system, were clearly influential in Julius's life and his final destination—prison.

In April 2000, three years after Julius had been in the fight at the Community Center that resulted in his dismissal from the program, I was watching the news and Julius came on the screen, holding his minister's hand like a little boy. They were walking to the courthouse so Julius could confess to murder. He shot and killed a rival gang member the night before and was going to turn himself in. As the camera flashed to Julius in handcuffs listening to the judge, his head was low, and I saw his little-boy face was trying to look brave. My mind flashed to him sit-ting in my car sensitively singing a love song out loud to the radio. I thought of the times we played basketball, and he would laugh. I pictured him reading to the young children at the Community Center. Now he was labeled a "murderer." I thought about the structures and processes that contributed to his being in that courthouse on that day. I remembered the things he told me and what his teach-ers and counselors told me about his life.

School violence and street violence will continue if we fail to address the in-stitutions and processes that shape these children's lives and give them so few alternatives that we increase the likelihood that they will become killers.

Julius was born to a drug-addicted mother who undoubtedly exposed him to drugs prenatally. Perhaps she used drugs to help herself deal with the pain of loss and poverty. Perhaps she herself was born to a drug-addicted mother. Maybe as a result of Julius's prenatal exposure, he was always quick to anger and had a short attention span. Possibly this exposure partly contributed to his own drug use. Julius did get to school as a child, but he learned at an early age that he was not a good student—he did not read well (he was never read to as a child he told me) and as a result never performed well on tests or other traditional forms of assess-ment we used in schools. He felt like a "dumb kid," and the structures around him validated that notion.

Julius lived alone with his mother until his younger sister was born three years later. They were poor and struggled to survive. Julius's mother got clean and sober when Julius was a teenager, and she became very religious and very involved in her church. She sent messages loud and clear to her son that he was a good-for-nothing. She tried to get him involved in church, but he knew he could never be as religious as she was or as she wanted him to be. Julius told me that his mother always prayed for him. "My sister," he told me, "is the good one—she's good in school and stuff." Clearly, in contrast, he was not.

The one thing Julius was good at was getting into trouble. He was a clown in class and would often be disciplined for being disruptive—a trick he learned to get out of class—which he hated because he had received multiple messages that he did not belong in school. He was so good at getting into trouble that he ended up at WANTS (placing him even farther behind academically with no hope of catching up to be able to receive a diploma), and ultimately he ended up involved in the criminal justice system. He was good at this system—or at least at finding himself involved in it.

Julius felt proud that he was involved with one of the most notorious gangs in the city. He made it very clear that he would do anything for his gang members and that they would do the same for him. He carried a gun because he knew that he was in danger of rival gang retaliation for crimes that he did not necessarily commit. He had been shot at several times during the time I knew him. He would matter-of-factly say to me, "I'll either end up dead or in jail." Frankly, I expected the former to happen first.

Julius had a few options—school, juvenile justice, religious involvement, gangs, family involvement. These options narrowed quickly when he realized that he was a failure in school. He did what we all do. He gravitated toward and ultimately chose the things he did well—and wanted to do them really well—gang involvement and criminal justice. He demonstrated his loyalty to his gang by shooting and killing a young man from a rival gang. This act ultimately resulted in his ending up—for the rest of his life—within the criminal justice system, a place where ironically he thought he would be safer, or at least alive. If he stayed on the streets, he knew he would be killed in retaliation for killing a rival. Did he have choices? Of course. Do all young men in his situation kill others? No, but it is surprising that this type of violence does not happen more often.

Structural violence takes subtle forms: placing poorer students at significantly higher numbers in special education classes, preparing students for incarceration or government dependence by giving inadequate resources for their education, incarcerating high percentages of African American men, creating a system in which dropping out of school is okay, and dropouts are not helped (or recognized before they drop out). These are just a few of the structural forms of violence students experienced. It is essential that we not only examine the obvious forms of physical personal violence, but also look critically at the structural violence that may contribute to groups of young people becoming victims and perpetrators of violence and ultimately being systematically removed from society. We need to consider how our policies, procedures, and institutions contribute to creating violent schools and society. We need to examine the ways that structural violence exists silently and prevents certain groups of children from realizing their full potential.

Final Thoughts on Structural Violence

Structural violence is less obvious than personal violence. Victims tend to blame themselves. Perpetrators often fail to see their role as perpetrators and often engage in victim-blaming. We need to examine structures in place that continue to support physical violence, as well as those structures that prevent individuals from reaching their full potential. When a child drops out of school before graduation, this is structural violence. Nearly all children can learn and should be able to master the concepts required to graduate from school with proper guidance and support. If students are dropping out, there are structural reasons. We need to examine the subtle forms of structural violence that continue to support drug dealing, gang violence, and subsequent incarceration of nearly half of the African American males between the ages of 16 and 25.

What existing structures prevent teachers from reaching more of their students? What are the structures that prevent students from feeling safe and protected in school and between school and home? How can we create a caring school environment that will allow students to acknowledge their myriad of confusing and difficult emotions without denial of student and staff affect.

How can we ensure that all teachers and students will have the essentials they need to learn at school including books, paper, and other supplies? How can we even out the playing field between poor urban schools and wealthy suburban schools?

We need to create caring school communities for all students where they can receive individualized instruction (when needed) that is culturally relevant. We need to create school communities that work with the local communities and families of their children to develop realistic strategies that have had demonstrated effectiveness. We need to acknowledge the silent but deadly effects of structural violence.

PART III

Solutions and Recommendations

CHAPTER 6

Conclusions, Implications, and Recommendations

As researchers, educators, and others attempt to determine which violence prevention and intervention programs might potentially work in a given culture, we need to start by asking individuals from various backgrounds and social locations within that culture how they define violence, how they make sense of violence in their lives, and how violence within their culture can be minimized if not eliminated. We need to determine what individuals in certain geographic locations are already doing successfully to prevent violence in their lives. We need to examine how new efforts might conflict with, dismantle, or render such existing systems ineffective. We need to know what the motivation is for buying into a new system. For example, do most people within a given culture live in fear of violence and want to feel safer walking down the street at night? We cannot simply identify "promising practices" and assume these will work in all environments, but we need to evaluate possible measures qualitatively. First, what are individuals currently in the location doing to prevent or reduce violence that most involved in the system believe works? Second, how might a selected "promising practice" interfere with existing structures or strategies already being used? Third, what can realistically be accomplished and internalized into this system? Fourth, what is the motivation for adopting a new strategy? This book is intended to facilitate a better understanding of the aforementioned questions and to make readers aware of the situations with which young people in certain environments have to cope. The hope is that readers will learn from these lessons—to ask, to observe, and to listen carefully to those most intimately involved in the environment they want to change.

Suggestions on building a school-wide approach to violence prevention were made to the staff at WANTS after literature on the topic was carefully reviewed, after gaining an insight of how people at WANTS perceived violence, and after analyzing what students, families, and staff did to keep themselves safe, although existing structures may have made it more difficult to achieve personal safety.

Promising Practices in the Literature

Loeber and Farrington (1998) conducted perhaps one of the most thorough investigations of promising practices for at-risk youths in their edited volume commissioned by the Office of Juvenile Justice and Delinquency Prevention entitled *Serious and Violent Juvenile Offenders: Risk Factors and Successful Interventions.* In their comprehensive review of the literature on serious and violent juvenile offenders, they identified the most promising practices for working with these young people. The most promising programs included multiple services such as personal counseling, tutoring, job skills training, family therapy, case management, mentoring, cultural education, and physical exercise (health and wellness training). Multimodal programs addressed law breaking, substance use and abuse, academic issues (including learning disabilities, literacy, and special needs), and family problems were also successful. Programs that required integration of schools with juvenile justice, mental health, and child welfare agencies, and included parents as well, had demonstrated success with young people.

Different strategies for violence prevention and intervention have shown success with different groups. The National Institute of Justice (Sherman, Gottfredson, MacKenzie, Eck, Reuter, & Bushway, 1998) identified the following programs for different groups: for infants and pregnant teenagers, frequent home visits by nurses and other professionals; for preschoolers, classes with weekly home visits by preschool teachers; for delinquent and at-risk youths, family therapy and parent training; for schools, organizational development for innovation, communication and reinforcement of clear consistent norms, and teaching social competency skills (e.g., skill streaming, prosocial skills, and so on), and critical thinking skills. For repeat offenders, special police monitoring and incarceration were the most promising choices. (See the Appendix A for programs that have been found to be "promising" or have "demonstrated success.")

Programs with demonstrated success or those described as "promising" have many common elements: conflict resolution, creating caring environments, anger management, teaching prosocial and problem-solving skills, consistent discipline, family involvement, community service and involvement, academic support, drug prevention, and drug intervention. These promising and demonstrated strategies guided the recommendations made to Lorenzo Hill and WANTS. However, it was important to take into account the very different cultures at Lorenzo Hill and

WANTS before making recommendations. (For a more detailed description of demonstrated and promising practices, see Williams, 2003, chapter 3.)

What Was Needed at Lorenzo Hill

At Lorenzo Hill, there was an identified need to reduce putdowns. This seemed to be the biggest problem for students, teachers, and administrators—mean treatment (through verbal abuse) and ostracism. The school chose the "No Putdowns" program. "No Putdowns" is a comprehensive school-wide prevention curriculum. It has been used since 1991 with elementary school children in grades K to 6 to reduce violence. Teachers or administrators are trained to employ the program as an integrated part of their existing curriculum or in addition to their existing curriculum. Teachers are given lesson plans, strategies for teaching skills to students, and training to use the materials. The program teaches students a variety of skills (awareness of putdowns, strategies for staying calm in stressful situations, ways to build confidence and self-worth, celebration of diversity, responses to stressful situations and how to choose the best one, ways to build others' self-worth, ways to demonstrate respect, and ways to encourage others). The use of the school-wide curriculum establishes an environment with a common language for teacher, staff, parent, and child interactions. There is a parental component.

For Lorenzo Hill decision makers, the decision to implement "No Putdowns" seemed straightforward. It was relatively inexpensive, and it could be infused into the traditional curricular areas. It seemed to address the main needs that teachers, students, and administrators identified.

The Needs at WANTS

At WANTS, the needs were greater and the decisions more challenging. There were so many needs and so few resources. The needs were prioritized. Among the top priorities was to find a safe place where students were not crossing gang boundaries. The school was moved to another location where students were not crossing into rival gang territory. More security officers were hired for the school. Students needed help to manage their anger so that they were not so quick to fight when they were provoked. Thus, they chose components of various programs based on the anger management competencies outlined in an earlier part of this book. These competencies were created out of a textual analysis of successful programs. There was a need to include caregivers and parents. Students needed help to transition back to their home schools, and consistent and fairly enforced discipline standards had to be established. The components were selected based on the needs of the students at WANTS. The parental component and discipline strategies were discussed in the previous chapter and, although these were a part of the strategies at WANTS, they will not be covered again here.

Learning by Case Example: WANTS

As director of the Violence Prevention Project at the local university, I officially formed a partnership with WANTS with the stated purpose of using our grant money to help them address the needs I had identified in my needs assessment. My goal with Catelyn Willey, the new principal (who came in the summer of 1998 with almost no warning because of budget cutbacks and administrative seniority) was to develop a comprehensive approach to violence prevention at the school based on the formal and informal data collected during the previous year. In the summer of 1998, we started to put the following plan in place. We used grant money for violence prevention in the following areas during the first year:

- direct conflict resolution and anger management training to all students;
- rethinking and developing a new community service component for students;
- in-service training with teachers and curriculum development to infuse anger management and conflict resolution into their existing curricula;
- parent outreach.

(See the end of this chapter for a complete checklist of items to consider when developing a school-wide approach.)

During that year, we also made plans to develop a comprehensive transition program for students returning to their regular schools, as well as strategies for working more closely with parents.

Before the start of the second year of my work at WANTS, I hired an experienced, popular, well-known trainer to teach anger management, prosocial skills, problem solving, communication, and conflict resolution skills to students. The emphasis was on teaching anger management strategies every day (each student once per week for two hours in a group setting).

As of January 25, 1999, there were 87 students on the roster and 12 teachers (four full-time), two full-time administrators, a school counselor, a part-time school psychologist, two hall monitors, a school nurse, a full-time secretary, and a police officer. This was nearly double the staff (it was double the number of full-time teaching staff) that had been at the school the previous year.

The school was moved at the beginning of the academic year (the start of its fifth year in existence) to the newly renovated and historically restored library in the business part of the city. The school relocated from the dilapidated former church school building. The new site had become available when the funding for the enrichment program that had been in the building was cut just before the start of the school year. The administration needed to fill the space with a program that would be able to move with virtually no notice; WANTS seemed the easiest and smallest program to move. There was much noise made by school board members and other vocal people within the district administration when the nicest building was being given to the "delinquents" when "elementary schools had rats and cockroaches and needed repair." Nonetheless, the school was moved, perhaps mostly because of ease, but it proved to be critical to improving the morale of staff and students. Suddenly, they felt that if they were worthy of such a beautiful space, they must be more important than they had thought. The physical environment of a school can make a huge difference in students' perceptions of themselves and their school.

As mentioned above, many needs had been identified during the yearlong examination using interviews, focus groups, observations, and surveys. For example, before the start of the 1998–99 academic year, WANTS had no consistent strategy to teach all students and staff skills such as anger management, conflict resolution, communication, and problem solving (alternatives to violence). We focused our efforts on providing classes in anger management and conflict resolution for all students in the school. Furthermore, we provided in-service and curriculum development work on these same topics with all of the teachers. In addition, we developed a parent outreach component. Before our partnership with WANTS, there was no strategy to involve parents in the school. We hired a part-time social worker to do parent outreach. We worked to create a parent advisory group and a system of regular communication with the parents.

The transition component of the intervention—when students were returned to their original schools—was being developed. We were in the process of examining the 14 other schools in the district and were assessing their transition strategies to reintegrate students who had been sent to WANTS. WANTS teachers and an additional "transition counselor" were hired to assist students with their transition back to their regular schools and to do family outreach. The schools were asked to help develop strategies to facilitate the transition process. The relationships formed during the first year would help us implement this strategy. However, our focus would be on our WANTS partnership and WANTS students.

The Need to Prioritize Solutions

Although we wanted to be able to contribute more at WANTS based on the needs we identified and the reality of limited resources (time, space, money, and personnel), we focused our contributions to the school on:

- direct teaching of communication skills, anger management, conflict resolution, and problem solving;
- integration of anger management, conflict resolution, and prosocial behavior skills training for students in the general curriculum through in-service work with staff;
- parent outreach and involvement;
- facilitation of the transition back to regular school for students and their families.

As programs for schools are selected and implemented, the responsible staff will be forced to recognize the limitations in terms of resources and will have to prioritize. However, the issue of resources should not be overemphasized because there are local, state, and federal grants available, particularly for schools to implement programs with demonstrated success. Having the data to show a need (as have already been collected in formal or informal strategies) will also help make a case for grant-funding agencies. A word of warning about external funds—when these funds dry up, often (as was the case at WANTS) so do the interventions. Therefore, it is important to institutionalize as much as possible the selected interventions, so that additional funding is not always critical for successful implementation.

Student Anger Management Training

All students at WANTS were required to attend one two-hour class per week on anger management, conflict resolution, problem solving, communication skills, and skill streaming (a prosocial skills program with demonstrated success in working with at-risk youths developed by Dr. Arnold Goldstein; see reference in Appendix A). The course ran the entire academic year and was taught twice daily at WANTS to small groups of less than 10 students.

The course started in September 1998, but because students entered WANTS on a rolling basis, the length of time of student participation in the intervention program varied according to the length of time they were assigned to WANTS (based on their superintendent's hearing) and the regularity of their attendance. Thus, some students had been in the class since the beginning of the school year and were still in the class while others, who attended the class at the beginning of the school year, returned to their regular schools. Still others started at some point later in the academic year (October, November, December, or January) and remained in the class until the end of the year. Most students were assigned to WANTS for one calendar year, but some students were assigned for one marking period. Although we identified this rolling admission and departure as problematic for teachers and students, this reality was viewed as one that could not be changed.

The results of a mid-term qualitative assessment and a formative evaluation were used to improve our interventions. For example, the anger management course needed to be more individualized—identifying students' needs when they entered the class and setting goals for skills they felt they needed to obtain.

Community Service and Carryover of Skills

On the other four days when students were not in anger management class, students were supposed to go to their community service placement site. Annie, whom I hired to teach the class, also coordinated the community service placements for students, following up with students and agencies. This task became burdensome, and students still were not attending their placements regularly. Students liked the idea of doing projects, but especially high school students wanted paid work experience. We worked with students who were old enough to work for pay to help them find paid work experiences when possible.

During the winter of my second year, Annie and I worked with the new principal to reconceptualize the community service component. Consistent with what some of the teachers mentioned in their interviews, we created projects for students that could be linked to their academic subject areas. Students were assigned roles in these 10-week projects. Annie and a graduate assistant helped organize the paperwork and oversee the assignments. We solicited volunteers from the university and the community to help.

During the fall of 1998 and spring of 1999, we piloted the first of several planned innovative community service projects for students at WANTS based on student interest. The school principal, Annie, and I developed lists of possible projects, such as a community newsletter, art projects, community gardens,

HIV/AIDS education, and day care. The school sought additional funding for these projects. These service projects provided an opportunity to observe students and to determine if they transferred the skills they learned in the course (anger management, conflict resolution, and so on) to other settings. It was also an opportunity to reinforce the prosocial skills they had learned in the class.

We noticed a great deal of change among the students in the pilot projects. One of the most successful projects was an art class where students learned to take others' perspectives and draw pieces of what they could see. Annie would coach students to use the skills in these environments and help students make connections to what they learned in the anger management course. Students loved the hands-on nature of the art class; attendance was very high, and students were very motivated. Annie trained some of the supervisors to recognize when students used the skills, and they were praised when they used the skills successfully—or even when they tried. The support of staff was essential to students practicing the anger management and conflict resolution skills outside of class.

WANTS Staff Training

Annie and I conducted training for teachers at WANTS during the summer of 1998. Returning teachers from the 1997–98 academic year were paid to participate in a three-day workshop where teachers learned anger management, judicious discipline, conflict resolution, communication, and problem-solving skills. They were also taught how to infuse these skills into their subject areas, i.e., math, English, social studies, science, business.

Curriculum infusion is a challenging task. Teachers were expected to write lesson plans infusing some of these components into their existing lesson plans. Jerry, the social studies teacher, was the first to complete the assignment, but then he quit WANTS. Paul completed the assignment after working with the university staff. He struggled with the task, as had Jerry, but ultimately he completed it. Ken, the business teacher, handed me six lesson plans that he already used, with no attempt to infuse the components. When I talked with him about this omission, he said, "Kim, it's like I've invited you into my house, and now you're trying to move in and take over." He ended up not revising the lesson plans. The other teachers never handed me any drafts of lesson plans.

Many of the teachers considered this idea as a burden, or an add-on, that was detracting from their scheduled tasks. I tried to explain how collaborative learning activities could be used to teach what they were already teaching, and that within collaborative learning groups, students could be taught anger management and conflict resolution. However, some teachers at WANTS were uncomfortable with alternative pedagogy. Discussion and lecture were the popular styles. The veteran teachers had created packets for students to work on independently. In these settings, teachers served in the role of tutor. These veteran teachers had developed strategies that they felt worked with this population of students and were reluctant to try the new techniques and subjects described in the workshop.

During the academic year, Annie and I conducted workshops with the entire staff: the administration, counselor, nurse, teaching assistants, teachers, hall monitors, and the police officer. We described the principles of anger management and conflict resolution, and encouraged teachers and other staff members to build these principles into their teaching or interactions with students, respectively. The staff members were very supportive and enthusiastic, with the notable exception of some veteran teachers, who often came late to these meetings and talked among themselves during the small group work. This form of resistance suggested to me that the veteran teachers felt they had found strategies that worked for them and did not want to learn others. Raji told me one day that the reason she did not look for jobs in the regular school is that she had already developed her packets for the WANTS students and would need to start again and do more work if she moved to a "regular school."

Attendance

Attendance rates at alternative education sites for at-risk youths have historically been low. At WANTS, the average daily rate of attendance was 60% during both years of my observations. Students were savvy and knew ways around the system, and thus many were able to avoid attending WANTS. Students who were 16 years old or older did not have to attend school of any kind, and many did drop out. The students who were under 16 would attend somewhat more regularly, but many were placed on probation for truancy—although it was rare that any kind of penalty would result.

Any program focusing on the needs of the students most at risk of violence and aggression needs to address the issue of attendance. Working with community agencies conducting street outreach and those who hire street outreach workers is a start. Furthermore, most schools have truancy officers. It is important to work closely with these individuals. In addition, the parent outreach should involve regular feedback about attendance. Parents need to be aware of their child's lack of attendance, and a partnership between the schools and parents needs to be formed to make sure students go to school on a regular basis. Mechanisms need to be put in place at schools so that the homes of regularly absent students—once they have been identified—will be called on days when these students are absent and if it becomes necessary that these students be picked up in the morning. These students are perhaps the most at risk of criminal behavior when they are not in school.

Aftercare and Transition

An examination of the comprehensive bibliography compiled by the Hamilton Fish National Institute (available at http://hamfish.org) about alternative education for violent youths shows that the aspect of alternative education most consistently neglected is the students' transition back to their home schools. At WANTS we found this to be the case as well. The transition back was largely ignored, and many students would ultimately drop out of school shortly upon their reentry into their home schools. Because of this disturbing scenario, we hired a graduate assistant to work with WANTS students when they returned to their regular schools to help them with the challenging transition back.

In the fall of 1999, WANTS teachers and others worked with students through their first year of transition on academic and social issues. Teachers provided academic support and made referrals to additional support as needed. They worked closely with the social worker to make appropriate referrals for the student and his or her family.

Issues of transition must be addressed for any student who is taken out of the mainstream classroom. This should include any time out of the classroom for poor behavior (suspension, expulsion, or even in-school suspension), time out for incarceration, or mental health treatment. Whenever a child is out of the classroom, plans need to be in place to help him or her reenter.

Pedagogy Using Media and Collaboration

Teachers are often reluctant to use videos and other forms of media in their classrooms. However, when done well and used to reinforce good teaching, these media forms—particularly videos—are very effective ways to capture the attention of challenging students. We need to develop better tools for students that capitalize on our myriad of media forms (computers, televisions, video, and so on). We need to acknowledge that students respond well to various forms of media and provide opportunities for students to interact with media forms as often as possible. Unfortunately, in poorer urban districts where these forms of media are perhaps even more necessary, the equipment is unavailable. This lack of resources requires teachers and administrators to be creative. Partnerships with local colleges or universities for undergraduate volunteers to work with young people on campus with different media forms and collaboration with local agencies for funding for supplies are two possible strategies. I do not mean to suggest that media be used to replace the work that teachers need to do to teach basic math and literacy skills but rather that these alternative forms of media be used to support more traditional strategies.

In addition to media, more collaborative forms of pedagogy need to be employed in the classroom. Developing a culture of cooperation rather than competition results in students learning how to create win–win situations instead of win–lose situations. Cooperative learning strategies have been shown to create less violent and less aggressive classrooms. Students learn to value other students as colleagues rather than competitors. This culture of cooperation creates the foundation for developing a caring school.

Creating a Caring Environment

Within the school-wide approach model, there needs to be a strategic way to teach care and how to build caring relationships. Nel Noddings's book, *Challenge to Care in Schools*, describes the importance of teaching students how to care and how to be cared for. She also discussed the importance of creating a caring school environment. She writes, "My description of a caring relation does not entail that carer and cared-for are permanent labels for individuals. Mature relationships are characterized by mutuality. They are made up of strings of encounters in which the parties exchange places; both members are carers and cared-fors as opportunities arise" (1992, p. 16). There were some examples of students who demonstrated care for each other and for teachers, and there were some examples of staff caring for students and other staff. Caring for one another needs to become a central component of any school environment—especially for students who are identified as being at risk of violent behavior.

Considering Prenatal and Postnatal Care as
Violence Prevention Strategies

It may seem strange to read about the importance of prenatal and postnatal care in developing a whole-school approach to violence prevention. However, we have to incorporate these notions into our thinking. A truly comprehensive approach to violence prevention addresses the needs of young people from the earliest possible point. At WANTS, there were pregnant and parenting teens with no guidance whatsoever about how to care for themselves during pregnancy or how to take care of an infant. I heard many stories of pregnant teens using drugs (particularly alcohol and marijuana) without thought to the impact on the fetus. I heard stories from social workers working with these young people after their infants were born. The social workers were concerned about how overly rough (almost abusive) these young people were with their newborns, and these young mothers admitted that they did not know how to hold or care for their babies. These babies are at risk of growing up and being aggressive or violent in school. More work is necessary to examine the links between the lack of parental attachment and children's violence. Furthermore, we need to better understand the connection between maternal drug use and resulting aggression in the offspring later in life. In the meantime, schools can be poised to be proactive by working with pregnant and parenting teens to be drug-free, positive, and caring role models for their children. Providing skills for parents to read to their children and spend quality caring time together is one way, but there are many. This approach is perhaps the earliest proactive strategy to reduce violence that schools can use. Schools cannot ignore this charge. If they are ignored, the long-term effects will be devastating.

Learning by Case Example: Lorenzo Hill

In contrast to WANTS, which had complex and multiple needs and required complex solutions, Lorenzo Hill's problems seemed more straightforward. They, like many schools, decided to purchase an existing, developed program. The "No Putdowns" program seemed to meet their needs. Choosing existing programs from the many programs that have had demonstrated success can be easier than constructing programs tailored to meet the specific needs of a specific school, but they may not meet all the needs or may even have inappropriate components or program elements.

The Forgotten Art of Evaluation

One of the main objectives of the projects at Lorenzo Hill and WANTS was to use evaluation to determine if the programs implemented there had a positive impact on students and staff. Evaluation is challenging and often shortchanged or omitted entirely. Any program dealing with school violence must be committed to determining whether or not the program meets its stated objectives. There are various approaches that can be useful in determining the success or failure of a program or components of programs. Qualitative approaches may include observations of key places in the school, focus groups with students or staff, interviews, journal writing, and open-ended surveys. Quantitative approaches may include experimental designs (as used with Lorenzo Hill with a pre- and post-test comparison and a comparison group not receiving the intervention) or statistical analyses that compare the differences before and after a program has been implemented. Surveys are often used for that purpose.

Evaluation at Lorenzo Hill

At Lorenzo Hill, I conducted a formal and informal analysis of the "No Putdowns" program to determine its effectiveness. Not all schools will have the time or luxury of conducting both formal and informal evaluations of their programs, but ideally these strategies when used together give us a good picture of what works and what does not.

Choosing a Comparison School or Group. One of the best ways to determine if a program works is to compare it before and after it is implemented to another similar group of students who do not have the program (a comparison group). Lorenzo Hill Middle School implemented the "No Putdowns" program during the fall of 1999. To serve as a comparison school, the neighboring Tug Hill School, which was of similar size, socioeconomic background, and racial makeup, was selected. I created the surveys from the objectives of the program and from questions that I had as a result of observations, focus groups, and interviews. Pre-tests were given before the start of the "No Putdownsprogram, and the post-tests were given at the end of the school year to both schools.

Qualitative Results. The results from observations, interviews, and focus groups at Lorenzo Hill indicated that students felt positive about the program and could see its results (students were nicer to one another, and there were fewer fights). Students acknowledged that they were more aware of their own use and others' use of putdowns. However, students also said that the more "popular students," albeit nicer in general, came up with new and creative putdowns of which teachers or administrators were not aware. The creative use of putdowns was an integral part of popularity, particularly for boys.

Teachers at Lorenzo Hill had mixed feelings about the program. Some of them felt insufficiently equipped to do the lessons (citing lack of time, familiarity with the material, poor student response, and the feeling that the program was not necessary or effective). Other teachers were positive, reporting that they liked that the program gave them a "common language to use with students" and that it offered some concrete ways for students to deal with conflicts without fighting. Veteran teachers tended to be the most skeptical, reporting that the students' attitude was "we do this anyway." Ironically, a couple of powerful veteran teachers at one school (which was initially in the study but was later dropped) bullied less experienced teachers into rallying the teachers' union to support them not to implement the program and evaluation. However, some teachers liked the program because it enhanced the students' social skills in terms of a common polite language and a common strategy in dealing with one another.

Administrators generally felt that there were fewer office referrals, that teachers were handling conflicts in the classroom more often, and students were less cruel to each other. Nevertheless, administrators acknowledged that some teachers complained about the program (particularly veteran teachers) and did not see a reason to have it. Administrators agreed that continuing to motivate teachers to use the lessons and reinforce the skills was one of the most challenging tasks to make the program successful.

Formal Survey Results. Because the survey questions required "yes" or "no" answers, statistical analyses using these kinds of variables were used to compare pretest and post-test results as well as assessing the similarities and differences with the comparison school. Statistical analysis is not always necessary, but if schools want to examine results for their statistical significance, then it becomes an important tool. Survey results for simple percentage changes in students' experiences and perspectives can be examined without the use of more complex statistics.

Lorenzo Hill Pre-test and Post-Test Comparison. The sixth grade at Lorenzo Hill participated in the study to determine whether a single grade within a school could successfully implement the "No Putdowns" program with positive results. Only the sixth grade of Lorenzo Hill Middle School implemented the "No Putdowns" program. Comparing Lorenzo Hill sixth-grade student survey results before the implementation of the "No Putdowns" program (administered in October 1999 to 128 students) to the student survey completed at the conclusion of the first year of the "No Putdowns" program (administered in May 2000 to 148 students), the following statistically significant differences were found:

There were significant *increases* in the number of students who reported "yes" on the following questions at the post-test:

1. Students in this school sometimes use putdowns
2. Students say mean things a lot in school
3. Do you sometimes put others down or say mean things to others in school?
4. Have others picked on you on the bus in the past two months?
5. Do some people think you're mean in school or on the bus?

At first glance, one might conclude the program actually caused more problems than it solved. However, focus groups and observations revealed that these increases were actually most likely an indication that students had become more aware of their own use and others' use of putdowns and mean behavior. They also became more aware of others' perceptions of themselves. These were goals of the program.

There were significant decreases in the number of students who reported "yes" to the following questions at post-test:

1. Putdowns hurt my feelings.
2. Do you feel safe in school?
3. Do you like school?
4. Do you like most of your classes?
5. Have you hit anyone at school or on the bus in the past two months?
6. Have you been hit in school or on the bus in the past two months?

Lorenzo Hill Compared to the Comparison Group. At pre-test, there were no significant differences between the comparison group (Tug Hill sixth-grade cohort, which did not have the "No Putdowns" program) and the experimental group (Lorenzo Hill sixth grade, which did have the "No Putdowns" program), except on the measure of students being "picked on" in school or on the bus where the numbers were significantly higher among the control group at pre-test. The other measures were not significantly different.

The most fundamental goal of the "No Putdowns" program was changing student behavior. Thus, the analysis here focused on the questions that dealt with school violence behaviors (victimization, ostracism, and perpetration). The post-test groups were compared, and the differences were not as dramatic without comparing the comparison group to the "No Putdowns" sites by grade level, indicating that the most significant changes in behavior happened at the higher grade levels, specifically the sixth grade. When comparing the sixth-grade population at Lorenzo Hill with the sixth-grade population at Tug Hill, there were significant differences between the two groups on the following variables at post-test, although there had been no significant differences at pre-test:

1. Students who said that they had been picked on in school or on the bus in the past two months (victimization) (Tug Hill 65%, Lorenzo Hill 38%)
2. Students who said they had been in a fight in school in the past two months (violent behavior) (Tug Hill 40%, Lorenzo Hill 18%)

3. Students who felt left out when groups played on the playground (ostracism) (Tug Hill 48%, Lorenzo Hill 32%)
4. Students who agreed that they had hit someone in the past two months (perpetration) (Tug Hill 29%, Lorenzo Hill 13%)
5. Students who agreed that they have been hit in school or on the bus in the past two months (victimization) (Tug Hill 50%, Lorenzo Hill 27%)

Even without sophisticated statistical analyses, we can see here the dramatic differences between the two groups after the first year of the intervention at Lorenzo Hill. Comparing percentages can be a powerful tool for schools that may not be able to conduct more sophisticated statistics.

Summary of Results

Increased Awareness of Putdowns by Self and Others. There was a significant increase in awareness of putdowns and cruel behavior, including one's own behavior and that of others that resulted in dramatic increases in the measures that asked students about their own and others' use of putdowns, such as saying mean things. Students felt that putdowns did not hurt their feelings as much at the time of the post-test as they did during the pre-test. The qualitative results supported these notions as nearly all students in interviews and focus groups said that they were more aware of their own use and others' use of putdowns and mean behavior as a result of the program.

DecreasedSatisfaction and Sense of Safety. At the end of the school year, Lorenzo Hill sixth-grade students felt significantly less safe in school and liked their classes and school significantly less than they did in the beginning of the year. Unfortunately, no post-test data were collected at the comparison school to determine if these feelings were a maturational function of the age and grade level, but it is interesting to note that students felt less safe and happy in school at the end of the year after the "No Putdowns" program. This association needs to be addressed by school personnel who may wrongly assume that because schools are safer, students feel safer.

The Good News: Actual Change in Violent Behaviors. What was significantly reduced at Lorenzo Hill were actual violent behaviors—experiences as both perpetrator and victim (hitting, being hit, fighting) had significantly declined by the post-test. These behaviors showed a significant reduction when compared to the sixth-grade cohort in the comparison school and when compared to the pre-test data at the experimental school site.

In conclusion, at Lorenzo Hill in the sixth grade, an increased awareness of putdowns and mean behavior resulted in increased reports of putdowns and mean behavior of self and others. Perhaps this increased awareness in problem behaviors was the cause of decreased perceptions of safety and satisfaction with school. Despite these perceptions, actual behavior related to violence was significantly decreased when compared to the sixth-grade cohort in the comparison school.

Conclusions From Data. The data from Lorenzo Hill Middle School demonstrated that there were significantly more reports of putdowns (probably because of increased awareness) and a reduction in perceptions of feeling safe in school and on the bus (again, probably because of increased awareness of putdowns). Despite these increases, there were significant reductions in violent behavior such as fighting and hitting when compared to the pre-test and to the cohorts in the comparison school.

The data indicated some dramatic gender differences among the topics that "No Putdowns" addresses for youths. Boys were more likely to report putdowns and mean behavior, and they also were more likely to be both victims and perpetrators of physical violence. Furthermore, boys were more likely to feel unsafe in school and on the bus and to be less satisfied in school. Girls were slightly more likely to experience ostracism, to be more aware of others' use of putdowns, and to indicate that putdowns hurt their feelings. There were no gender differences for fighting. In addition, girls may experience many types of harassment—particularly various forms of sexual harassment—that neither "No Putdowns" nor the evaluation specifically addressed. More work needs be done to determine the impact of this program, specifically on sexual harassment and other issues for girls.

Recommendations and Implications Based on the Data. Visible success of any program intended to decrease violence in schools is essential to keeping it going, getting more support, and sometimes getting much-needed recognition. Research data can assist in making recommendations for additional needs. The sixth-grade results at Lorenzo Hill Middle School demonstrated that the program had an impact without being a school-wide intervention. Clearly, the qualitative data showed that children felt that the sites where others had not been through the program (the bus, the cafeteria, and the hallways when they intersected with other grades that had not had "No Putdowns") were areas where putdowns and problem behavior needed to be addressed. Ideally, the program should be implemented as a school-wide or district-wide intervention. However, if this option is not available, the data indicate that the program can be successfully implemented also on a smaller scale. Of course, only those students are the beneficiaries of the program who actually experience it.

The "No Putdowns" program at Lorenzo Hill demonstrated success at reducing some of the most problematic behaviors in schools today (hitting and fighting), particularly among the students for whom these behaviors are the most challenging (the sixth grade). Despite a reduction in these problematic behaviors, students felt less safe. The qualitative data suggest that these reports were possibly connected to an increased awareness in one's own and others' use of putdowns. Although the program was probably responsible for a decrease in violent behaviors, but by like token it may also have been the cause for students feeling less safe in school and on the bus. Awareness of any problem often makes those who are most at risk of experiencing the problem more fearful. School violence is only one such problem. More analysis needs to be conducted to unravel some of these questions.

These results indicate what works in school environments to reduce violent acts such as hitting and fighting. A program can meet its stated objectives and have other issues that need to be addressed. More work needs to be done to determine the long-term impact on school-wide programs such as "No Putdowns" and the components that have demonstrated success in reducing violent behaviors.

Evaluating Effectiveness at WANTS

At WANTS, there was a formal approach to evaluation. A formal, nationally tested survey was used before the start of the intervention and at the end of the year. These results give us some idea of the kinds of feedback we can get from more formalized surveys.

Pre-Test and Post-Test Results at WANTS

The National School Crime and Safety Survey was administered in September 1998 to students at WANTS. Pre-test and post-test surveys were used in conjunction with other informally collected data. In the alternative school, 43 students in grades 7 through 12 (72 % of the students were in grades 7–9, 35.7% were males, and 64.3% were females) completed the pre-test questionnaire. At the conclusion of the formative year, 41 students completed the post-test (11 of whom had completed the pre-test)–73.2% in grades 7–9; 55% were male, and 45% were female.

Only 38% of students reported that they agreed or strongly agreed with the statement "I can keep from getting really angry." The post-test data indicated that significantly more students (52%) could keep from getting very angry, suggesting that they thought they had become better able to handle their anger since they came to the school. In addition, 60.7% of students who took the post-test revealed that they had become better able to deal with conflicts with their friends, acquaintances, and family without becoming violent since they came to the alternative school. This result was significantly higher than the results for those taking the pre-test who reported that they could not refrain from getting very angry. Approximately 64% of students agreed or strongly agreed with the statement that they would get into a fight if someone disrespected them at the time of the pre-test, compared with 14.7% of students taking the post-test. This discrepancy demonstrated a significant reduction in the number of students who reported a willingness to fight because they were disrespected.

It was one of the goals of teaching school staff how to include anger management into their curriculum to improve students' ability to manage their anger. Students reported an increased ability to recognize their anger cues and to handle their anger without becoming violent. The second major goal of the program was to reduce the number of everyday student fights that resulted from feeling "disrespected" (a major cause of fights in the school). This number was dramatically reduced. Finally, one major goal of involving the faculty and staff in the anger management curriculum development was to reduce the number of students who felt disrespected by school staff. This goal was not achieved, as there was not a significant change between those in the pre-test group and those in the post-test group.

Upon completing the anger management course and after experiencing the benefits of courses with an infused anger management component, students were asked to report on their ability to manage their anger and handle conflict. Only 11 of the 41 respondents had completed the pre-test because of high student turnover during the school year. Nearly half (45.5%) had been at the alternative school since January 1999 and participated in the program since then. Most of the students had several months of the interventions before taking the post-test.

At the post-test, most of the students (86.2%) believed that they were good at listening to others, and 41.4% thought they had become better listeners since they came to the alternative school. Most of the students (more than 75%) answered positively that they thought they were good communicators (i.e., could recognize their own and others' body language and could get others to listen to them without threatening them). Nevertheless, most of the students reported that when somebody made them angry, they wanted to fight (55.6%), even though most students (92.9% and 75%, respectively) reported that they could recognize when they were getting angry and knew what to do to calm themselves when they became angry. Although 51.7% reported that they had become better able to handle their anger since they came to the alternative school, only 20.7% said they usually walked away from an argument, 39.3% said that they usually tried to talk to the person with whom they were in conflict, and 82.8% said that they usually would physically fight if they were having a fight or argument. At the end of their time at the alternative school, many students attributed their improved ability to handle conflict and anger to their time at the school where they learned anger management directly and had these skills reinforced in their traditional curricula.

The School Environment and Staff Perspectives

Throughout the school year, assessment was conducted by analyzing field notes collected during observations of and interviews with staff and students for emerging themes. I examined field notes for themes related to students' and teachers' reactions to the programs as well as students' changes in violent and aggressive attitudes and behaviors. Classroom observations and interviews with students and teachers were used to gather data about the daily working of the school and the interventions.

At WANTS, preceding curriculum infusion, teacher training, and comprehensive efforts to reduce violence in the school, student and staff reports of the school were profoundly negative. Interviews, observations at staff meetings and classes, and focus groups yielded much evidence of frustration and dissatisfaction with the school. The year after implementing the intervention strategies, most students reported that they liked the school very much and felt comfortable and secure there. All of the students interviewed felt that the teachers were very supportive and attempted to help them and work with them. However, as one student stated, "[The school] is very easy." Few students felt they had to work very hard. This lack of academic rigor placed them far behind their peers when returning to the regular schools.

Interviews were conducted with staff, students, and parents, and observational data were collected. Compared to the previous year, students all said that they liked the school and felt comfortable and safe. Students were interviewed before their return to their regular schools. Despite liking their experience at the school and feeling as if they "learned their lesson," most were excited to return. However, many parents wanted their children to stay as long as possible because the school provided smaller classes and more individualized attention. Most of the parents described their children as having difficulty in school but thought they were doing better academically and socially in the more intimate setting. Teachers noticed a difference too. They said there was more of a feeling of community in the school than the previous years when teachers would come in, teach their classes, and leave. Now teachers would come in early and stay late. They attended activities. The tone at staff meetings was no longer one of hostility and frustration—it had become one of collaboration and fun.

Staff Survey Results. Staff at WANTS completed a post-test created by the Hamilton Fish National Institute with questions about their experiences in the school and their perceptions of the interventions. Teachers, administrators, and other school staff (n=16) were given a survey at the conclusion of the first year of the intervention. Most teachers prior to the intervention complained that students rarely treated adults in the school with respect. At the end of the first year, only 13.3% of the staff agreed with the statement "Students rarely treat school personnel with respect." All of the staff agreed that school personnel were respectful to students, and all except 13.3% felt that students received appropriate punishment for infractions.

Compared to the previous school year when the school was located in one of the more notorious sections of the city, all staff at the end of the intervention year (when the school was located in the heart of the downtown business district) reported feeling moderately to very safe in the building during and after class hours.

Nearly 90% of staff reported that they were moderately to highly satisfied with the violence prevention activities (direct anger management and staff training), 93.3% felt that violence prevention knowledge among student participants improved among student participants, and 73.3% felt that violence-related attitudes and beliefs among the student participants improved. More than 93% of staff felt that relationships between student participants in the anger management project had improved. All staff members said they would recommend the interventions to other schools.

The overwhelmingly positive staff ratings of the school and the intervention indicate that during the first year of the intervention, there was a dramatic improvement in the overall attitude of staff at the school. Some of this improvement may be attributed to the anger management training of students and staff and the work with teachers on infusion, but there were many changes happening in the school simultaneously. First, the new building was a beautifully restored historical library compared to the previous site which was a dilapidated former Catholic school. Second, there was a change in leadership—the school received a new principal who was a 35-year veteran of the district and had the power to get changes that teachers wanted done. Third, the administration supported the programs and thus, the teachers were more involved with the interventions and in supporting them. Fourth, there were more full-time staff added, including more teachers. There had previously been no police officer or security guard. During the year of the intervention, they had hired a full-time police officer and security guard. This made staff and students feel safer. In addition, all staff and students mentioned the presence of the anger management trainer who modeled the behavior she taught. She was respectful of students and staff and worked with them to resolve conflicts nonviolently. Her room became a safe haven for students and staff alike—where all were expected to be respectful and kind.

Clearly, no intervention exists in a vacuum. There are always other factors at work. However, it is important to recognize how individuals make sense of these factors and their impact on their lives. Students and teachers alike felt better about being at the school.

Lessons We Can Learn

Evaluation takes time, but time is a commodity that teachers or administrators often do not have. However, it is important to make time to evaluate what we do to see if our programs are working—or what parts of our programs are working. Not all types of evaluation can be used in all cases. Sometimes it may be possible to use mostly informal strategies such as observing students, speaking with students in interviews or focus groups, or creating and administering informal surveys. Sometimes formal strategies such as those used at Lorenzo Hill (including a comparison school) or WANTS (using a nationally developed survey) are appropriate or sometimes a combination of formal and informal strategies, as was the case at both WANTS and Lorenzo Hill, are the ones to use. The goal is finding out what has changed as a result of an intervention. Collecting information before the start of a program (which also gives a picture of the needs of the students) and collecting information after the intervention has been underway for at least a year should yield some constructive feedback. Evaluation should not be used as a punitive device to scrap a program entirely, but it should provide constructive, critical feedback that can inform and ultimately improve the practice. Investing in a program that is consistently not yielding any successful results is a greater waste of time. It would be useful to know if, year after year, there are no positive results. Similarly, it would be helpful to know if a program is improving relationships among students and reducing violent behavior, as was found at Lorenzo Hill and at WANTS.

Sometimes a good strategy for busy teachers or administrators is to team up with a teacher-educator at a local college or university interested in school issues related to violence or evaluation. Collaboration to help with the sometimes seemingly overwhelming task of evaluation is helpful and may prove to be mutually beneficial for the collaborators. In addition, most grant-funded violence-prevention activities require evaluation and built-in money to hire an outside evaluator. Hiring outside evaluators when possible is very helpful for lifting the burden of responsibility from the staff. Nevertheless, individuals in the school should be involved closely with the evaluator to make sure she or he is using appropriate strategies and providing useful reports and feedback about programs and components.

Final Words of Encouragement

Violence presents a complex and challenging problem for schools. There are schools with children who have little or no hope for a future in a world in which they can feel safe and can be positive, contributing members. Children need hope and be able to believe that they can have bright futures. They need to see schools as an important vehicle to arrive at these futures. They need to feel as though they belong in school—that they are important members of their school community.

Clearly there are differences among schools and the types of personal and structural violence within them. There are differences within a school culture about what constitutes violence. Violence happens at all types of schools, although all schools are not equal in the amount and type of violence they experience. Horrific acts of violence have taken place at wealthy suburban schools, and there are daily horrors that happen at urban schools. Violence in some form seems to exist in every type of school. However, whether a school is poor, wealthy, suburban, rural, urban, small, large, and so on influences the perceptions of violence among the staff and students—what is problematic, what is tolerated, what is the threshold of violent behavior, and what is the solution. When Lorenzo Hill and its school district were focusing on eliminating hitting, bullying, ostracizing, and verbal cruelty, WANTS and its school district were trying to deal with weapon carriers, physical attacks, and gangs.

Each school has its obstacles and its strengths. Clearly the problems are as different as are the solutions. We need to avoid a one-size-fits-all approach to violence prevention and intervention. Each school needs to identify through a thorough assessment procedure, including both traditional (e.g., surveys, opinionnaires) and authentic measures (e.g., observations, interviews, focus groups), the problems surrounding violence. For some schools this may include doing some digging to examine aspects of violence that are often hidden and accepted as a part of going to school (e.g., sexual harassment, bullying, and ostracizing).

For readers who are interested in implementing a school-wide approach to violence prevention, here is a quote from Frederick Douglass's speech in 1857 that I cite when I speak to practitioners about developing a school-wide approach:

If there is no struggle, there is no progress. Those who profess to favor freedom, and yet deprecate agitation, are men who want crops without plowing the ground. They want rain without thunder and lightning. They want the ocean without the awful roar of its many waters. This struggle may be a moral one; or it may be a physical one; or it may be both moral and physical; but it must be a struggle. Power concedes nothing without a demand. It never has and it never will.

It has become a struggle to keep our schoolchildren safe. We must listen to the words of children to hear how they are socially constructing violence. We must take the information gained from listening to tailor our strategies to meet the needs of children. We must struggle and demand for the sake of the safety and healthy development of all children.

Promising and Demonstrated Violence Prevention Programs

An expert panel for *Safe and Drug-Free Schools* found the following programs to be "exemplary" when applying their rigorous criteria of excellence:

Safe, Disciplined, and Drug-Free Schools Expert Panel Exemplary Programs (2001)

Athletes Training and Learning to Avoid Steroids (ATLAS) Linn Goldberg, M.D. Professor of Medicine and Principal Investigator for the ATLAS Program Oregon Health Sciences University ATLAS Program 3181 SW Sam Jackson Park Road (CR 110) Portland, OR 97201 Phone: (503) 494–6559 Fax: (503) 494–1310 E-mail:goldberl@ohsu.ed http://www.ohsu.edu/som-hpsm/info.htm	**Project Northland- Alcohol Prevention Curriculum** Ann Standing Hazelden Information and Educational Services 15251 Pleasant Valley Road PO Box 176 Center City, MN 55012 Phone: (800) 328-9000 Ext: 4030 Fax: (651) 213-4577 E-mail:astanding@hazelden.org http://www.hazelden.org
CASASTART Lawrence F. Murray, CSW Senior Program Associate The National Center on Addiction and Substance Abuse at Columbia University (CASA) 633 Third Avenue, 19th Floor New York, NY 10017 Phone: (212) 841–5208 Fax: (212) 956-8020 E-mail:lmurray@casacolumbia.org http://www.casacolumbia.org	**Project T.N.T.-Towards No Tobacco Use** Sue Wald ETR Associates (Education, Training, & Research Associates) 4 Carbonero Way Scotts Valley, CA 95066 Phone: (831) 438–4060 Ext: 164 Fax: (831) 438–4284 E-mail: wals@etr.org http://www.etr.org

Life Skills Training	Second Step: A Violence Prevention
National Health Promotion Associates, Inc.	Curriculum
141 South Central Avenue, Suite 208	Committee for Children
Hartsdale, NY 10530	Client Support Services Department
Phone: (914) 421-2525	2203 Airport Way South, Suite 500
Fax: (914) 683-6998	Seattle, WA 98134
E-mail: training@nhpanet.com	Phone: (206) 343-1223; (800) 634-4449
http://www.lifeskillstraining.com	Fax: (206) 343-1445
	E-mail:info@cfchildren.org
	http://www.cfchildren.org
OSLC Treatment Foster Care	**Strengthening Families Program:**
Patricia Chamberlain, Executive Director	**For Parents and Youth 10-14**
Oregon Social Learning Center Community	Virginia Molgaard
Programs	Institute for Social and Behavioral Research
160 East 4th Avenue	2625 N. Loop, Suite 500
Eugene, OR 97401	Iowa State University
Phone: (541) 485-2711	Ames, IA 50010
Fax: (541) 485-7087	Phone: (515) 294-8762
E-mail:pattic@oslc.org	Fax: (515) 294-3613
http://oslc.org	E-mail:vmolgaar@iastate.edu
	http://www.extens
Project ALERT	
G. Bridget Ryan	
725 S. Figueroa St., Suite 1615	
Los Angeles, CA 90017	
Phone: (800) 253-7810	
Fax: (213) 623-0585	
E-mail:info@projectalert.best.org	
http://www.projectalert.best.org	

Available online at:
www.ed.gov/offices/OERI/ORAD/KAD/expert_panel/2001exemplary_sddfs.html

Reprinted from the U.S. Department of Education.

The Safe, Disciplined, and Drug-Free Schools Expert Panel (2001) found the following programs to be "promising" based on the rigorous criteria they used in categorizing programs:

The Safe, Disciplined, and Drug-Free Schools Expert Panel Promising Programs

Aggression Replacement Training Arnold P. Goldstein (deceased) Professor Emeritus of Education and Psychology, and Director Center for Research on Aggression Syracuse University 805 South Crouse Avenue Syracuse, NY 13244 Phone: (315) 443-9641 Fax: (315) 443-5732	**Open Circle Curriculum** Pamela Seigle, Executive Director Reach Out to Schools: Social Competency Program The Stone Center, Wellesley Centers for Women Wellesley College 106 Central Street Wellesley, MA 02481-8203 Phone: (781) 283-3778 Fax: (781) 283-3717 E-mail:pseigle@wellesley.edu http://www.wellesley.edu/opencircle
Aggressors, Victims, and Bystanders: **Thinking and Acting to Prevent Violence** Erica Macheca Center for School Health Program Education Development Center, Inc. 55 Chapel Street Newton, MA 02458 Phone: (617) 969-7100 Fax: (617) 244-3436 E-mail: emacheca@edc.org http://www2.edc.org/thtm/	**PATHS Curriculum** **(Promoting Alternative Thinking Strategies)** Carol A. Kusche, Ph.D. PATHS Training, LLC 927 10th Avenue East Seattle, WA 98102 Phone: (206) 323-6688 Fax: (206) 323-6688 E-mail: ckusche@attglobal.net http://www.prevention.psu.edu/PATHS or http://drp.org
Al's Pals: Kids Making Healthy Choices Susan R. Geller, President Wingspan, LLC P.O. Box 29070 Richmond, VA 23242 Phone: (804) 754-0100 Fax: (804) 754-0200 E-mail:sgeller@wingspanworks.com http://www.wingspanworks.com	**Peers Making Peace** Susan Armoni, Executive Director PeaceMakers Unlimited, Inc. 2095 N. Collins Blvd., Suite 101 Richardson, TX 75080 Phone: (972) 671-9550 Fax: (972) 671-9549 E-mail:Susan.Armoni@pmuinc.com http://www.pmuinc.com

All Stars (Core Program)
William B. Hansen, Ph.D.
Tanglewood Research, Inc.
7017 Albert Pick Road, Suite D
Greensboro, NC 27409
Phone: (336) 662-0090
Fax: (336) 662-0099
E-mail:billhansen@tanglewood.net
http://www.tanglewood.net

PeaceBuilders
Michael I. Krupnick, President
Heartsprings, Inc.
P.O. Box 12158
Tucson, AZ 85732
Phone: (520) 322-9977 (877) 4-PEACE-NOW
Fax: (520) 322-9983
E-mail: mik@heartsprings.org

Child Development Project
Dr. Eric Schaps, President
Developmental Studies Center
2000 Embarcadero, Suite 305
Oakland, CA 94606-5300
Phone: (510) 533-0213
Fax: (510) 464-3670
E-mail: Eric_Schaps@devstu.org
http://www.devstu.org

Peacemakers Program: Violence Prevention for Students in Grades Four through Eight
Jeremy P. Shapiro, Ph.D.
Applewood Centers, Inc.
2525 East 22nd Street
Cleveland, OH 44115
Phone: (216) 696-5800 Ext: 1144
Fax: (216) 696-6592
E-mail:jeremyshapiro@yahoo.com

Community of Caring
Brian J. Mooney
Community of Caring, Inc.
1325 G Street NW, Suite 500
Washington, DC 20005
Phone: (202) 824-0351
Fax: (202) 824-0351
E-mail: contact@communityofcaring.org
http://www.communityofcaring.org

Positive Action Program
Dr. Carol Gerber Allred
Positive Action, Inc.
264 Fourth Avenue South
Twin Falls, ID 83301
Phone: (208) 733-1328 (800) 345-2974
Fax: (208) 733-1590
E-mail:paction@micron.net
http://www.positiveaction.net

Creating Lasting Family Connections
Ted N. Strader, Executive Director
Council on Prevention & Education:
Substances, Inc. (COPES)
845 Barret Avenue
Louisville, KY 40204
Phone: (502) 583-6820
Fax: (502) 583-6832
E-mail:tstrader@sprynet.com
http://www.copes.org

Preparing for the Drug-Free Years (PDFY)
Dan Chadrow
Developmental Research and Programs, Inc.
130 Nickerson St., Suite 107
Seattle, WA 98109
Phone: (800) 736-2630 Ext: 162
Fax: (206) 736-2630
E-mail:moreinfo@drp.org
http://www.drp.org

Facing History and Ourselves
Terry Tollefson, Ed.D.
Director of Human Resources and
Evaluation
Facing History and Ourselves National
Foundation, Inc.
16 Hurd Road

Primary Mental Health Project
Deborah B. Johnson
Children's Institute
274 N. Goodman, Suite D103
Rochester, NY 14607
Phone: (716) 295-1000 (877) 888-7647
Fax: (716) 295-1090

Brookline, MA 02445 Phone: (617) 232-1595 Fax: (617) 232-0281 E-mail:Terry_Tollefson@facing.org http://www.facing.org	E-mail:djohnson@childrensinstitute.net http://www.pmhp.org or http://www.childrensinstitute.net
Growing Healthy Director of Education National Center for Health Education 72 Spring Street, Suite 208 New York, NY 10012-4019 Phone: (212) 334-9470 Fax: (212) 334-9845 E-mail:nche@nche.org http://www.nche.org	**Project STAR** Karen Bernstein University of Southern California Norris Comprehensive Cancer Center 1441 Eastlake Avenue, Room 3415 Los Angeles, CA 90089-9175 Phone: (323) 865-0325 Fax: (323) 865-0134 E-mail:karenber@usc.edu
I Can Problem Solve (ICPS) Dr. Myrna B. Shure, Professor MCP Hahnemann University Department of Clinical and Health Psychology 245 N. 15th St. MS 626 Philadelphia, PA 19102-1192 Phone: (215) 762-7205 Fax: (215) 762-8625 E-mail:mshure@drexel.edu http://www.researchpress.com	**Responding in Peaceful and Positive Ways (RIPP)** Melanie McCarthy Youth Violence Prevention Project Virginia Commonwealth University 808 W. Franklin Street, Box 2018 Richmond, VA 23284-2018 Phone: (804) 828-8793 Fax: (804) 827-1511 E-mail:mkmccart@saturn.vcu.edu http://www.wkap.nl/book.htm/0-306-46386-5
Let Each One Touch One Mentor Program Vicki Tomlin, Ph.D. Denver Public Schools 4051 S. Wabash St. Denver, CO 80237 Phone: (303) 796-0414 Fax: (303) 796-8071 E-mail:vtomlin@dnvr.uswest.net	**Say It Straight Training** Paula Englander-Golden, Ph.D. Professor and Director University of North Texas, Department of Rehabilitation P.O. Box 310919 Denton, TX 76203-0919 Phone: (940) 565-3290 Fax: (940) 565-3960 E-mail: golden@unt.edu
Linking the Interests of Families and Teachers (LIFT) Dr. J. Mark Eddy, Researcher Oregon Social Learning Center 160 East 4th Avenue Eugene, OR 97401 Phone: (541) 485-2711 Fax: (541) 485-7087 E-mail:marke@oslc.org http://www.oslc.org	**SCARE Program** D. Scott Herrmann, Ph.D. Tripler Army Medical Center/Child Psychology Services One Jarrett White Road TAMC, Hawaii 96859-5000 Phone: (808) 433-2738 Fax: (808) 433-1801

Lions-Quest Skills for Adolescence Greg Long Quest International 1984 Coffman Road Newark, OH 43055 Phone: (740) 522-6400 Fax: (740) 522-6580 E-mail:gregl@quest.edu http://www.quest.edu	Seattle Social Development Project Development Research and Programs, Inc. 130 Nickerson Street, Suite 107 Seattle, WA 98109 Phone: (206) 286-1805 Fax: (206) 286-1462 E-mail: moreinfo@drp.org http://www.drp.org
Lions-Quest Working Toward Peace Greg Long Quest International 1984 Coffman Road Newark, OH 43055 Phone: (740) 522-6400 Fax: (740) 522-6580 E-mail:mailto:gregl@quest.edu http://www.quest.edu	SMART Team (Students Managing Anger & Resolution Together) Kris Bosworth, Ph.D. Smith Endowed Chair in Substance Abuse Education The University of Arizona, Department of Educational Leadership Smith Prevention Initiatives, College of Education P.O. Box 210069 Tucson, AZ 85721-0069 Phone: (520) 626-4964 Fax: (520) 626-6005 E-mail:boswortk@u.arizona.edu http://www.drugstats.org
Michigan Model for Comprehensive School Health Education Don Sweeney Michigan Department of Community Health School Health Unit 3423 N. Martin Luther King Blvd. Lansing, MI 48909 Phone: (517) 335-8390 Fax: (517) 335-8391 E-mail:sweeneyd@state.mi.us http://www.emc.cmich.edu	Social Decision Making/Problem Solving Linda Bruene-Butler The University of Medicine and Dentistry University Behavioral Health Care Institute for Quality Research and Training 335 George Street New Brunswick, NJ 08901 Phone: (800) 642-7762 Fax: (732) 235-9277 E-mail:SPSWEB@UMDNJ.EDU http://www2.umdnj.edu/spsweb/news.htm
Minnesota Smoking Prevention Program Ann Standing Hazelden Information and Educational Services 15251 Pleasant Valley Road P. O. Box 176	Teenage Health Teaching Modules Erica Macheca Center for School Health Programs Education Development Center, Inc. 55 Chapel Street Newton, MA 02458

Center City, MN 55012 Phone: (800) 328–9000 Ext: 4030 Fax: (651) 213–4577 E-mail:astanding@hazelden.org http://hazelden.org	Phone: (617) 969–7100 Fax: (617) 244–3436 E-mail:emacheca@edc.org http://www.edc.org/thtm
	The Think Time Strategy J. Ron Nelson, Ph.D. Research Professor University of Nebraska, Lincoln Center for At-Risk Children Services Barkley Center Lincoln, NE 68583–0738 Phone: (402) 472–0283 Fax: (402) 472–7697 E-mail:rnelson8@unl.edu

Available online at:
www.ed.gov/offices/OERI/ORAD/KAD/expert_panel/2001promising_sddfs.html

The Hamilton Fish National Institute on School and Community Violence conducted a meta-analysis of promising practices and comprised the following list of
successful practices:

Results from the Hamilton Fish National Institute on School and Community Violence's Meta-analysis of Programs with Demonstrated Success

The Anger Coping Program (middle and early secondary school program) *Contact information:* John Lochman, Ph.D. Department of Psychology University of Alabama Box 870348 Tuscaloosa, AL 35487 Tel: (205) 348-5083 Fax: (205) 348-8648 E-mail: jlochman@gp.as.ua.edu	**The Brainpower Program** (late elementary program) *Contact information:* Cynthia Hudley, Ph.D. Graduate School of Education University of California at Santa Barbara 2210 Phelps Hall UCSB Santa Barbara, CA 93106-9490 Tel: (805) 893-8324 Fax: (805) 893-7264 E-mail: hudley@education.ucsb.edu
The First Step to Success Program (Kindergarten program) *Ordering Information* Sopris West 4093 Specialty Place Longmont, CO 80504 Tel: (800) 547-6747 Fax: (303) 776-5934 www.sopriswest.com	**Good Behavior Game** (early elementary program) *Contact information:* Sheppard G. Kellam Department of Mental Hygiene Johns Hopkins University School of Hygiene and Public Health Prevention Research Center Mason F. Lord Building, Suite 500 5200 Eastern Avenue Baltimore, MD 21224 Tel: (410) 550-3445

I Can Problem Solve (Elementary school program)	Kid Power Program (Elementary school program)
Contact information:	*Contact information:*
Myrna Shure, Ph.D.	Mike Bennett
MCP Hahnemann University	River Region Human Services, Inc.
245 N. 15th Street	330 West State Street
MS 626	Jacksonville, FL 32202
Philadelphia, PA 19102	Tel: (904) 359-6571, ext. 135
Tel: (215) 762-7205	Fax: (904) 359-6583
E-mail: mshure@drexel.edu	E-mail: rrhsmike@msn.com
Metropolitan Child Area Study (violence and substance abuse adolescents)	**Teaching Students to be Peacemakers**
Contact information:	*Contact information:*
Patrick H. Tolan, Ph.D.	Linda Johnson
Institute for Juvenile Research	Interaction Book Company
Department of Psychiatry	7208 Cornelia Drive
University of Illinois at Chicago	Edina, MN 55435
Chicago, IL 60612	Tel: (612) 831-7060
Tel: (312) 413-1893	Fax: (612) 831-9332
Fax: (312) 413-1703	
E-mail: Tolan@uic.edu	
Peer mediation program	**Tools for Effective Violence Prevention:**
Contact information:	**School Security**
Donna Crawford, Executive Director	For more information, contact:
National Center for Conflict Resolution	Kenneth S. Trump, President and CEO
Education	National School Safety and Security
110 West Main Street	Services Corporate Headquarters
Urbana, IL 61801	P.O. Box 110123
Tel: (217) 384-4118	Cleveland, OH 44111-2950
Fax: (217) 384-4322	Tel: (216) 251-3067
E-mail: crawford@nccre.org	Fax: (216) 251-4417
www.nccre.org	KENTRUMP@aol.com
	www.schoolsecurity.org

Positive Adolescent Choices Training (PACT) *Contact information:* Betty R. Yung, Ph.D. School of Professional Psychology Wright State University Ellis Human Development Institute 9 N. Edwin C. Moses Boulevard Dayton, OH 45407 Tel: (937) 775-4300 Fax: (937) 775-4323 E-mail: betty.yung@wright.edu	**Think First** (for Secondary School students) *Contact information:* Jim Larson, Ph.D. Coordinator, School Psychology Program Department of Psychology University of Wisconsin - Whitewater Whitewater, WI 53190 Tel: (414) 472-5412 Fax: (414) 472-1863
Violence Prevention Curriculum for Adolescents *Contact information:* Education Development Center, Inc. 55 Chapel Street Newton, MA 02458-1060 Tel: (800) 225-4276 www.edc.org	

Reprinted from www.hamfish.org

Checklist for School-wide Approach

Issues to consider when developing a school-wide approach to violence prevention:

1. Identify and create programming for students most at risk of violence (intensive case management, social skills training, etc.) tailored to meet their individual needs.

2. Address multicultural education needs in curricula and in school activities.

3. Develop programs that teach caring and help create a caring school environment where caring is modeled and rewarded.

4. Create a discipline program that is consistent, fair, and that all students and staff understand.

5. Design and implement pedagogy that is cooperative and collaborative instead of competitive that incorporates ways that students learn best.

6. Create opportunities to teach conflict resolution, anger management, empathy, and problem solving to all staff and students (directly and using curriculum infusion).

7. Use peer mediation as a prevention strategy (including peer–peer, parent–child, teacher–student, gangs, and other members of the community in mediation practices) that is embedded within the culture of the school.

8. Encourage parental involvement (including outreach, home visits, regular communication between teachers and parents, parent education programs).

9. Involve community members (including tutoring and mentoring programs, GED programs).

10. Design constructive alternative education sites for some students who fail to thrive in traditional classrooms that addresses individual needs with appropriate resources.

11. Implement transition programs for all students new to a building including those from alternative education sites as well as any time a student is removed from or returned to class.

12. Address environmental issues such as:
    One entry and exit with greeter
    Security in hot spots, including teachers
    Prevention of weapon concealment in clothes and packs
    No graffiti
    Clean and welcoming building

13. Provide or be able to refer to reputable drug education and treatment (or appropriate referrals) for students and parents.

14. Collaborate with all major stakeholders in child's life.

15. Provide activities, including academic enrichment during after-school hours.

16. Design and implement strategies to identify and address academic needs—especially poor literacy among students and their families.

17. Provide prenatal care and post-care for at-risk parenting teens (including counseling, education, and prevention programs).

18. Put comprehensive evaluation plans in place
    Qualitative components (interviews, observations, and focus groups)
    Quantitative components (pre-test, post-test, comparison groups)

Adapted from Williams, 2003, pp. 90–91.

APPENDIX C

A List of References for School Violence Prevention

The following is a nonexhaustive list of resources useful for planning school violence prevention.

Assessment Instruments

Achenbach, T. M. (1991). *Teacher's report form.* Burlington: University of Vermont Department of Psychiatry.
Brown, L., & Leigh, J. (1986). Adaptive behavior inventory. Austin, TX.: Pro-Ed.
Taylor, R. T. (2000). Assessment of exceptional students: Educational and psychological procedures. Boston, MA: Allyn and Bacon.
Walker, H. (1983). Walker problem behavior identification checklist. Los Angeles: Western Psychological Services.
Walker, H., & McConnell, S. (1995). Walker-McConnell scale of social competence and school adjustment. San Diego: Singular.

Books

Anderson, E. (1999). Code of the street: Decency, violence, and the moral life of the inner city. New York: W.W. Norton.
Apple, M. (1993). Official knowledge. New York: Routledge.
Berman, S., & LaFarge, P. (Eds.). (1993). *Promising practices in teaching social responsibility.* New York: SUNY Press.
Burstyn, J. N. (Ed.). (1997). *Educating tomorrow's valuable citizen.* Albany: SUNY Press.
Burstyn, J. N., Bender, G. , Casella, R., Gordon, H. W., Guerra, D. P., Luschen, K. V., Stevens, R., & Williams, K. M. (2001). *Preventing violence in schools: A challenge to American Democracy.* Mahwah, NJ: Lawrence Erlbaum.

Canada, G. (1995). *Fist, stick, knife, gun: A personal history of violence in America.* Boston: Beacon Press.

Carlsson-Paige, N., & Levin, D. E. (1987). *Who's calling the shots? How to respond effectively to children's fascination with war play and war toys.* Philadelphia: New Society.

Darling-Hammond, L. (1997). *The right to learn: A blueprint for creating schools that work.* San Francisco, CA: Jossey-Bass Publishers.

De Bono, E. (1990). *Lateral thinking: Creativity step by step.* New York: Harper and Row.

Delpit, L. (1995). *Other people's children: Cultural conflict in the classroom.* New York: New Press.

Eckert, P. (1989). *Jocks and burnouts: Social categories and identity in the high school.* New York: Teachers College Press.

Epp, J. R., & Watkinson, A. M. (1996). *Systemic violence: How schools hurt children.* London: Falmer Press.

Foley, D. (1990). *Learning capitalist culture.* Philadelphia, PA: University of Pennsylvania Press.

Gathercoal, F. (1997). *Judicious discipline.* San Francisco, CA: Caddo Gap Press.

Goldstein, A., & McGinnis, E. (1997). *Skillstreaming the adolescent: New strategies and perspectives for teaching prosocial skills.* Champaign, IL: Research Press.

Goodwillie, S. (Ed.). (1993). *Voices from the future: Our children tell us about violence in America.* New York: Crown.

Gootman, M. (2001). *The caring teacher's guide to discipline: Helping young students learn self-control, responsibility, and respect.* Thousand Oaks, CA: Corwin Press.

Grundy, S. (1987). *Curriculum: Product or praxis?* New York: Falmer Press.

Hamburg, D. A. (1994). *Education for conflict resolution.* Report of the President, Carnegie Corporation of New York.

Hernandez, A. (1998). *Peace in the streets: Breaking the cycle of gang violence.* Washington, DC: Child Welfare League of America.

Hoffman, A. M. (1996). *Schools, violence, and society.* Westport, CT: Praeger.

Isenberg, J. P., & Rains, S. C. (1993). Peer conflict and conflict resolution among preschool children. In: *The annual review of conflict knowledge and conflict resolution: The role of formal education in conflict resolution.* Vol. 3. J. Gittler & L. Bowen (Eds.). New York: Garland.

Lappe, F. M., & DuBois, P. M. (1994). *The quickening of America: Rebuilding our nation, remaking our lives.* San Francisco, CA: Jossey-Bass.

Loeber, R., & Farrington, D. P. (1998). *Serious and violent juvenile offenders: Risk factors and successful interventions.* Thousand Oaks, CA: Sage.

Noddings, N. (1992). *Challenge to care in schools.* New York: Teachers College Press.

Prothrow-Stith, D. (1991). *Deadly consequences: How violence is destroying our teenage population and a plan to begin solving the problem.* New York: Harper Perennial.

Reardon, B., & Nordland, E. (Eds.). (1994). *Learning peace: The promise of ecological and cooperative education.* Albany: SUNY Press.

Williams, K. M. (1998). *Learning limits: College women, drugs, and relationships.* Westport, CT: Bergin and Garvey.

Williams, K. M. (2003). *The PEACE approach to violence prevention: A guide for administrators and teachers.* Lanham, MD: Scarecrow Press, Inc.

Journal Articles

Burstyn, J. N., & Stevens, R. (1998). Education in conflict resolution: A whole school approach. *Nexus: Journal of Peace, Conflict and Social Change, 1*(1), 1–15.

Crary, D. R. (1992). Community benefits from mediation: A test of the "peace virus" hypothesis. *Mediation Quarterly, 9*(2), 241–252.

Galtung, J. (1969). Violence and peace. *Journal of Peace Research,* 167–191.

Harris, I. M. (1990). Principles of peace pedagogy. *Peace and Change, 15*(3), 254–271.

Johnson, D. W., Johnson, R. T., Dudley, B., Ward, M., & Magnuson, D. (1995). The impact of peer mediation training on the management of school and home conflicts. *American Educational Research Journal, 32*(4), 829–844.

Kingery, P., Coggeshall, M., & Alford, A. (1999). Weapon carrying by youth: Risk factors and prevention. *Education and Urban Society, 31,* 309–333.

Reinhart, M. (1995). Understanding the concept of peace: A search for common ground. *Peace and Change, 20*(3), 379–396.

Rist, R. (1970). Student social class and teacher expectations: The self-fulfilling prophecy in ghetto education. *Harvard Educational Review, 40,* 411–451.

Williams, K. M. (2002). Determining the effectiveness of anger management training and curricular infusion at an alternative school for students expelled for weapons. *Journal of Urban Education, 37*(1), 59–76.

Teaching Strategies/Curricula

Carpenter, S. (1977). *A repertoire of peace-making skills.* Consortium of Peace Research, Education and Development.

Consensus Building Institute. *Program for young negotiators.* (Contact Person: Bruce B. Richman, Associate Director, 131 Mt. Auburn Street, Cambridge, MA 02138.)

Creating safe and drug free schools: An action guide. (1999). Office of Juvenile Justice and Delinquency Prevention, Department of Justice, Washington, DC.

Families and schools together (FAST). University of Wisconsin-Madison, 1025 West Johnson Street, Madison, WI 53706. Phone: 608-263-9476, Fax: 608-263-6488.

Institute for Mental Health Initiatives. (1991). *Anger management: The RETHINK method.* Distributed by Research Press, 2612 N. Mattis Avenue, Champaign, IL 61821.

Kreidler, W. (1984). *Creative conflict resolution.* Glenview, IL: Scott Foresman.

Kreidler, W. J. (1990). *Elementary perspectives 1: Teaching concepts of peace and conflict.* Cambridge, MA: Educators for Social Responsibility.

Kreidler, W. J. (1994). *Conflict resolution in middle schools.* Cambridge, MA: Educators for Social Responsibility.

Kreidler, W. J. (1994). *Teaching conflict resolution through children's literature.* New York: Scholastic Professional Books.

Lieber, C. M. (1998). *Conflict resolution in the high school.* Cambridge, MA: Educators for Social Responsibility.

Mundy, L., & Wissa, E. (1993). *Help increase the peace: A manual for facilitators.* American Friends Service Committee, e-mail: hippuyp@igc.apc.org

NO PUTDOWNS PROGRAM MATERIALS. CONTACT, Inc., 315-251-1400 or CONTACT-Syracuse, Inc. , 3049 E. Genesee St., Syracuse, NY 13244.

National Coalition Building Institute (NCBI) (contact person: Sherry Brown). Available online at www.ncbi.org.

O'Toole, M. (2001). FBI threat assessment report. *U.S. Federal Bureau of Investigation* at http://hamfish.org/pub/fbiss.pdf (accessed July 2, 2002).

Prutzman, P. M., Burger, L., Bodenhamer, G., & Stern L. (1978). *The friendly classroom for a small planet.* Wayne, NJ: Avery.

Resolving Conflict Creatively Program. Contact information: Jennifer Selfridge Project Director 23 Garden Street, Cambridge, MA 02131, email: jselfridge@esrnational.org. More information available online at www.esrnational.org.

Schmidt, F., & Friedman, A. (1990). *Fighting fair, Dr. Martin Luther King Jr. for kids.* Miami, FL: Grace Contrino Abrams Peace Education Foundation.

Sleeter, C. E., & Grant, C. A. (1994). *Making choices for multicultural education: Five approaches to race, class, and gender.* 2nd ed. Englewood Cliffs, NJ: Merrill/Prentice-Hall.

Stomfay-Stitz, A. M. (1993). *Peace education in America, 1928–1990: Sourcebook for education and research.* Metuchen, NJ: Scarecrow Press.

Tolan, P., & Guerra, N. (1994). What works in reducing adolescent violence: An empirical review of the field. Center paper for the Center for the Study and Prevention of Violence, July, at Boulder, Colorado.

Readings from Internet Resources

Association for conflict resolution. http://www.acresolution.org.

Early learning, timely response: A guide to safe schools. http://www.ed.gov and http://www.air-dc.org/cecp.

First annual report on school safety. Office of Juvenile Justice and Delinquency Prevention. http://www.ed.gov.

Hamilton Fish National Institute on School and Community Violence, with reports of promising and demonstrated practices and National School Crime and Safety Survey. www.hamfish.org.

Indicators of school crime and safety. http://nces.ed.gov or http://www.ojp.usdoj.gov.

Office of Juvenile Justice and Delinquency Prevention. www.ncjrs.org/ojjdp. Participant Packet from the White House Conference on School Safety information on FAST, RCCP, PAL, and San Diego's comprehensive program.

Safe and Drug-Free Schools, with several links to other resources and readings and list of exemplary practices with links to contact names. www.ed.gov/offices.OESE/SDFS.

What works, research in brief. National Institute of Justice. www.usdoj.gov.

The PEACE Approach to Violence Prevention Framework

Personalize the experience of violence: Begin with your own perspectives and definitions of violence and what counts as violent. These personal experiences are critical in shaping our understanding of violence and what we notice about it. This first step helps us understand our personal biases and the importance of our personal experiences.

Examine experiences of students in the school. Teachers, administrators, researchers, and others, after exploring their own perspectives on violence, are invited to explore how students in their particular school make sense of violence. What acts do they notice? What do they take for granted? Through a series of possible strategies (interviews, observations, formal and informal surveys, and focus groups), we need to gain a picture of what concerns students most regarding issues of violence.

Advocate for students based on their needs. Once the needs are identified, the next step is to advocate for these needs. Part of advocacy includes educating oneself about the components of programs with demonstrated success and determining which components will best suit the needs of students.

Choose and implement program components. With the decision makers in the school, choose and implement program components that seem to be most appropriate, given the needs of your students. Examples of particular programs and components are given using two different case studies.

Evaluate effectiveness. Finally, critically important but often left out, is evaluating how effective the intervention is. Was violent behavior less frequent? Do students feel safer? Are they more aware of the impact of cruel treatment? In a nutshell, were the identified needs met? Two examples of evaluations of the interventions implemented at the case study sites are described (Williams, 2003, pp. ix-x).

References

Bastian, L., & Taylor, B. (1995). *School crime*. U.S. Department of Justice, Bureau of Justice Statistics, 1991 (NCJ-131645).

Brydon-Miller, M. (1993). Breaking down barriers: Accessibility self-advocacy in the disabled community. In: Peter Park et al. (Eds.). *Voices of Change: Participatory Research in the United States and Canada*. Toronto: OISE Press, 125-143.

Canada, G. (1995). *Fist, stick, knife, gun: A personal history of violence in America*. Boston: Beacon Press.

Corvo, K. N., & Williams, K. M. (2001, Fall). Substance abuse, parenting styles, and aggression: An exploratory study of weapon carrying students. *Journal of Drug Education, 47*(3), 1-13.

Delpit, L. (1995). *Other people's children: Cultural conflict in the classroom*. New York: New Press.

Douglass, F. (1857) Black classic voices at
http://www.duboislc.org/BlackClassicVoices/BlackStruggle.html (Accessed April 5, 2004).

Epp, J. R., & Watkinson, A. M. (1996). *Systemic violence: How schools hurt children*. London: Falmer Press.

Frank, B. (1987). Hegemonic heterosexual masculinity, *Studies in Political Economy, 24*, 159-170.

Effective violence prevention programs. (2001). *Hamilton Fish National Institute on School and Community Violence* at http://hamfish.org/pub/evpp.html (Accessed June 8, 2002).

Garmezy, N. (1991). Resiliency and vulnerability to adverse developmental outcomes associated with poverty. *American Behavioral Scientist, 34*(4), 416-430.

Goldstein, A. P., & McGinnis, E. (1997). *Skillstreaming the adolescent: New strategies and perspectives for teaching prosocial skills*. Champaign, IL: Research Press.

Hernandez, A. (1998). *Peace in the streets: Breaking the cycle of gang violence*. Child Welfare League of America, Inc.: Washington, DC.

Kachur, S. P. (1996). School associated violent deaths in the United States, 1992 to 1994. *Journal of the American Medical Association, 275*(22), 1729-1733.

Loeber, R., & Farrington, D. P. (1998). *Serious and violent juvenile offenders: Risk factors and successful interventions*. Thousand Oaks, CA: Sage.

Mansfield, W., Alexander, D., & Farris, E. (1991). Teacher survey on safe, disciplined, and drug-free schools, fast response survey system, FRSS 42, U.S. Department of Education, National Center for Education Statistics (NCES 91-091).

Martineau, S. (1996). Dangerous liaison: The eugenics movement and the educational state. In: J. R. Epp, & A. M. Watkinson (Eds.). *Systemic violence: How schools hurt children.* Bristol, PA: The Falmer Press.

NO PUTDOWNS PROGRAM. CONTACT, Inc. (315) 251-1400 or CONTACT-Syracuse, Inc., 3049 E. Genesee St., Syracuse, NY 13244.

Noddings, N. (1992). *Challenge to care in schools.* New York: Teachers College Press.

Nolan, M. J., Daily, E., & Chandler, K. (1995). *Student victimization at school.* U.S. Department of Education, National Center for Education Statistics, 1995 (NCES 95-204).

Sherman, L. W., Gottfredson, D., MacKenzie, D. L., Eck, J., Reuter, P., & Bushway, S. D. (1998). *Preventing crime: What works, what doesn't, what's promising.* Washington, DC: National Institute of Justice: Research in Brief, U.S. Department of Justice, Office of Justice Programs.

Smith, D. (1987). *The everyday world as problematic: A feminist sociology.* Boston, MA: Northeastern University Press.

Tolan, P., & Guerra, N. (1994). *What works in reducing adolescent violence: An empirical review of the field.* Center Paper for the Study and Prevention of Violence: University of Colorado, Boulder.

U.S. Bureau of Justice Statistics (2001). Crime characteristics: School violence at http://www.ojp.usdoj.gov/bjs/cvict_c.htm (Accessed April 19, 2004).

U.S. Department of Education, National Center for Education Statistics. (1998). *School actions and reactions to discipline issues.* nces.ed.gov/pubs98/violence.

U.S. Department of Education, National Center for Education Statistics 1997, Fast Response Survey "Principal/School Disciplinarian Survey on School Violence FRSS 63.

Walker, H. (1995). *The acting out child: Coping with classroom disruption.* Longmont, CO: Sopris West.

Williams, K. M. (1998). *Learning limits: College women, drugs, and relationships.* Westport, CT: Bergin & Garvey.

Williams, K. M. (2001). Determining the effectiveness of anger management training on students at an alternative school for weapons expulsion. *Journal of Urban Education, 37*(1), 60-75.

Williams, K. M. (2003). *The PEACE approach to violence prevention: A guide for teachers and administrators.* Lanham, MD: Scarecrow Press.

Index

acceptable violence, 43, 46, 51, 70, 71
addiction, 79
age, 53, 69
aggression, 79, 80
AIDS, 78, 157
at-risk, xvi, xvii, 4, 7, 25, 151
attendance, 15, 59, 75, 95, 100, 141, 156, 157, 159

basketball, 23, 26, 55, 63, 75, 80, 101, 126, 137, 143
blackmail, 117, 121
bullying, xiii, 42, 45, 96, 140, 163

Canada, Geoffrey, 40
caring relationships, ix, 56, 126, 161
college, xiv, xv, xvi, xviii, 8, 16, 73, 100, 101, 120, 135, 136, 173
community, vii, xiv, xvii, xxiv, xxv, 22, 23, 54, 56, 63, 70, 82, 85, 128–130, 132, 133, 141, 143, 159, 171, 173
Community Center, 24, 82
community service, 10, 22, 26, 58, 81, 104, 105, 107–110, 112, 114, 115, 129, 152, 153, 156, 157
conflict resolution, xvii, 110, 115, 116, 151–158
criminal justice system, 96, 134, 143–145

curriculum, 16, 18, 32, 71, 77, 110, 127, 128, 152–155, 169, 170
curriculum infusion, 158

death, xiii, xv, 26, 41, 50, 73, 75, 78–80, 87
definition, viii, xvi, 1, 37, 38, 40, 62, 70, 118, 119
disabled students, 68
discipline, 2, 5, 15, 60, 66, 117, 130, 132, 152, 153, 157
disrespected, 13, 85, 86, 169
disruptive students, 15, 116, 117, 120
drug use, xviii, 74, 75, 137, 138

emotion, xv, 45, 61, 72, 80, 83
ethnographic research, ix, 7, 34, 65
Ethnography, ix
Eugenics, 92
evaluation, 131, 162, 163, 172
    qualitative approaches, 162
    quantitative approaches, 162

family, xix, xx
fighting, xiii, xv, xvii, xviii, xix, xx, xxii, xxiv, 13–15, 23, 40, 42, 45, 48, 50, 60–63, 80–84, 86, 96, 97, 99, 100, 111, 122, 126, 127, 136, 137

fights, xiii, xvii, xviii, 4, 5, 11, 14, 26, 28, 38, 39, 51, 60, 61, 81, 86, 137, 140, 142, 163, 169

firearm, 5, 6, 95

football, xxi, 67, 68, 101, 126

frontin' it, 17

gangs, vii, xiv, xv, xviii, xix, xxiv, 3, 5, 11, 15, 25, 28, 33, 40, 43, 46, 50, 51, 54, 57, 64-66, 97, 102, 132, 135, 137, 143, 144, 173
girls and gangs, 65

gender, vii, 1, 8, 12, 13, 39, 53, 56, 58, 66-68, 70, 71, 167

girl fights, 60, 61

grief, 20, 40, 72, 73, 75, 76, 78, 79, 86, 87

guns, xi, xix. *See* weapons

harassment, vii, 37, 59, 61, 66, 86, 139, 141, 167

homosexuality, 64, 84, 86

illegal drugs, xviii, xxiv, 4-6, 27, 28, 29, 37, 38, 46, 48, 50, 66, 73-75, 79, 82, 83, 94, 134, 137, 138, 140, 143, 161

incarceration, 135

individualized instruction, 105, 119, 120, 133, 146

instructional media/materials, 111

intimate relationships, xviii, 11, 61, 64, 96, 137

jail, xx, 8, 24, 25, 46, 50, 79, 81, 95, 112, 135-137, 144

juvenile detention, xx, 8, 26, 45, 47, 48, 95

key Informants, 16

literacy program, 23, 150, 174

Lorenzo Hill, ix, xiii, xxii-xxiv, 29, 30, 33, 38-40, 53, 54, 59, 60, 62-64, 66, 68-72, 86, 87, 91, 93, 94, 135, 141, 142, 152, 162-68, 172, 173

loss, 40, 41, 72, 73, 74, 75, 77, 78, 79, 86, 87, 125, 144
loss of infants, 79

low expectations, 128

masculinity, 62, 63, 64

mediation, viii, xx, xxi, 11, 14, 136

mothering, 122, 123, 124, 125, 132

neglect, 123

No Putdowns, xxiv, 29, 32, 39, 71, 152, 162-68

observations, viii, xxiv, 2, 3, 16, 17, 21, 24, 27-29, 58, 95, 103, 104, 108, 111, 118, 127, 131, 133, 154, 159, 162-64, 170, 174

Office of Juvenile Justice and Delinquency Prevention, xxv, 3, 151

ostracizing, vii, xiv, xxii, 38, 54, 71, 173, 174

pain, xiv, 15, 21, 40, 72-78, 112, 144

parent outreach, 153, 155, 159

parental alcohol and other drug use, 29

parents, vii, x, xii, xxv, 20, 30, 32, 45-49, 51, 58, 73, 74, 77, 78, 96, 112, 116, 126, 130, 135, 136, 151, 153-55, 159, 162, 170. *See family*

peer mediation, xx, xxi, 11

personal violence, viii, xi, xxii, 3, 33, 37-40, 42-44, 50, 51, 53, 69-71, 86, 87, 145

physical abuse, 46, 49

popularity, xiii, xv, xix, xxiii, 7, 13, 17, 29–32, 54, 59, 63, 64, 67, 83, 85, 92, 116, 137, 138, 154, 158, 163

poverty, xiii, xiv, xv, xxiii, 8, 11, 33, 34, 48, 53, 54, 72, 76, 82, 83, 93, 100, 141–144

pregnancy, ix, xiii, xviii, 65, 75, 77, 84, 135, 140, 141, 151, 161

prenatal and postnatal care, 161

privilege, xi, xiii, xiv, xv, xxi, 76

program evaluation, 131

promising practices, viii, 2, 34, 150, 151, 152

race, xxi, 53, 54, 57, 59, 70, 86

respect, xii, xviii, xxiv, 11, 13, 17, 21, 42, 49, 54, 85, 86, 119, 125, 152, 171

retaliation, xxi, 40, 73, 78, 79, 81, 83, 144, 145

school shootings, ix, 3

self-protection, 49, 99

sexual abuse, 37, 48, 51, 96

sexual harassment, vii, 38, 61, 70, 86, 167, 174

sexuality, 63

sexual molestation, 48

Smith, Dorothy, viii, ix, x, 33, 134

social construction of violence, vii, xi, 1, 38

social location, vii, xi, xxiv, 1, 8, 33, 37–39, 53, 71, 86

special education, 34, 41, 94, 142, 145

salaries, 112

stress, 19, 72, 75, 76, 80, 81, 123, 127

structural violence, viii, ix, xxi, xxii, xxiv, 1, 3, 33, 87–141, 145, 146, 173

suicide, 75

surveys, 162

symbolic violence, 92

systemic violence, viii, 92, 93, 117

teacher-mothers, 122, 123, 125

theoretical framework, viii

threats, 3, 37, 69, 139

thug, 26, 40–45, 62, 99

transition, 10, 98, 153–155, 159, 160

trial and error, 16, 18, 115, 118, 119

U.S. Department of Education, 4

victimization, xxii, 19, 20, 45, 81, 86, 92, 96, 132, 145, 166

violent offenders, 38

WANTS, vi, ix–xi, xvi, xxiii, xxiv, 1, 2, 6–11, 16–33, 37–142, 144, 150, 152–162, 168, 170–173

weapons, vii, ix, xxiv, 1, 4, 6–9, 11, 14, 15, 18, 27, 38, 40, 42, 45, 47, 49, 50, 51, 56, 60–62, 65, 66, 82, 92, 94–104, 113, 126, 130, 131, 138, 141

zero tolerance, viii, ix, 4, 6, 7, 9, 47, 50, 92–94, 97–99, 143

Studies in the Postmodern Theory of Education

General Editors
Joe L. Kincheloe & Shirley R. Steinberg

Counterpoints publishes the most compelling and imaginative books being written in education today. Grounded on the theoretical advances in criticalism, feminism, and postmodernism in the last two decades of the twentieth century, Counterpoints engages the meaning of these innovations in various forms of educational expression. Committed to the proposition that theoretical literature should be accessible to a variety of audiences, the series insists that its authors avoid esoteric and jargonistic languages that transform educational scholarship into an elite discourse for the initiated. Scholarly work matters only to the degree it affects consciousness and practice at multiple sites. Counterpoints' editorial policy is based on these principles and the ability of scholars to break new ground, to open new conversations, to go where educators have never gone before.

For additional information about this series or for the submission of manuscripts, please contact:

> Joe L. Kincheloe & Shirley R. Steinberg
> c/o Peter Lang Publishing, Inc.
> 275 Seventh Avenue, 28th floor
> New York, New York 10001

To order other books in this series, please contact our Customer Service Department:

> (800) 770-LANG (within the U.S.)
> (212) 647-7706 (outside the U.S.)
> (212) 647-7707 FAX

Or browse online by series:

> www.peterlangusa.com